Beauty Matters

Civics Lessons from an Olmsted Village

BENJAMIN SELLS

SPRING PUBLICATIONS

THOMPSON, CONN.

Published by Spring Publications
Thompson, Conn.
www.springpublications.com

First edition 2022 (1.1)

Cover art © 2022 by Margot McLean

Library of Congress Control Number: 2022951153

ISBN: 978-0-88214-989-9

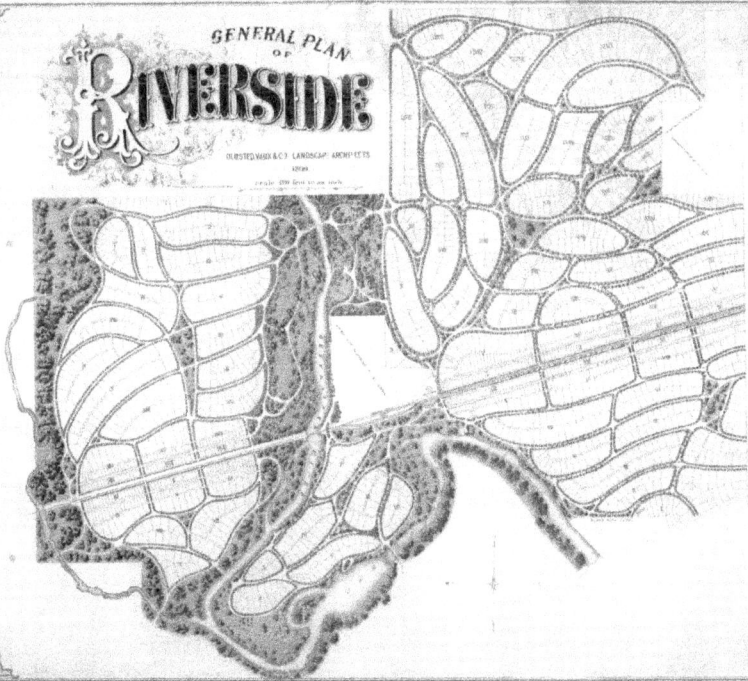

GENERAL PLAN
OF

RIVERSIDE

OLMSTED VAUX & CO. LANDSCAPE ARCHITECTS
1869

CONTENTS

TO BEGIN

My premise is straight-forward—beauty is a civic necessity. Beauty inspires and sustains community and is essential to politics and governing. Beauty gives rise to love, and without love, there would be no community, no society, and no culture. It is the binding and ordering powers of beauty that draw humans together to achieve things that they could never achieve as individuals. And so, in the beating heart of every village, town, and city lies the foundational presence of beauty.

This book tells the story of how as village president of Riverside, Illinois, I attempted to put the idea of beauty as a civic necessity into practice. To tell this story, we will look at beauty in relation to politics, ethics, and nature. These ideas lie at the beginning of our Western minds and are inextricably bound together. To the ancient Greek mind, politics and ethics were two sides of the same coin, both striving for "the good," which was itself aligned with beauty. So, too, politics was seen as part of nature, even as deriving from nature. The connection between politics, ethics, and nature persists all through our Western religious, philosophical, and scientific traditions. Our approach will flirt with, but will not be seduced by, these traditions. Instead, we will explore how beauty inspires and animates how we think about, and more importantly how we *imagine,* politics, ethics, and nature.

Riverside is a small suburb just west of Chicago. Its claim to fame is that it was designed by the landscape architect Frederick Law Olmsted in 1869. He designed it with beauty and nature in mind, and over forty percent of the village is public green space of forests, parks, and landscaped triangles. There are only two straight roads in town, and they parallel the train tracks that were laid to bring stressed out city workers to a village in the forest designed to be serene and rejuvenating. All of the other streets are curvilinear, following the contours of the land and the Des Plaines River that snakes its way beside the village. Riverside was declared a National Historic Landscape District in 1972, and its residents are both proud and protective of its historic legacy and natural beauty.

Olmsted's landscape design was not incidental and was not intended to be merely decorative. The fact that Riverside has more public green space per capita than any city or town in the United States was deliberate. Olmsted believed that beauty was critical for social well-being and for democracy itself, and he wanted to design public places that would encourage people to come together in nature to help improve society and grow democracy through engagement and interaction. He landscaped Riverside to be a place that inspired reflection, contemplation, and conversation, qualities easily lost in the bustle of big-city life.

Long before Olmsted, though, the place that we now call Riverside was recognized by indigenous people as special. An ancient sand beach cuts through the town, just inches beneath the surface soil. The beach is from the ancestral Lake Chicago, precursor of Lake Michigan. Indigenous people lived all along this ridge, and one park in Riverside, named Indian Gardens, was both a settlement and a burial ground. Europeans came to the area that became Riverside because of the Chicago Portage, a marshy area that connected Lake Michigan to the Des Plaines River and then on to the Illinois and Mississippi Rivers. The Chicago Portage was thus the connecting point that allowed canoe travel from the Atlantic Ocean to the Gulf of Mexico. The Chicago Portage was essential during the fur trade era, and it is because of the Chicago Portage that Chicago exists. In the early part of the nineteenth century, what we now call Riverside and Lyons were the population center of what would become the metropolis of Chicago.

The historic aspects of Riverside, its unusual curvilinear streets, and the gas street lights that still remain throughout most of the village, are all loved by the people who live here. But more than anything it is Riverside's natural beauty that holds the imagination of its residents. Our urban forest abounds with wildlife and there is a rich and deep respect for the flora and fauna that surrounds us here, just ten miles from the concrete and skyscrapers of downtown Chicago. There are many multi-generational families here but also a vibrant mix of young families who move to Riverside to raise their children. We are not as diverse a community as I would like, but my hope is that will change over time. There is a strong volunteer spirit within the village, and residents are quick to help those in need. It is a safe community often likened to the fictional Mayberry, but it is nonetheless only a few miles from a major city and so must have public safety services ready to meet modern realities.

I was elected village president in 2013 after serving as a village trustee for six years. Local politics in Riverside is genteel compared with the toxic partisanship on display in much of American political affairs. There are no long-standing political parties, and all of our elected positions are volunteer positions. Every now and then we will have opposing slates and contentious elections, but for the most part a local community caucus vets and recommends candidates and those candidates are usually elected. Having said that, the actual governing of the village is as complex as any other municipality. One of the things that makes local government enjoyable is that even in a small community the deeper aspects of policy and decision making are as profound as in larger cities or even at the state and federal levels. In some ways they can be more complex because of the closeness between decisions and policies and their immediate impact on the populace. Local elected officials are not removed from their constituents but see them daily on the street, and in our stores and restaurants. When a resident calls the village president it is the village president who answers the phone. None of our elected officials even have an office.

When I was elected village president, I had two core missions that are not usually associated with politics or governing. One was to make Riverside more beautiful, and the other was to care for its soul. For eight years I governed guided by those two ideas and ideals, beauty and soul. For me, a village is more than the sum of its parts. It cannot be defined either by the residents who live here, physical structures like houses and buildings, its location and geography, or even its history. I take Riverside to be first an image. As an imaginal presence, Riverside includes all of the things I just listed, but it also is inhabited by invisible presences, memories, dreams, reflections, ideas, and fantasies. It has a life of its own that cannot be reduced to its component parts. It has a destiny given with its unique place in the world, a trajectory toward becoming more beautiful by becoming more richly present and more fully revealed. As an image it longs to be realized by finding its proper place in the greater world, by relating to and respecting the other images with which it shares a common home. I call this context of relations by and among images an ecology of imagination because another premise of this book is that a village or city is as much a part of nature as a seashore or a forest.

To make Riverside more beautiful, then, meant more than sprucing up the place with pretty things. It meant nurturing an ecology of imagination where the image of Riverside could not only better connect and relate with its surrounding communities and natural areas but also grow downward, reaching deeper and deeper into the mystery that lies within every image. We can see analogies to this in some people as they grow older. They seem to become more content with themselves, more fully formed and articulated, more solid somehow, more beautiful. In things that are truly beautiful, there is no distinction between interiority and display; they are exactly, precisely as they appear to be. Although we too often associate beauty with youth and its form of vitality, the beauty I mean is the beauty of something that simply appears as what it truly is. Socrates was said to be beautiful not because of a handsome visage, but because he was fully present as who and what he was. Beauty brings with it a vitality of animal awareness that directly perceives things as they are. Beauty grants us an unwavering certainty in a supporting world where one's place exists as a given, free from self-doubt. This is what beauty provides to the world. According to the Greeks, it was Aphrodite, the goddess of beauty, that made all things visible, including the gods. It was she who made the world available to the senses, making all things at once sensate, sensual, and sensible.

If beauty is at the heart of Riverside's appearance as an image in a broader ecology of imagination, then soul is its animating force, the propelling power that gives it life and guides its destiny. Really, we should not move too quickly to even talk of beauty and soul separately because they so readily bond together. Plotinus said Aphrodite *was* soul (*Enneads* 3.5.4),[1] and in the old tale by Apuleius, Psyche (*anima*, soul) was known first by her beauty that rivaled even that of Aphrodite. So, at least in my mind as a civic leader, when I attended to beauty I was caring for soul and vice versa.

---

1. All citations of Plotinus are from *The Enneads*, translated by Stephen MacKenna (Burdett, N.Y.: Larson Publication, 1992).

If these themes seem esoteric or odd when talking of politics and governing, that is because we have repressed beauty and so no longer see it as a practical reality. We have estranged beauty to the wilderness and the art gallery and in so doing we have also estranged ourselves from our proper place in the world. Crafting a well-worded ordinance, conducting an orderly and collaborative meeting, and designing and crafting the repair and maintenance of streets, sewers, and public buildings are all essentially aesthetic acts. Budgets are statements about the ideals and values of the polis. Parks and recreation extoll the beauty inherent in nature and play. Civil discourse, mutual trust, communal sharing of goals—all of these arise first from beauty because it is beauty that creates love, and it is love that creates community. Beauty is not only *a* civic necessity, it is *the* civic necessity.

To our modern, especially urban, minds, beauty is usually thought of as superficial, as only skin deep. It conjures connotations of narcissism and vanity. Soul is, for most of us, a religious notion, or perhaps is taken to refer to our personal subjectivity, our inner "self" that is available to each person only through introspection and reflection. As for politics, it has become a pejorative, the arena of selfish ambition and machinations, every game a zero sum. It is difficult for us to feel the essential connection between beauty, soul, and politics. One aim of this book is to redeem these old and noble words.

We can see the result of our current ways of thinking all too clearly. When we repress beauty and lock soul within individual humans, we deny beauty and soul a proper role in politics. In so doing we deprive beauty and soul a communal existence, and we condemn politics to a brute and ugly isolation. The toxic partisanship that poisons so much of politics today is an aesthetic disorder, a pathology arising from our misshapen ideas of beauty, soul, and politics. The turbulence and chaos that we are experiencing result from a lack of the ordering power of beauty, which traditionally gave stability to the cosmos.

At this point I offer no definitions of beauty or soul. Demands for definition, as we will see much more fully in the pages to come, are power plays, attempts to restrict and control the spontaneous creativity of the imagination, which has always been the active organ of beauty and soul. Definitions want to limit and put an end to things, which is what "define" means in its etymological roots. This entire book is an exposition on the meanings of beauty and soul. So, as we begin, I ask that you take whatever ideas and notions you have about beauty and soul and consider them in the context of what you are reading. We do not have to agree about what beauty and soul mean, and indeed I think that they exist beyond meaning. They are not creations of the mind but rather are what allows the mind to proceed. Discussions about beauty and soul always spark multiple ideas, stories, and myths. Their inherent diversity, the way they draw things together and reveal multiple facets through contrast and composition, their power to inspire, animate, and persuade—all of these things point to their essential place as civic necessities.

One final thing as we begin is a note on the language of this book. I follow the great psychologist James Hillman in his idea that there is *"a poetic basis of mind."*[2] That means that language, one of the mind's great gifts, is inherently imaginative, that it proceeds through images, fantasy, and poetic associations. To speak about politics, ethics, and nature in terms of beauty and soul requires poetic, artful, and aesthetic language that speaks in terms of images. I ask, then, that you do not take my words literally but that you hear them poetically as images that seek to see through our current ways of thinking to find the fantasies they express and the myths to which they belong. To do this we will look carefully at the words we use, often looking to their etymological roots for clues of their mythic and imaginative significance.

I will refer often in this book to invisible powers, to gods and myths, and to ancestors as necessary for a fuller understanding of politics, ethics, and nature. These words have religious connotations, and, indeed, they are intended to evoke our religious sensibilities. But in my meaning they are not words that ask for belief or faith. I refer to them because beauty and soul always take us beyond ourselves, implicating mysteries and powers that outstrip human capacities of understanding. To refer to Aphrodite as the goddess of beauty, for example, is to emphasize the

---

2. James Hillman, *Re-Visioning Psychology* (New York: Harper and Row, 1975), xi: "Here I am suggesting both *a poetic basis of mind* and a psychology that starts neither in the physiology of the brain, the structure of language, the organization of society, nor the analysis of behavior, but in the processes of imagination."

transpersonal nature of beauty, its autonomous status within psychological life, arising not from human subjectivity but as an inhuman power that constitutes and informs all that is. Aphrodite has the power to deepen our appreciation for even the most common of things, but she also has the power to raise our eyes to the heavens in all of its starry magnificence. Like the other gods, she neither asks for nor needs our belief—but we neglect her at our peril.

If our language is poetic and mythical, then so, too, our attitude toward ideas will follow a different path, one less taken. This book does not propose a theory. I am not amassing evidence and I am not asking that you agree with any set idea or believe in any ideology. I am not asking you to choose between sides, or to declare any ideas true or false. Choices that exclude and limit options, and declarations about veracity leave too much out and so do not belong to an imagining, poetic mind. Instead, I ask that we entertain ideas, that we consider them both seriously and playfully, appreciating both their complexities and their pleasures. I ask that we allow invisible friends to have their voice, and that we sense life and soul in things that we too often and too quickly proclaim inanimate.

Lastly, the language of this book is intended to be subversive, just as the book itself is intended as an act of civil disobedience. I want us to disturb our usual habits of thought, rebel against confining and divisive ideologies, and upset the economic cart to restore the value inherent in the many things of the world. It is time to restore the polis to its proper place in beauty and soul.

PART I

Beauty and Politics

ONE

By Nature a Political Animal

O ne of Aristotle's most famous statements is that "man is by nature a political animal."[1] He believed that humans have a natural desire to come together, whether in search of a partner or spouse, the creation of a family household, the binding together of numerous households to estab-lish a tribe or village, or the larger congregation of villages that results in cities and states. Aristotle considered this last form of human bonding, the polis, to be the highest form of human interaction. He thought that the household exists primarily for procreation and basic survival, and that villages contributed to common defense and sharing of resources. But the polis offers the greatest opportunity to the human as a political animal because the polis provides the communal support necessary for humans to flourish and reach their highest potential. Although the polis "comes into existence for the sake of life, it exists for the good life.[2]

In the first part of his sentence about humans being political animals, Aristotle says that "the city-state is a natural growth."[3] Although we moderns tend to think of nature as "out there" and separate from the city, Aristotle argues that cities are themselves the result of the human's natu-ral political propensity, that the city is an essential part of human nature and therefore of nature itself. Indeed, he goes so far as to assert that the polis is *prior* in nature to the village, household, or even the individual. As political animals we cannot be fully realized outside of the polis. Aristotle states that an individual "who is incapable of entering into partnership,

---

1. Aristotle, *Politics,* translated by H. Rackham, Loeb Classical Library 264 (Cambridge, Mass.: Harvard University Press, 1932), 1253*a*9.
2. Ibid.
3. Ibid.

or who is so self-sufficing that he has no need to do so, is no part of a state, so that he must be either a lower animal or a god."[4]

When we listen to Aristotle's claim today, we do so under the influence of millennia of religious, philosophical, and scientific traditions that run contrary to his view. The various words—human, nature, political, animal—all are so heavily weighted in our Western minds that we find it hard to get to the core meaning and value of what he is saying. We are so burdened by intractable mental habits, so trapped in unyielding currents of tradition that it is difficult for us to grasp the content and power of Aristotle's claim.

Although our history admits to many eddies and backwaters, places where we attempt to push against the flow of tradition, we cannot help but be born into a milieu of thoughts and ideas that seem so fundamental that we no longer can even see them as thoughts and ideas. They have become fundamentalisms, ideologies that are no longer thought about but only accepted and believed. And because they are no longer available to our conscious reflections, they have become the places where we are most unconscious. Where we are the most certain, where we no longer feel the need for thought, is where we are most un-knowing, the most ignorant of our own core beliefs. The ideas we don't know that we have are the ones that most certainly have us.

Let us begin with three of the words used by Aristotle—human, nature, and animal. The prevailing view of ourselves as humans and our relation to nonhuman animals comes to us largely through a Christian lens. We are told that we are exceptional, different in kind from the other animals, that only we were made in God's image, and that we have dominion over the nonhuman animals and indeed over all other aspects of God's creation. Western philosophy from its beginnings has reinforced and perpetuated this idea of human exceptionalism by declaring that only we have a rational soul and that we stand alone at the top of the *Scala Naturae*. Despite Charles Darwin's protestations that humans and nonhuman animals differ in degree, not kind, our prevailing religious, philosophical, and scientific traditions have maintained a steady control over our anthropocentric view that we are radically unlike nonhuman animals. Over and over again, we find some trait—speech, logic, rationality, imagination, emo-

---

4. Ibid., 1253*b*5.

tion—that we claim sets us apart from nonhuman animals and that makes us different in kind, not degree.

The Christian separation of humans from nonhuman animals, indeed from nature itself, has persisted through our philosophical and scientific traditions. Rene Descartes and his followers are prime architects of this wall, declaring that nonhuman animals are mere automata, living robots that lack thought, feeling, emotion, imagination, and even the capacity for pain. Later scientific traditions perpetuated these religious and philosophical claims, denying that nonhuman animals were conscious in any meaningful way. Nonhuman animals were conceived to be creatures of blind instinct, incapable of reflection and acting only on the basis of biological needs. They might join together to hunt, or bond together to procreate, but those were simply means to an evolutionary end to survive and reproduce. Their hunts were without camaraderie and their bonds were without love.

We do not have to be Christians or have ever even heard of Descartes to nonetheless be carried by their currents. The notion that humans are separate from and superior to nonhuman animals is the currency of our realm and we spend it daily without realizing its devaluing effect on humans, nature, and our fellow animals. It is certainly true, especially in science, that the capabilities of nonhuman animals are receiving increased respect. But we still struggle under the yolk of anthropocentrism and false claims of human exceptionalism.

"Nature," as used in Aristotle's claim, is not the all-encompassing, abstract "capital-N Nature" of our contemporary minds.[5] It is not the nature that we imagine as "out there" in the wilderness of mountains and plains and forests. Aristotle uses the old meaning of nature, as in the nature of something in particular. So, when he says that humans are by nature political animals, he means that we are essentially political animals,

---

5. Jedediah Purdy wonders if perhaps part of the human-nature separation comes from taking "nature" abstractly as a "coherent system of principles that somehow adds up to a whole and orders all the material activity of the universe, at all scales, living and nonliving." This is what he refers to as "capital-N Nature." Quoted in Ross Anderson, "Nature Has Lost Its Meaning," *The Atlantic,* November 30, 2015 (online at *https://www.theatlantic.com/science/archive/2015/11/nature-has-lost-its-meaning/417918/*).

that the core reality of our being is as a political animal. Here "nature" refers to a style of being. This further suggests that it is only through embracing and appreciating ourselves as political animals that we can be fully realized, fully human. To deny our political animality is to deny our essential humanness. Politics from this perspective is not just something that humans do, politics is what makes us what we are. Politics is an ontological necessity.

Aristotle studied and wrote extensively on nonhuman animals, including insects. His method of careful observation has led some to consider him to be "the father of comparative psychology, as well as the founder of the other biological sciences and of natural history in general."[6] Although he considered humans to be political animals, he did not think we were the *only* political animals. He believed that at least some nonhuman animals also possessed varying political capabilities. So, when Aristotle uses "political animal" in regard to humans and other gregarious animals, he founds this idea in terms of his biological and zoological work. For Aristotle, *politics belongs to biology and zoology,* it is a *natural* activity carried out by human and nonhuman animals alike. Politics is essential to the natural world of which we are a part.

In his *Historia animalium* (History of Animals), possibly one of his oldest biological works, Aristotle distinguishes between different types of animals. He says that some animals are gregarious and that others are solitary, that some form groups and others do not. Even among gregarious animals, not all join together in ways that rise to Aristotle's meaning of being political animals. Aristotle defines political animals as those who join together for some common function.[7]

Despite this recognition that some nonhuman animals were capable of political interaction and cooperation, Aristotle nonetheless claimed

---

6. C.J. Warden, "The Development of Modern Comparative Psychology," *The Quarterly Review of Biology* 3, no. 4 (December 1928): 486.

7. "The social animals are those which have some one common activity, and this is not true of all the gregarious animals." Aristotle, *History of Animals,* vol. 1, translated by A.L. Peck, Loeb Classical Library 437 (Cambridge, Mass.: Harvard University Press, 1965), 488*a*10. For a discussion of Aristotle's distinction between "higher" and "lower" political animals, see Cheryl E. Abbate, " 'Higher' and 'Lower' Political Animals: A Critical Analysis of Aristotle's Account of the Political Animal," *Journal of Animal Ethics* 6, no. 1 (Spring 2016): 54–66.

exceptional status for humans because according to him only we have rational souls. He also considered humans to be the *most* political animal because of our unique capacity of speech and the advantages that speech offers us over nonhuman animals:

> Speech serves to reveal the advantageous and the harmful and hence also the just and unjust. For it is peculiar to man as compared to the other animals that he alone has a perception of good and bad and just and unjust and other things of this sort; and partnership in these things is what makes a household and a city.[8]

This view of humans as qualitatively different from nonhuman animals because of our rational minds and our dexterity of speech persists to this day and remains the dominant view in our habitual minds. Contrary to this view, however, there are strong countercurrents in contemporary cognitive ethology that dispute claims of human exceptionalism.[9] According to a growing body of research, there is little doubt that many animals have the capacity for sophisticated communication.[10] There is also a growing view that nonhuman animals also display behaviors that seem to exhibit an ability to distinguish between good and bad, just and unjust.[11]

---

8. Aristotle, *Politics*, 1253a10–11.

9. See, e.g., Donald R. Griffin, *The Question of Animal Awareness: Evolutionary Continuity of Mental Experience* (New York: The Rockefeller University Press, 1976) and his *Animal Minds* (Chicago: The University of Chicago Press, 1992); Frans B.M. de Waal, *Are We Smart Enough to Know How Smart Animals Are?* (New York: W.W. Norton, 2016).

10. See, e.g., Jack Bradbury and Sandra Vehrencamp, *Principles of Animal Communication* (Sunderland, Mass.: Sinauer Associates, 1998).

11. See, e.g., Mark Bekoff and Jessica Pierce, *Wild Justice: The Moral Lives of Animals* (Chicago: The University of Chicago Press, 2009); Mark Bekoff and Jessica Pierce, "Wild Justice Redux: What We Know about Social Justice in Animals and Why it Matters," *Social Justice Research* 25, no. 2 (2012): 122–39; Sarah F. Brosnan, and Frans B.M. de Waal, "Monkeys Reject Unequal Pay," *Nature* 425 (2003): 297–99; Robert Solomon, *A Passion for Justice: Emotions and the Origins of the Social Contract* (Lanham, Md.: Rowman & Littlefield, 1995); Robert Sussman and Audrey Chapman, *The Origins and Nature of Sociality* (New York: Aldine De Gruyter, 2004); Robert Sussman, Paul Garber, and Jim Cheverud, "Importance of Cooperation and Affiliation in the Evolution of Primate Sociality," *American Journal of Physical Anthropology* 128, no. 1 (2005): 84–97.

What is most relevant for our concerns is that it is politics that holds together the other ideas of human, nature, and animal. Politics is a biological and zoological activity based on communal action, mutual respect, and differentiations between good, bad, just, and unjust. Notice that Aristotle says that partnerships are arrived at through the *perception* of good, bad, just, and unjust and that these partnerships are what make a household or a city. But on what basis are such "perceptions" made? How do we distinguish between good, bad, just, and unjust? My contention is that these perceptions are based on essentially *aesthetic* responses. Indeed, I maintain that beauty lies at the heart of all four ideas of human, nature, politics, and animal. Yes, we are by nature political animals, but first we are by nature *aesthetic* animals.

By restoring ideas about humans, nature, politics, and animals to the realm of beauty we can begin to find ways of steering the ship of state out of the traditional currents in which it has been trapped. If humans by our very natures are intimately connected to politics and nonhuman animals through beauty, if beauty is the common foundation that makes partnerships of all kinds possible, then politics is an essentially aesthetic activity carried on in varying degrees by a wide range of creatures. Beauty erases the divide between human and nonhuman animals and restores us to our proper natural place in the cosmos.

For the ancient Greeks, the various forms of human partnerships and groupings took place within a broader mythical context. Their idea of a household, for example, included invisibles like gods and ancestors. Their animal companions, that they called "familiars," were also included in the household. The people in the household were not isolated individuals but were constituted by the household itself, each person a communal being. We find similar ideas among indigenous peoples. In many cultures, family and tribe take precedence over the individual, and often the concept of an individual in our meaning doesn't even exist—there is no "I." Instead, a person is unique because they interiorize the broader community through a unique set of relationships with that community. The family or tribe coalesces in each of its members in particular ways, just as the invisibles, gods, spirits, and ancestors each find different foci in each member. Each person is both unique and communal such that there is no isolated "I." To tell you who I am I must tell you *a story,* a story of where I come from, what animals imbue my spirit, to which ancestors I am particularly connected. There are no autobiographies, only stories of mythical relations.

All human groupings exist somewhere. They are grounded in specific places, and these places are also home to countless other animals and beings of all sorts, visible and invisible. For animistic and polytheistic peoples, rock formations and plains are places where spirits reside. For many indigenous cultures, animals were themselves divine, not representations of divinities, mind you, not symbols of divinity, but divinities directly present in animal form. So, too, the ancestors were there in the air, water, earth, and fire. The ground on which houses and villages were built was not fungible property to be owned and hoarded, but rather a place of living memory, a place where the blood and ashes of the past provided the nutrients that sustained daily life. All of these things, the animals, spirits, gods, ancestors, memories, and dreams, the rocks and trees and soil were part of the polis and for the polis to survive and flourish they all needed to be included in discussions and decisions about current, political affairs.

A story from Riverside. Our village sits alongside the Des Plaines River. It is truly a village in the forest, and we have many forest neighbors here: deer, fox, coyote, beaver, squirrel, and woodchuck to name but a few. Several years back, coyotes began to be seen more frequently in our village, perhaps because of increased efforts to restore the natural health of the river (we removed a dam that had created a dead zone in the river upstream from the dam), and the resulting increase in biodiversity helped to support more predators like coyotes and foxes. In the beginning, people were alarmed by the increased sightings of coyotes. Rumors and misinformation flooded social media with tales of coyote attacks, the risk to family pets and small children, and the like. There were calls for police to shoot the coyotes, or to hire professional trappers and hunters to relocate or kill the coyotes. For a number of residents, the coyotes were getting too close, too much at home in backyards and village streets.

What was difficult for some residents to accept was that the backyards and streets belonged to the coyotes, too. There was no scientific justification for the lurid tales and chain rattling about dangers from the coyotes. What was needed was a *political* response based in nature, a response that acknowledged and respected the coyotes' presence and importance to our village, in terms that recognized their ecological, aesthetic, and spiritual contributions to communal life. So, we went to work crafting a coyote policy based on science and an appreciation about the needs of both the coyotes and our residents. Research, consultation with outside experts, town halls, and extensive efforts to educate our residents about the actual lives, habits, and dangers of coyotes all coalesced into what became a cutting-edge policy for how to engage urban coyotes.[12]

One of the most telling aspects of the policy was that it was *our* behavior, not the coyotes, that needed changing. They are wild animals that don't distinguish between parks, forest, and backyards. If we wanted them to learn the difference, we had to teach them. Hiding behind a curtain clutching little Muffin wasn't going to cut it. We humans had to establish our boundaries just like the coyotes did in their world. And so, residents were taught how to haze coyotes in ways that required no violence or close interaction with the coyotes. Residents were taught not to leave food in their backyards for feral cats, which only attracted the coyotes. Although people remained rightly cautious in the presence of a coyote, they were now more willing to shout and wave their arms, shooing the coyote back to its part of our shared habitat.

Curiously, as the policy began to take hold, the calls to the police dropped, the tales of roving packs of coyotes mostly ceased (coyotes almost always hunt alone), and fears about pets and children being snatched from backyards waned. Now, years later, our residents have a different relationship with the coyote. Now people post photographs of coyotes on social media that include remarks about how beautiful they are. If people see a coyote with mange, they now express more concern about its well-being than fear. And, for their part, the coyotes have learned over time to keep their distance from their two-legged, loud, and arm-waving neighbors. The pact we have with the coyotes has become one of mutual respect and appreciation for our shared home. We have reached a political accord that benefits both species.

---

12. This policy was mainly driven by the research and work of Dr. Jill Mateo, a professor at the University of Chicago (online at *https://www.riverside.il.us/DocumentCenter/View/3105/Coyote-Policy-11-7-2018?bidId=*).

But what about the original sudden increase of sightings by residents of coyotes? It is possible that they had increased in numbers because of an improved habitat, but we don't know that for sure. Were there in fact more coyotes or was there some other reason that we suddenly started seeing them more frequently? Many Native American stories about the coyote deem it a Trickster. Some describe how the coyote stole fire from the sun and gave it to humans to benefit us. Was there a beneficial trick being played in the coyotes' appearance? This was in pre-Covid times when many residents were not paying a lot of attention to our natural environment. Oh, we bragged about Riverside's National Historic Landmark status and the importance of Olmsted, our central creation myth, but for the most part we were not conversant with the animals who lived among us. I cannot help but wonder if Coyote appeared to attract our attention, trying to rekindle some fire in us, to make us pay more attention to what really mattered, that nature was not "out there" but right here, alive and wild in our backyards and streets. Perhaps we initially feared Coyote because fear is appropriate when confronted with divinity, but once we acknowledged and respected its place among us, we in turn received a blessing.

If politics is what holds the ideas of human, nature, and animal together, then the word itself deserves a closer look. It comes from *politikon,* which in turn comes from *polis,* meaning city. "The word *polis* means in its etymological roots and cognates: throng, crowd, runny, connected for instance with *palude* (swamp), pour, flow, fill up, flood, overflow, swim, an innately plural meaning, e.g., poly, many."[13] The intimate connections of these roots and cognates of politics vivify and animate our ideas of human, nature, and animal. Polis is the flow of the many images that constitute us, the throng and crowd of ideas, fantasies, and visions that appear both in dreams and in the city streets with their overflowing flood of people that run and pour through them. We swim in their mix, part of the many that is the polis. Concrete and steel belie the swamp of moist earth that lies below (New Orleans and Chicago were literally

---

13. "Man is by Nature a Political Animal: Patient as Citizen," in *Uniform Edition of the Writings of James Hillman,* vol. 2: *City & Soul,* edited by Robert J. Leaver (Thompson, Conn.: Spring Publications, 2018 [2006]), 56.

built on swamps). Our souls are reflections of the polytheistic and polysemous soul of the polis that is inherently diverse and that fills us up with
possibilities and portents. Each human is a polis realized by their animal
nature that is fulfilled by the broader polis, microcosm and macrocosm
reverberating together just like the old ideas said. The polis releases us
into our deeper and broader being. Perhaps that is why so many people
dream of going to the city, drawn to the polis as that place where they can
achieve their potential and fulfill their destiny. How misguided we are
when we retreat to the wilderness, climb the mountain, or look within to
find ourselves when what we seek lies in the natural habitat of the political animal, the throbbing, pulsating polis.

If our souls are constituted by the polis, then to serve and care for our
souls we must first serve and care for the polis. The proper site for psychotherapy (*psyche-therapeia*) as soul-care, then, would no longer be the
quiet consulting room with drawn curtains, that most apt metaphor for
how we tend to think of the soul as isolated, withdrawn, and interior, but
rather the places where humans come together by the nature of our animal sensibilities, in our homes, villages, and cities. Soul-making happens
in the streets, in architecture and urban design, in the hustle and bustle
of commuter trains and crowded sidewalks at lunchtime. John Keats
famously wrote "Call the world if you Please 'The vale of Soul-making.'
Then you will find the use of the world."[14] But we have for too long mis-
construed his meaning. The use of the world is not for *our* soul-making,
but rather the *world*'s soul-making. This connects politics to the old idea
of an ensouled world, an *anima mundi.*[15]

It is not accidental that in our contemporary world the word "soul" was
tied directly to community, especially the black community. Soul food,
soul music, soul brothers and soul sisters all refer to that something extra,
a feeling, flavor, scent, beat, or rhythm that enriches communal bonds and
keeps them connected to ancestors. Soul-making takes place in the public

14. Letter to his brother George Keats, April 28, 1819, in *The Letters of John Keats, 1814–1821,* edited by Hyder Edward Rollins, 2 vols. (Cambridge, Mass.: The Har-vard University Press, 1958), 2: 102.

15. For an introduction to the idea of *anima mundi,* see James Hillman, *"Anima Mundi*: Return of the Soul to the World," *Spring: An Annual of Archetypal Psychology and Jungian Thought* (1982): 71–93.

sphere far more than in private contemplation. Soul needs the proliferation of images that the city provides, the diversity, the sights and smells,
the dangerous shadows, and the shocks to white-bread homogeneity. Soul,
like nature, abhors a vacuum, but this time the vacuum we create by turning away from the polis is a lack of images, a silencing and hollowing of
imagination. Yes, we each reverberate with images that we experience as
interior, but it is precisely this feeling that misleads us into thinking that
those images belong to us and can be subsumed within our own subjectivity. But the city will not permit such a reduction because it is so thoroughly not personal. The skyscrapers and alleyways, the shops with their
windows and awnings and displays, the polished businessperson and the
busker on the subway platform—they are as unneedy of our introspections
as are the mountains and valleys, the overstory and its underlings, and the
animals that inspirit there. Wherever in the sweep of nature we may go,
politics is a primary way, a *via regia*, of caring for soul.

We have been taught and trained, indoctrinated really, to think that
if we seek peace then we must find it in quiet solitude, in the absence
of tension or conflict. But peace of soul will not be achieved through
religious transcendence, philosophical explanations, scientific abstractions, or mediative practices that seek to eliminate the spontaneous flow
of images that irrepressibly fill the imagination, pushing aside the placa-
tions of the mind. Peace is not "inner" but is rather a political manifestation that belongs to the polis and that can only be achieved by appreciating, respecting, and coming to terms with the images found there. Please
note the move—it is *we* who must come to terms with *them*, the psyche's
naturally produced images, we who must give up our insular and isolating ways to once again be penetrated and enlivened by their imaginative
power and grace. Peace is not dull or static, the mere absence of conflict,
but is a divine presence (the Greeks called her Eirene). We will meet
Eirene again later, along with her sisters Dike, and Eunomia, and their
powerful mother Themis.

To care for anything means to help it become more beautiful, more
fully what it longs to be, by providing the support it needs to realize
its fate, its destiny. This kind of care requires more than concern and
encouragement, more than a regimen of policies and procedures, more
even than a sense of duty or responsibility. This kind of care requires

love. And nothing inspires love like beauty. When something is beautiful, we are drawn to it, and often come to love it. When we love something, we want to take care of it, to protect it, to make things possible for it that would not otherwise have been possible without our love and attention. This gives new life to the old saying that "politics is the art of the possible." It is through beauty that we help the polis attain what is possible by helping it to embrace a more encompassing vision about what it is and what it can be. The more this vision takes shape, the more deeply it is imagined, the more beautiful the polis becomes and the more it reveals its possibilities.

If our nature as political animals rests on aesthetics, then the main work of politics is to make the world more beautiful. Every aspect of politics would have to include aesthetic considerations. Artists would be as important in policy discussions as lawyers or engineers, and indeed lawyers and engineers would view their own work as necessarily including aesthetic dimensions. The very nature of political engagement would change as we attempt to find more beautiful ways to work through the disagreements and differences of opinion that are inevitable in public life. Instead of oppositions and conflicts we might see contrasts, different shades of meaning and understanding. Perhaps our political language would become more poetic, a return to the importance of rhetoric, and the artful use of metaphors. Just think how ugly our current political discussions are, how malformed, lacking in grace and so full of spite and innuendo. This is not just a matter of bad manners and insults. If we are by nature political animals, then when our politics are ugly, *we* are ugly. This ugliness weakens our animal natures and perpetuates the separation we feel from each other, from the other animals, and from nature itself.

This last point is critical. Plotinus wrote that "let the Soul fall in with the Ugly and at once it shrinks within itself, denies the thing, turns away from it, not accordant, resenting it." (*Enneads* 1.6.2) On the one hand, this instant, intuitive rejection of the ugly is a powerful aid because it elicits and energizes our animal response. Indeed, the rejection of the ugly might be one of the bases for how we perceive the good, bad, just, and unjust. But its harmful psychological effect, its *pathos,* is that we withdraw from the world and turn inward, which is what our controlling religious, philosophical, and psychological traditions unfortunately already want us to do. When we turn away from the world, soul loses the essential nourishment that the world provides. Better to stand firm and fight back against the ugly, meeting it face to face, and responding to its degrading and demeaning ways with aesthetic courage that lifts us out of the muck. This is the proper response of a political animal, an animal response that trusts its outrage in the face of the ugly, using its skill, cunning, and power to restore the polis to beauty. We need to remember that ugliness in the polis is a home invader, it seeks to come into where we live and deface its walls, weakening our foundations, making us more prone to collapse. It is bad enough not to recognize ugliness because that shows how anesthetized we have become, but to be apathetic in the presence of ugliness, to recognize its challenge and then turn away, is far worse. We cannot afford aesthetic cowardice. By failing the beauty of the polis, we betray our own souls.

As political animals, then, we must learn, or relearn, that our aesthetic instincts are our surest guides when it comes to life within the polis. Street smarts extend beyond knowing which sections of town to avoid. We instinctively know that if something is ugly it will not benefit the polis regardless of the promise of lower costs or increased efficiencies. Indeed, these latter two culprits lay at the base of so much ugliness. We are so used to our political discussions being dominated by economic concerns or bureaucratic definitions of productivity that we allow them to overpower our aesthetic sensibilities to discern the good from the bad, the just from the unjust. But I remain convinced that those sensibilities are still there, bred in our animal bones, given with the visceral wisdom of the heart, which for eons was recognized as the central organ of aesthetic and erotic perception. That is why the heart swells and the pulse quickens when touched by beauty and love, and why the heart shrinks and breaks when ugliness prevails. Only through beauty can we restore our natures as political animals by having the unrelenting courage to insist that political judgments at their core are first aesthetic discernments. Politics is the art of making beauty and thereby making soul, and only through beauty and soul can we more fully realize the polis. And only when the polis is properly served can the political animals that live there also partake in the aesthetic splendor of an ensouled world.

TWO

Self and Community

If we are by nature aesthetic and political animals, if we naturally desire beauty and joining together, then why is our current politics so ugly and so fraught with division? We don't have to look far to see how ugly and extreme our current political state of affairs has become. In cable news, talk radio, social media, and at the family dinner table, fundamental, and fundamentalist, lines are drawn, and conversations quickly deteriorate to arguments and accusations. At the same time, the quest for personal identity seems to be more and more desperate and the different concepts by which people can define themselves seem to proliferate daily.[1] And through it all there are demands at the extremes for purity of ideology and unwavering allegiance to inflexible and unwavering principles. All choices are either/or, for or against. To be with me you must agree with me completely. Failure to strictly adhere to the faith means condemnation and expulsion from the tribe.

I think that our politics are in disarray because of how we think about ourselves as individuals and especially of how we think about the "self." The Western idea of the self, and especially as it is conceptualized in the United States, is that each person is an individual that has, or rather *is,* an interior, subjective reality that is available only to that person's individual reflection and introspection. According to this belief, and that is what it is—a belief—I know myself in a way that is unattainable by you. Even though we share a common language, you can still never know my innermost thoughts and feelings the way that I know them. The "self" that I am belongs only to me and so can only be defined by me. Descartes

---

1. For a history of the modern meaning of "identity," see Gerald Izenberg, *Identity: The Necessity of a Modern Idea* (Philadelphia: University of Pennsylvania Press, 2016).

said, "I think, therefore I am," and the Western Self says, "I am what I think I am." Popeye as metaphysics.

This way of thinking about the self necessarily leads to the idea of "others" that are defined precisely as not me. And, just as I cannot be known to them in the same manner that I know myself, so, too, they remain ultimately a mystery to me, existentially separate and apart. Philosophy and psychology have long struggled with the strained relationship between self and others but what is significant for us is how this belief in a secret self plays out given our nature as aesthetic and political animals.

It is one thing to say that you cannot know my inner thoughts and feeling in the same manner as I do. Certainly, you are not privy to the words I "hear" inside my mind. But it is quite another to claim that my personal view of myself is the only correct view of who and what I am, or that my personal sense of myself is superior to and deserves priority over the views of others. And yet that is the American way of individualism. The individual, usually described as "rugged," is the lone hero who walks to his own drummer, unmindful and uncaring about what others might think of him. I don't care what other people think, we say, as if this is a statement of individual courage and moral standing instead of political depravity. My identity is what I say it is because only *I* get to say who and what I am. As an individual self I remain locked away within my personal subjectivity. It is my unalienable right to be alone.

And yet we all have known people who were radically wrong in their personal view of themselves. We have known people who thought of themselves as good people although their actions showed them to be selfish and uncaring. In fact, if we reflect for even a moment, we will likely recall times in our own lives when others have pointed out things to us about ourselves that were contrary to our sense of ourselves, perhaps painfully so. One of the great benefits of psychotherapy, and indeed friendship, is to have another person help us to see through the fantasies that we have about ourselves, and to reveal the lies that we tell ourselves. Each of us carry unfounded self-criticisms and doubts that haunt and restrain us, illusions and delusions of grandeur, narcissistic reflections, and paranoid suspicions. And yet we insist on proclaiming that our secret self is the only true self and that only I can determine who I am. We believe, to use Aristotle's term, that we are "self-sufficing" and exist separate from the polis and indeed from nature itself. It is up to us as free-willed, self-made, and self-actualized individuals that we choose to join with others in common cause. The individual comes first, and it is through individual choice that society is created. But even if we choose to join a community, or partake in what we call "interpersonal relationships," we always retain the option to turn away and retreat into our essential insularity, not no human an island, but every human an island.

I have a different view. I think that the voices we hear in our minds are not trustworthy precisely because we hear them in our minds. Even though the voices we hear are many and varied, even though they are often in disagreement, and even though they often seem to come out of nowhere, we still insist that they arise from within our individual self and that they belong to me, to my mind. We have no other way of thinking or imagining these voices that we hear. They *must* be mine because whose else could they be? And even though the voices be many, they must ultimately be subjected to my singular individuality—*e pluribus unum*. This inability to imagine the individual differently, this deep repression of what we actually experience as the soul's autonomy and power, is at the heart of our discontent. It is our *idea* of the individual, subjective self that is disordered. And because we have isolated the self from the world by proclaiming it a secret possession of the subjectivized individual, we cannot help but hear only the echoes of our own beliefs. Philosophy calls for us to "Know thyself," but then has us look exactly where thyself cannot be, in a mind abstracted from the world, each individual adrift and wandering alone amidst the dead fields of *res extensa,* listening to us talk to ourselves, a sure sign of madness.

This deranged idea of the self and individual as inner, isolated, and secret leaves us unable to imagine a truly social context for our lives and our being. When we divide the world into subjective and objective poles and then declare the self to belong to the former, we merely parrot Descartes's catastrophic error. This definition, reduction really, of a person to a subjective self that is separate from an objective world proclaimed soulless and dead runs contrary to our nature as political animals. As political animals we must be intimately engaged with the world as mutually ensouled. My soul can then no longer be reduced to a single idea of personal individuality, or identity, or self. It becomes unclear where my soul ends and the world soul, the *anima mundi,* begins.

When we separate soul from the world by declaring it a personal possession, we deprive soul the substantiality it must have as a worldly presence. In return, as individuals we become unable to sense and appreciate the soul of the world that shines forth in each thing. This numbing of the soul in its response to the world is a beauty disorder, and when we lose our ability to perceive and appreciate beauty, we lose our ability to love, the erotic impulse that is the source of our deep desire to form bonds with one another, to be political animals. The idea of an isolated individual possessing a secret self and a private soul thus becomes a self-fulfilling prophecy resulting in the very isolation it predicts.

I am suggesting that we are not isolated selves and that we are not solely, or even mainly, constituted by the thoughts, feelings, and emotions that we have posited as an inner reality called the Self. The Self is an illusion that requires us to look for concepts by which we can conjure a sense of identity. Because the idea of a subjective self denies our nature as political animals, we must then try to find replacements for the nature that we deny. The problem is compounded when we imagine the self in terms of wholeness, homogeneity, unity, and sameness (the etymological meaning of "identity"). We talk of the self as our core, and so to find ourselves we must be centered, balance, aligned—all of those things that psychotherapy and meditative practices say that we should be. But in that little "should" lies a demon. The idea of the self contains a hidden a moral claim about how we should be according to standards determined by the idea of the self. This self-referential circularity reveals in conceptual form how the idea of the self defends against all other ways of imagining a person and their relationship to the greater world. The idea of the self circles the wagons, closes the doors, and draws the shades, determined to stay subjective, interior, and alone.

By defining ourselves as isolated individuals having a centralized self, we repress our natures as political animals. Because we do not conceive of ourselves as inherently pluralistic, as a community of images that cohere to present our unique form to the greater world, we must therefore attempt to find that diversity through the illusion of individual choice. And so we begin collecting groups to self-create an identity—white, male, heterosexual, Irish, Catholic, Democrat. Or we self-identify with ideologies and beliefs, buttressed by core principles and values that establish where we stand. And because we imbue these choices with the power to create and sustain our identities, we must zealously guard them against any doubt or challenge. *It is our misshapen idea of the individual as a secret self that is at the heart of our cultural and political tribalism and that fuels our fundamentalist rage.* The proliferation of labels and categories generated by the idea of individual identity is trying to show us that no number of labels and categories can ever generate a real identity because identity as undifferentiated unity is not real. The symptoms are trying to direct us to their own resolution by showing us that we need different ways of imagining who and what we are. Identity wants sameness, and so we listen to the same voice over and over again, what Descartes called the *cogito* and Freud called the *ego,* and we call the *self.* The result is a tyranny over the many voices that actually constitute soul, a repression of the polis that claims us that then returns as the ugliness that dominates our politics and derails our attempts at community.

So long as we think of ourselves as isolated, singular, individual selves we can never truly belong anywhere. That is the tension we feel when we keep adding more groups to the list that we think defines us. We are trying to do what by nature we long to do, to join together in common cause, held by bonds of affection, and the sharing of communal spirits and ancestors. But because of how we have defined ourselves we remain paranoid and unable to truly connect. The repression of our nature as political animals is so deep that we actually fear that if we drop the walls that we have made for ourselves that we will lose ourselves, become dissolved into the cosmos, ransacked by the invading hordes that wait beyond the walls. Is this not the fear of every tyrant, every centralized form of government? To share power or to let in the many can lead only to chaos. The answer is to tighten the grip. The answer is war.

Our identities, if they exist at all, do not belong solely, or even mainly, to us. We exist most fully in the imaginations of others, and others know far more about us than we know about ourselves. We are not centered but eccentric, each of us odd, unusual, and therefore beautiful. Although we might think that we hear only one dominant voice within, that is because we have chosen to listen only to that one voice. If we quiet that voice, we will hear a vibrant community of voices having all manner of viewpoints. Even more powerfully, when we dream, we encounter the vast richness of images that pervade our soul. In Greek myth, although a story might be about a particular god or goddess, the rest of the pantheon was always there by implication. So, too, for us the myriad fantasies, dreams, reflections are always ongoing even if we are not consciously aware of them. We are not aware of their influence, but others can see them expressed in our faces and flitting behind our eyes. It is the polis that sees our animal presence far better than we can. Only others can ever see all of us at once. Our so-called personal view is always partial, always limited by our perspective, like looking in a mirror. That is why we exist more fully in our reputations than in our private thoughts about ourselves. Only others can witness our lives, watch our actions, read our characters, and discern our styles. It is the imagination of us by others that affords us the possibility of being who and what we are. And so, to not care about what other people think or say about us is to not care about the only source that can help us realize our natures as political animals. To know thyself we must open ourselves to the imaginations of others. If we look to what the world asks of us and how others respond to us, then we learn about what we afford the world and what we can contribute to the polis. To find who and what we are requires less introspection and more extrospection.

Instead of a singular, private individuality defined by the self through its choices, what if we were to imagine our souls as communities, full of ancestors, memories, fantasies, personified presences, dreams, animals, places, ideas, values, and reflections? As W. H. Auden, wrote, "We are lived by powers we pretend to understand."[2] It is the soul's spontaneous creation of fantasy that coalesces in us as individuals, allowing us to appear to the imaginations of others, and that is felt as destiny. We do not have souls, soul has us. Here I suggest that each person is a polis that is intimately connected with the greater polis that lies beyond the person in the inhuman reaches of the soul.

If we pay attention to our "inner" imaginings, we will find that some aspects seem to endure over time, that we hear familiar voices that have been with us for as long as we can remember. Other images are transient, staying only for a while, like a dream that fades so quickly upon waking.

---

2. "In Memory of Ernst Toller," in *The Collected Poetry of W. H. Auden* (New York: Random House, 1945), 125.

Still others are wholly strange, radically different, seemingly not of ourselves at all but having an autonomy and power that cannot be reduced to any idea or feeling that we might have about ourselves. This is the natural diversity that we see mirrored in the greater world, a diversity not of our making and not subject to our dominion. And yet our interior community is inseparably engaged with and at least partly constituted by the greater polis. From this perspective, what we want to call individuality is the unique, idiosyncratic manner in which these two communities mutually interact. Imagining the soul as at least partly the interiorization of the polis includes the *anima mundi,* thereby restoring soul to politics and politics to soul.

But what about those familiar, enduring images that stay with us over time to the extent that they seem to be uniquely ours? They do seem to be remarkably consistent. Certainly, the ideas that I have as an elder are better formed and crafted than those of my youth, just as my mature character is more refined than that of my younger years. But there is nonetheless something familiar about them, something that has been there from the beginning, a kind of impulse or impetus that has carried and pushed and pulled me along, a sameness that has remained through the vagaries of life, a sameness that perhaps even loves me. The Greeks called this enduring tutelary spirit that is given with a person's life the *daimon.* Here is another way of imagining the sameness that we seek to reduce to personal identity—sameness not as definition but as destiny. My sameness is how my unique, odd, eccentric, and peculiar soul endures through and outside of time, how it comprises my longings and irresistible passions, how it shows me what I must do and what I must avoid. It is what the mentor, or the parent, or the friend sees in us far more clearly than we can see, and usually before we can see. Our mortal attempt to define the self cannot help but pale before the soul's destiny, which is more than human and even outstrips the gods. Not even the gods of the great pantheon were privy to the threads of Fate. Our destiny is born of soul, revealed through life, and resolved in death.[3]

------

3. For an extended discussion of the idea of the *daimon* and soul's destiny, see James Hillman, *The Soul's Code: In Search of Character and Calling* (New York: Random House, 1996).

I share this call of destiny with the other members of the polis. I like to imagine that the other voices that I hear within have their destinies, too, which I have somehow been graced to participate in and enjoy. They don't belong to me, but they are here with me. We are joined together, fellow political animals alive within a shared polis, seeking to flourish, to not only live but to live well. That is why it is so critical that we listen to the images that inhabit and visit us, that we remain alert for the influence of the ancestors who can teach us so much about the responsibility of answering our call, as well as attending to the aspirations of the generations yet to come, because they will someday turn to us in memory, asking for our guidance.

When I was elected village president, I suddenly felt fuller. I think sometimes politicians get full of themselves because they mistake the source of this fullness. They think that the fullness comes from within themselves, that they are big shots. But the fullness comes from without. The citizens of the polis are the source and enduring energy of the public official's sense of fullness. The polis is the source of all authority and power and in return for this temporary loan the official is granted the opportunity to craft the polis in the most beautiful manner possible. As president I was both responsible *for* the residents and their well-being and responsible *to* the residents to provide the best political leadership that I could. It was a partnership. It was my job as the titular leader of the village to help the broader community imagine Riverside more fully in terms of its destiny, its longing, and what it was striving to become.

To do this I read history about our village and the surrounding region, took walks through the forest and along our streets, watched birds, talked with residents in the aisles of the local grocery store, thought about the ancient beach that once cut through the village, and imagined the indigenous people who called this place home long before the first Europeans arrived in the seventeenth century. And I thought, too, about the generations to come, represented by the young families who move to Riverside to make a home and raise their children. I was an elder who would someday be an ancestor, just as those young families would grow to be elders and watch the cycle renew. The living people of a polis come and go, but there is a deeper image of a polis that endures through time as it passed from hand to hand. Each generation has the opportunity, in its own time, to increase the beauty of the polis and thereby deepen its soul. It is a sacred trust.

A polis is not a collection of individual, isolated, selves that come together purely through personal choice. A polis is an ecology of imagination, a diverse array of images that cohere to create a habitat that does more than merely sustain the lives of the people who come together to contribute to the polis. People as political animals come together for more than just security or survival or selfish genes. A polis exists to blossom, to echo the calls of ancestors, to propitiate the gods and spirits of the place, to honor the animals who grace it with their presence, and to reveal and display itself more and more beautifully over time.

The revelation of soul and intensification of beauty that occurs when a polis is properly attended to by its members requires proper vessels to contain it. Some of these vessels are the ideas that we use to think about the polis. Ideas like good and bad, just and unjust, beauty and ugliness, have been the around for millennia and are the source of endless philosophical debates. Other ideas seem to slip into our thinking about the polis with less reflection and get applied by rote. We have touched in passing how economics, efficiency, and productivity so often become the habitual standards by which political and policy decisions are made. The default judgments in those ideas are that cheaper is better than expensive, faster is better than slower, and more is better than less. Two related ideas that are often similarly applied to the polis without much thought are growth and development. Growth is taken to be good, and development is considered necessary to insure a vibrant polis. These last two ideas, that belong as much to psychology as to politics, deserve a closer look.

In the natural world, perpetual growth does not exist. Even the universe, according to the cosmologists, will only expand to a certain point before receding. Unimpeded growth is cancerous, revealing itself in the polis as urban sprawl and soulless subdivisions. Development, too, becomes problematic when it is conceived linearly or in terms of constant progress. Constant growth and development as perpetual progress are unnatural ideas that are as inappropriate for the polis as they are for the soul. Like all natural things, the polis ebbs and flows, things come and go, live and die. The red leaves of autumn are as necessary as the green sprouts of spring. It is natural for the polis to sometimes lie dormant and even regress. Heraclitus wrote that the "soul has its own principle of growth," and so we must be careful of trying to impose our ideas of growth and development on the polis.[4] The polis is both historical and outside of history, the way a painting appears all at once and we cannot tell which brush stroke came before the next. That is why political life is so endlessly fascinating and mysterious. Politics keeps us in the vale of soul-making, contributing daily to the *anima mundi* as it is presented in our particular place and time, and helping the polis to manifest its destiny. And yet, at the same time, we can never know how things will turn out. All we can do is strive for beauty.

The more a person can appreciate and contribute to the beauty of a community and feel its aesthetic uniqueness, the more fully realized the community will become and the more the person will feel a sense of belonging. It is important to remember that community is always tied to a particular place that is neither abstract nor transcendent. That is why ideologies cannot make community, because they are by nature displaced and free-floating and therefore prone to excess. Ideologies both exclude others while at the same time being inherently imperialistic. Because they believe in their righteousness, they seek to constantly expand their control and influence. In this sense ideologies are antithetical to community.

Real community grounds the soul by giving it a place to put down roots and to flourish. Just as the polis affords people possibilities and potentials they would not otherwise have, so, too, people afford the polis opportunities to be more deeply and fully realized. Psyche or soul has always been associated with depth and deepening; it belongs to the valleys and shades, not to the peaks and arid brightness. And so, a community must grow *down* if it is to grow up, just as the deepening of soul over time contributes to maturity, wisdom, and fullness of being. As political animals we can contribute to this deepening by honoring and maintaining the polis in all its aspects, visible and invisible. We can care for the land that supports our homes and buildings and nourishes the flora and fauna, land that also contains the bodies and memories of our ances-

---

4. Philip Wheelwright, *Heraclitus* (Princeton, N.J.: Princeton University Press, 1959), 58.

tors. We can find better ways to live in concert with our natural environment, reducing our negative impact on the greater world. And we can maintain and beautify our public facilities and infrastructure, not only to allow for their continued use by us, but to demonstrate *to them* our shared respect for their importance.

In Riverside we have a large park called Swan Pond that sits right beside the Des Plaines River. It is in a flood plain and is naturally a wetland. At some point, however, many of the native plants were removed and a section of Swan Pond was turned into a soccer field. It of course continued to flood in heavy rain events, so the soccer field was sometimes underwater. The cost of mowing the soccer field added to the overall maintenance cost for the park, which was also mowed but not quite as manicured as the soccer field was. The entire situation was, to me, untenable. We were trying to force a natural wetland into being something it wasn't. To make matters worse, an earlier village board had constructed a narrow asphalt path alongside the river that was barely wide enough for two people to walk on side by side. The asphalt path regularly failed during the floods as the ground was washed out from underneath it.

As the rain events and their accompanying flooding increased, we finally decided that enough was enough. We brought in consultants to work with our village forester on reestablishing the area as a natural wetland. A careful selection of native plants was chosen, and an initial planting plan was designed. It took a few years to get established, but now Swan Pond is increasingly what it is naturally meant to be. We still mow small paths so that residents and visitors can walk through the grasses and plants. During the summer, the entire area is buzzing with dragonflies, pollinators, butterflies, and grasshoppers. You can see them hovering and glistening in the sunlight. Frogs are back, along with other critters that thrive in the wetland. It's a magical place and one of the loveliest spots in the village.

Next, we decided to deal with that ugly asphalt path by replacing it with something new. We were fortunate to have a very skilled public works director who also shared our aesthetic desire to construct something that was both beautiful and engineered in a way to withstand the floods. He advocated strongly for an exposed aggregate concrete that he said would better complement the natural setting. We also widened the path to ten feet, which would not only allow for greater pedestrian and cycling use, but would, if necessary, allow emergency vehicles to have access to the riverfront. To address the inevitable flooding, the path was engineered with deeper footing to prevent erosion. And lastly native limestone was brought in to build terraced access points in low areas where the river first flowed into Swan Pond during a flood. These areas provide access for fishing and canoe launching in good weather, and facilitate the ingress and egress of flood waters, thereby further protecting the new path.

The path itself meanders and flows alongside the river as if an extension of it, and the exposed aggregate has a warmth and visual interest that delights the eye. The result is that both residents and visitors from surrounding communities have flocked to walk and bike the path with the river on one side of them and a beautiful wetland on the other side. Entire families stroll together on the wider path and its undulating form pulls the eye forward to scan the trees to which hawks, osprey, and eagles have returned. Even residents who had initially been opposed to the new path came to the village board to express their pleasure with how beautifully it had turned out. Swan Pond feels reborn.

By devoting ourselves to doing right by Swan Pond and working to restore its natural integrity, we were rewarded with a stronger sense of community. Swan Pond is perhaps the only natural setting in our village where we get to greet a diversity of visitors from other communities through a shared love of natural beauty. Children play, skipping rocks, while elders sit in the sun and watch the river flow by. The renovation of Swan Pond is a source of civic pride and an example of how beauty contributes to social interaction. And from the beginning it was specifically conceived and intended as an aesthetic communal act dedicated to restoring a part of the polis that had been inadvertently misused. Swan Pond is happy again.

To help complement the new path, we had our public works department clear a path along the riverfront so residents and visitors alike could walk the entire length of the river in Riverside. By drawing people to the river that was our namesake I hoped also to rekindle an appreciation for it as our spiritual focus. The river was more than just a natural happenstance. Olmsted saw this when he imagined our curvilinear streets. And the indigenous people who came before turned to the river and all that it provided for sustenance that went beyond food and water.

None of this was cheap. But because of the energy and interest the project created, the village government and staff were able to pay for it almost entirely with grant funding. Nonetheless, we never allowed the cost to overshadow the greater goal. Yes, a brushed concrete path would have been less expensive, but our public works director kept emphasizing how the appearance of such a path would be radically different. Brushed cement was too uniform, too plain and uninteresting, and therefore unbefitting the place. Great care was taken in the landscape design to ensure the native plantings would thrive, and we knew that the engineering for the path had to address the impact of repeated flooding—but as we addressed these practical concerns the focus for the entire project was always beauty.

Another small example: We have a small log cabin in a park known as Indian Gardens that is used for private parties, scout meetings, and the like. The area was named Indian Gardens because it was settled by indigenous people long before Europeans showed up. Some sections of Indian Gardens were burial grounds. We worked with a local artist to create a map of Riverside that showed the location of the settlements and burial grounds, along with the names of the tribes that had settled there. Also on the map are places that were significant in Riverside's early history, a trading post present before Riverside's founding, river fords used by indigenous people and later settlers to cross the river, an old orchard now covered with homes and lawns. Because the cabin is used primarily for gatherings of children, we wanted to have a colorful, interesting way of drawing their attention, and imagination, to the people who were here long ago. It was our way of giving the ancestors a visible presence, a way of educating our children of their unseen heritage. Educate means to "lead out," and the goal was to lead their young, vibrant imaginations out into their natural surroundings and to show them that nature contains not only plants and animals, but also spirits and memories. Again, this was a direct use of aesthetics to propitiate the soul of the place, to honor the dead and vivify their presence as ongoing participants in our community.

As a community, one way we declare what matters to us is by how we allocate and spend our tax dollars. Every village budget is a quantified testament of shared values, whereby we put numbers to our ideals. Budgets are spiritual documents despite their secular garb of charts and graphs. We allocate our communal funds to ensure that all parts of the community receive the attention they deserve. And these allocations will change with circumstances and needs, the community necessarily arranging priorities differently over time. This is similar to how the ancients attended to the gods—none could be neglected but there were times when some took precedence over others. When we maintain our communities, we pay homage to the gods that the ancients said were in all things. That is why maintenance is such a vital part of communal life. The etymology of "maintain" is to hold in the hand, or, more likely, to hold *by* the hand. When we maintain the visible and invisible structures of our community we move together, hand in hand, toward a common destiny. There is nothing so mundane that it is not also sacred. It is only when we fail to imagine things fully that we lose sight of their radiance, their divine beauty.

Here we expand and deepen the meaning of community by emphasizing the importance of care and devotion over duty and obligation. Community ultimately rests on love, and when you love something, you want to take care of it, and to help it become more fully beautiful through your attention and appreciation. Each person within a community will have their own unique ways of contributing to this care according to their talents, attributes, and abilities. It is this communal sharing of care and devotion that we feel as belonging. And note that these are selfless acts, freely given without hope of reciprocity or personal benefit. *The path to community begins with leaving the self behind.* "Real community," Hillman once said, "does not develop out of the neediness of individuals, but rather out of their desire and ability to contribute."[5]

How different this is from having to sign onto agendas, or pledge allegiance to ideologies, or profess tenets of faith! The devotion we give to the polis is freely given because the polis deserves it. We care about it because it is worth caring about. We love it because it is beautiful and so

---

5. "The Soul of the Matter: James Hillman in Conversation with Wes Nisker," *Inquiring Mind* 11, no. 2 (Spring 1995) (online at *https://www.inquiringmind.com/article/1102_8_hillman-soul-of-matter/*).

attracts our love and ignites our desire to attend to its becoming. Each of our destinies includes our service to the polis, and it is only through the selfless giving of that service that community may flourish and our common destinies be revealed.

THREE

The Aesthetic Citizen

As citizens we are accustomed to accepting certain duties and obligations. We obey the law, pay taxes, serve on juries, and the like. But what are our aesthetic responsibilities? If the polis is best served through beauty and the deepening of soul, then our aesthetic responsibilities are of paramount importance. What does it mean to be an aesthetic citizen? What would aesthetic citizenship, activism, advocacy, or protest look like?

The first step toward aesthetic citizenship is perhaps the most difficult—paying attention. We are so used to introspection and self-interest that it is hard to sustain an outward gaze and to appreciate what is going on around us. Paying attention means opening our senses to the greater world, feeling its sensuality and being embraced by its inherent intelligibility. The things of the world are constantly presenting themselves to us with great particularity, each thing a unique presence with specific qualities and characteristics. Whether it is the morning sky that portends the day, or a dripping faucet that slowly erodes our patience, the world calls upon our senses, asking to be attended to.

I have written elsewhere that "We are by nature aesthetic animals that exist to appreciate beauty, to create beauty, and to be beautiful. That is all the world asks of us. Nothing more is required."[1] With this as a backdrop, an aesthetic citizen therefore exists to appreciate the polis, and, to the extent of their talents and abilities, to increase its beauty. One way an aesthetic citizen can increase the beauty of the polis is by maintaining and cultivating their own beauty through civil and decorous conduct. Few things brighten a person's beauty more than displays of kindness and respect toward their fellow citizens. This dedication to beauty is at the heart of aesthetic citizenship.

---

1. Benjamin Sells, *Return to Beauty: Restoring the Ecology of Imagination* (Putnam, Conn.: Spring Publications, 2022), 11.

Attending to the world aesthetically means paying close attention to things as particulars, each thing having its own integrity and unique characteristics. Just as important, however, and politics certainly teaches us this, is paying attention to the relationships among things. All things exist in relationship with others, and it is by carefully and lovingly paying attention to those relationships that we find out what things are like, what their capabilities and potentials are, and what they afford and make possible for the greater world. Hillman wrote that an image always implicates "a precise context, mood, and scene," and we can apply this imaginal perspective to how we care for the polis through our aesthetic sensibilities.[2] By imagining the polis we are able to both appreciate the particularity and integrity of its many members while also holding them together within a broader context, feeling the communal power that they entail.

This latter point is important. Appreciating other members of the polis as fellow aesthetic citizens inspires a move beyond tolerance to actually taking pleasure in the many differences the polis offers. Tolerance is always begrudging (its etymology means "to bear or endure"), whereas appreciation draws us to a desire for diversity and pluralism. Appreciation leads to delight and welcoming embraces, to enjoying the multiple viewpoints, lifestyles, and cultures that make the polis interesting and invigorating. An aesthetic citizen savors a polis of many tastes, textures, smells, and styles. The more varied the menu the better.

Paying attention to things also includes paying attention to our individual aesthetic reactions and responses. An aesthetic citizen learns to trust their animal responses, whether we are drawn to something or repelled by it. This is not a matter of subjective opinion, but an instinctive response that precedes subjectivity. And this instinctive response is not limited to physical objects, but is there in how we encounter ideas, policies, organizational structures, urban design—all of the various things that go into making and sustaining a polis. What is important here is to not limit the nature of our responses to intellectual or conceptual responses. Aesthetic responses are animal responses, they are fully

---

2. James Hillman, "An Inquiry into Image," *Spring: An Annual of Archetypal Psychology and Jungian Thought* (1977): 62.

embodied, bred in our bones, felt in our hearts, rumbling in our gut, and reacted to in our muscular reflexes. Aesthetic responses are not ephemeral but grounding, not abstract or transcendent but sensually, immediately present.

It might help here to recall that "aesthetic" comes to us from the Greeks. *Aisthesis* goes back to *aiou* and *aisthou* that both mean "to perceive" and have the root meaning of "taking in," "breathing in," "gasp," and "struggle for breath."[3] Although modern translators equate *aisthesis* with "sense perception," that meaning "cannot be understood without taking into account the Greek goddess of the senses [Aphrodite] or the organ of Greek sensation, the heart, and the root in the word—that sniffing, gasping, breathing in of the world."[4] This kind of aesthetic response is the quick up-taking of breath, the *ahhh* we express when we encounter a wild animal in the woods, or recognize a familiar face when traveling far from home. Aesthetic citizenship is by nature Aphroditic, in service to beauty. One of Aphrodite's epithets is Aphrodite Pandemos, which means "common to, or of all the people." According to Pausanias, when Theseus united the scattered villages into the Athenian city-state, he established the cults of Aphrodite Pandemos and of Persuasion and erected statues of them.[5] According to this view, it is Aphrodite's beauty and sensuality that gives rise to our natures as aesthetic and political animals. It is thus through devotion to beauty that we best serve the polis.

Aesthetic citizenship is an ongoing process and cannot be limited to a narrow understanding of politics and the polis. Politics extends far beyond electoral politics or the halls of government. Politics exists wherever we engage the world aesthetically. That means that politics cannot be limited to our interactions with people but must naturally extend to all aspects of daily life. Our relationships with nature, the other animals, and our human-made objects are all aesthetic and therefore political.

---

3. Richard Broxton Onians, *The Origins of European Thought: About the Body, the Mind, the Soul, the World, Time, and Fate* (Cambridge: Cambridge University Press, 1989), 74 and n. 6.

4. James Hillman, *The Thought of the Heart and the Soul of the World* (Thompson, Conn: Spring Publications, 2021 [1992]), 35.

5. Pausanias, *Description of Greece,* vol. 1, translated by W. H. S. Jones, Loeb Classical Library 93 (Cambridge, Mass.: Harvard University Press, 1918), 109.

When we engage ideas, or imagine, dream, and reflect we are giving form to our political natures. And so, it matters greatly how we relate to the greater world because our actions necessarily implicate and affect the polis, for both good and bad.

The buzzing fluorescent lights that desecrate so many workplaces, the ice water that deadens our palates before we have our first bite of dinner, the blitzkrieg of consumerism and the daily barrage of advertising, the loss of greater vision by focusing on tiny screens, flowing conversation reduced to thumb-tapped texts—all of these serve daily to weaken the polis. Part of our responsibility as aesthetic citizens is to stand up against such offenses and to call them out for their trespasses. Two examples come to mind. Many years ago, I was having dinner with James Hillman at a restaurant in Santa Barbara, California. It was toward the end of our meal, and we were chatting when a young server came to the table and reached for James's plate while asking "are you still working on this?" That was a mistake. James bristled and replied, "I do not *work* on my dinner, I enjoy it." The second example comes from my friend Thomas Moore, the author of *Care of the Soul* among many other wonderful books. I heard Tom on an interview when he was on the book tour for *Care of the Soul* and the interviewer commented that with all of the interviews and book signings that Tom was doing that "his batteries must be low." Tom did not like that and rather pointedly said "I don't have batteries."

In neither case did the people asking the questions mean any harm or disrespect. But therein lies the problem. Both questions betray a style of imagining that is contrary to beauty and soul-making. The first question shows how unconsciously ingrained in our thinking are images of economics and productivity, such that we "work" on a meal. The second shows how often we liken ourselves to machines instead of animals. When we think of consciousness or memory in terms of computers, we make a similar mistake. These metaphors reveal habits of the mind that are ugly and inappropriate, and both James and Tom were right to call them out. In both instances their responses were aesthetic and political at the same time, and in their own ways James and Tom were practicing psychotherapy on the polis, trying to free it from unconscious biases that work contrary to beauty and soul-making. Their responses were acts of aesthetic activism and protest.

The instinctive bristling of both James and Tom is instructive for aesthetic citizenship. One of the ways we repress beauty within the polis is by associating beauty solely with pleasure and pleasantries, as if beauty is all pretty faces and sunsets. This view denigrates the great power inherent in aesthetic responses. Outrage and anger, too, are aesthetic responses that boil up to resist ugliness and injustice. Aesthetic citizenship has no allegiance to the status quo, but instead is constantly on the lookout for better, more beautiful ways to more fully realize the polis and its possibilities. And when it finds those ways, it is ready to advocate, push, and, if necessary, demand that they be given voice. Beauty has always had the ability to stir the emotions and heat the blood and so it is naturally suited to rousing people up to resist what it finds to be inappropriate or unduly restrictive. Aphrodite was beautiful, yes, but she could also be fearsome if riled up.

When we start paying attention to things and appreciating their interactions and relationships with other things, we quickly come to see that the world is incredibly diverse and complex. That means that our political sensibilities need to match this diversity and complexity, like treating like. Aesthetic citizenship therefore inherently resists ideologies that would attempt to limit the spontaneous creativity that has always been associated with the soul. An aesthetic citizen is innately wary of attempts to reduce diversity or pluralism. Instead of trying to make one out of the many, aesthetic citizenship wants to foster and encourage the many, always asking for more perspectives and viewpoints. Not a melting pot but a gumbo, all of the ingredients working together while retaining their individual nuances and flavors. Homogeneity cannot sustain a polis, which by its very nature is multiple, varied, and many-colored. It is no accident that the history of segregation, red lining, discrimination, and voter suppression is so characterized by ugliness. The ignorance, hate, and bigotry they reflect are of course affronts to human dignity and equality, but they are also aesthetic offenses that attempt to deny and restrict the inherent diversity and beauty of the polis.

Aesthetic citizenship champions diversity and pluralism and seeks to foster an inclusive, welcoming community. It finds beauty in providing equal access to opportunities and resources and is especially interested in reaching out to those on the margins. Policies that systematically exclude some members, or that justify income, racial, or gender inequality are to be rejected on aesthetic grounds. Beauty intensifies a being's presence and integrity. Ugliness diminishes what it touches. This is another aspect of aesthetic citizenship—it is inherently participatory. When we pay attention to things aesthetically, we become involved with them. The Swiss zoologist Adolf Portmann once wrote that "to observe means to study every detail lovingly, to dwell upon these minute structures, not to be rushing from one thing to another with a hasty glance as it catches the eye."[6] This erotic component of aesthetic citizenship leads us to ask others to similarly participate in community and to ensure that there are safeguards in place to encourage and facilitate their participation. Aesthetic citizenship favors policies that promote participation in the polis.

Note, too, in Portmann's nice statement that the kind of observation he is describing "dwells" and does not rush from one thing to another in haste. This slowing of attention is one of the gifts of beauty. It asks us to linger, pause, caress. Aesthetic citizenship offers an alternative to the cult of always being busy and the crazy drive of manic productivity. The constant drive to do more and to do it quickly runs contrary to aesthetic citizenship. Little wonder that studies indicate that attention deficit disorder is on the rise in the United States. Aesthetic citizenship would look for ways to slow things down to provide the time that attention needs to dwell. Appreciation, concentration, and focus all require patience and time. Just think of how we become still in the presence of beauty—a fox appears in the woods and we freeze in place, or we stand still before a work of art, allowing it to penetrate our imaginations in silence.

When I ran village board meetings, I was always aware of the pace of the dialogue and debate. Careful deliberation takes time, and it is important to allow periods of silence during such discussions. Allowing silence creates a lacuna, an unfilled gap, like the necessary quiet between notes of music, that allows a place for minds to meet and thoughts to occur. I would extend this idea to aesthetic citizenship. As citizens we need to

---

6. Adolf Portmann, *Animal Forms and Patterns: A Study of the Appearance of Animals,* translated by Hella Czech (London: Faber and Faber, 1948), 23.

have places in the polis that are dedicated to being still and quiet, places where we can listen to silence. Continuous chatter and a constant torrent of information fray the fabric of consciousness, disordering attention and disrupting memory, both of which are essential for the polis.

An aesthetic citizen also would insist that education pay as much attention to imagination as to the rational mind. Art, literature, history, language, science, philosophy, mathematics—the so-called liberal arts—are critical to learning how to pay attention to and appreciate things. Indeed, by educating and deepening our natural aesthetic sensibilities the liberal arts help us to become more human. Perhaps that is why some of these subjects are also referred to as the "humanities." Instead of harnessing education to the demands of predatory capitalism and hyper consumerism, aesthetic citizenship would nurture the imagination in all of its many forms. Educating and sophisticating aesthetic sensibility would be the guiding principle of curricula at all levels. This emphatically would include vocational education. The wisdom of Sophia originally referred to the skills of a craftsperson, carpenter, sculptor, and seafarer. "Sophia originates in and refers to the aesthetic hands of Daedalus and Hephaistus who was of course conjoined with Aphrodite *and so is inherent to her nature.*"[7] (Emphasis added.) From the perspective of aesthetic citizenship, there is no divide between liberal arts and vocational education. They are just different ways of attending to beauty and helping to craft the polis.

Aesthetic citizenship also favors and welcomes complexity over simplicity. When we appreciate something, we find that there is always more there than first met our eyes. That is why we can return again and again to a favorite book or song or work of art. When we look again, when we "re-spect," we find some subtlety revealed or some new connection made. And so, an aesthetic citizen distrusts simple answers and is suspicious of issues that are presented in a simplistic manner. An aesthetic citizen expects and welcomes complexity, is interested in the intricate, twisted, and knotty ways in which things manifest themselves. The life of the polis is messy, its issues are complicated, and they require careful attention and

---

7. Hillman, *The Thought of the Heart,* 34.

reflection. Knee-jerk answers and from-the-hip solutions rarely match the depth and complexity that policy considerations require. (Note that "policy" derives from "polis" and so, too, is in service to beauty.) This is not a call for unnecessary obscurity, but a warning that attempts to overly simplify matters can miss shadings in meaning. Not only the devil is in the details. That is why it can take so long to put words to a policy, ordinance, or contract. It takes time to consider the various angles, to imagine different scenarios, and to hear from various viewpoints. One of the functions of government is to slow the speed by which decisions are made, the way a governor on an engine keeps it operating within a proper range of speed. This can be frustrating for those who want quick answers, but it is a necessary aspect of aesthetic citizenship.

I have said that ideologies cannot create community. A defining aspect of ideologies is that they have ready answers that are applied somewhat indiscriminately to complex issues and problems. Ideologies have a penchant for simplifying issues into either/or choices. Ideologies also tend to fundamentalism, to being certain and unwavering in their beliefs. Aesthetic citizenship always leaves possibilities open. It doesn't mind revisiting issues already decided to see if there is a better way, and it is inherently suspicious when it hears "but we've always done it this way." This doesn't mean that an aesthetic citizen lacks firm ideas or is wishy-washy. Indeed, the kind of open-minded perspective I am suggesting requires considerable intellectual courage and tenacity. It is easy to be certain. But to always have a kernel of doubt about even your most cherished beliefs creates a kind of ideational tension that better serves the ongoing flow of the polis. That is why aesthetic citizenship seeks to move beyond the horned dilemmas perpetuated by ideological puritanism. The aesthetic citizen is interested in the animal beneath the horns, the visceral, complex, muscular life of the polis.

One way to keep an open mind is to remember that there is a story within every issue, a philosophical consideration in every policy decision. If the gods are in all things, then the life of the polis is imbued with myth. Learning to listen with an ear attuned to story, fiction, and myth is an indispensable attribute of aesthetic citizenship. Indeed, there are few things more useful in educating an aesthetic citizen than reading mythology. The stories of the gods are the stories of every polis, full of comedy and tragedy, epic battles of divine wills, touching tales of love and beauty, webs of deceit, and wise compromise among equals. Learning to listen for the mythical dimensions that are hidden in the everyday stories of the polis helps us know how we might adjust our approach or tone in the appropriate manner. When a person enquired of the Delphic oracle, which had an important role in both individual decisions and decisions affecting the polis, the proper question to ask was, "to what god or hero must I pray or sacrifice to achieve such and such purpose?"[8] Learning to perceive the invisible forces at work in seemingly mundane issues is an important part of aesthetic leadership.

Aesthetic citizenship blends careful attention, sophisticated maintenance, deep listening, an educated imagination, reflective silence, and overt activism. All of these came together when Riverside was faced with what turned out to be quite a hot-button issue—video gambling. The Illinois state legislature had legalized video gambling but had also allowed an "opt out" provision for local municipalities if they wanted to ban video gambling machines in local establishments. The video gambling machines provided a significant financial boost for restaurants, and several of our local restaurants expressed a desire to install at least a few machines. The issue of whether to allow video gambling in Riverside started at a slow simmer, but over time came to a rolling boil.

My initial reaction was, why not? The state legislature had made video gambling legal, and I did not object to gambling on moral grounds. I figured adults had a right to spend their money however they wanted to so long as it was legal. Some residents were strongly in favor of allowing the gambling machines because they were already going to surrounding communities that allowed them. Other residents were strongly opposed on moral grounds, declaring gambling was addictive and wrong. The opposing views quickly hardened, and the debate became acrimonious, especially so among those who opposed the machines on moral grounds.

What happened next was what was interesting. The village board had several meetings to discuss the issue and there was a large turnout of residents who wanted to make their arguments for and against allowing video gambling. Those in favor tended to make the legal/economic argu-

---

8. H.W. Parke, *Greek Oracles* (London: Hutchinson, 1967), 87.

ment that video gambling was legal and would be an economic benefit for local businesses. Those opposed tended to do so on moral grounds. But there was a third group that made a different argument—yes, video gambling was legal and would have an economic benefit for some businesses, they said, but it wasn't appropriate for Riverside. Their argument wasn't that video gambling was immoral or wrong, but that it was ugly, that it was incongruent with Riverside's overall image. Riverside prides itself on being a bit like the fictional Mayberry, a place retaining a nostalgic view of wholesomeness and rural charm. The idea of loud and gaudy video gambling machines in local restaurants that catered heavily to family dining was just out of place, said this group of residents. It just wasn't Riverside.

As these residents spoke, I began to change my perspective. As an elected official I thought much more about how I had to balance my personal view with the views of the larger polis. This was at its base an aesthetic decision. In the end, the village board voted to not allow video gambling. Interestingly, the issue reappeared several years later with even more heated exchanges. Once again there were the polar, and polarizing, extremes with the majority of residents falling in between. This time the village board decided to put the question up to a referendum. Almost 80% of voters rejected allowing video gambling in Riverside.

Throughout the debate an interesting rhetorical detail emerged. The folks that wanted to allow the machines consistently referred to the issue as "video gaming," while those opposed used the term "video gambling." Gaming had such a nice sound, all fun and recreation. Gambling was gambling, full of vice and wickedness. This is how an aesthetic debate expresses itself, in images and metaphors that try to portray the issue in qualitative terms. It might include moral implications, but it is not in the first instance a moral debate. It is about whether something enhances or detracts from the image of the polis. I still believe that there is nothing inherently immoral or unethical about video gambling, but I also believe that the majority of our residents were correct that it did not belong in Riverside.

A similar example had to do with fishing and picnicking. For years there had been ordinances on the books that prohibited fishing in the Des

Plaines River or picnicking in our parks. I found both laws ridiculous. Our village was named Riverside, and our pride and joy was the abundance of public green space, and yet at some point the village had made it illegal to enjoy them. The simple fact was that this was the shadow side of Riverside's Mayberry fantasy. The point of these laws, which were never enforced, was to keep "others" out of our village. Although proponents argued that they were there to prevent littering or to protect our parks, they were in fact based in classism and bigotry. When I brought the issue up and made the case that these laws were ugly and inappropriate, and indeed completely contrary to the Riverside that we aspired to be, the village board unanimously agreed, and the laws were repealed. The next spring, we had our first annual Kid's Fishing Derby, an event that has now become much beloved by young and old alike.

Video gambling, fishing, and picnicking probably seem like trivial issues to get riled up about, but these are exactly the kinds of issues that call for aesthetic activism on the local level. I can point to countless issues at the state and federal levels that deserve similar aesthetic review, but I want to make the case for aesthetic citizenship in our daily lives. It is important that we protest against ugliness in all of its forms wherever we encounter it. Rudeness and racism are of a magnitude different, but both are aesthetic offenses that need to be immediately and actively challenged. Aesthetic citizenship requires active participation, civil disobedience, petitions, marches, and megaphones. But it also manifests with each citizen, how we ornament ourselves and our homes, how we conduct ourselves in relation to other people, other animals, our natural habitat. An aesthetic citizen treats others with respect, kindness, and compassion, but is also ready and willing to challenge a callous act, a hateful word, or an ugly innuendo.

Paying attention to things and relationships, embracing diversity, welcoming complexity, encouraging participation, and resisting ideologies are all essential components of being an aesthetic citizen. As we have seen, aesthetic citizenship takes place throughout life and in every imaginable scenario. But there is one aspect of aesthetic citizenship that deserves special mention—volunteerism. When one volunteers their time and talents, they express the deepest values of aesthetic citizenship.

The act of volunteering is by nature selfless, we volunteer not because of what we can get but because of what we can give. Volunteerism displays the polis in its finest potential as people come together in common cause to advance a greater good, a good beyond special interest that asks for nothing in return. Volunteerism is freedom incarnate, an embodied act of free will. The word itself comes from the Latin *voluntarius,* meaning willing or of one's own choice, and this in turn derives from Latin noun *voluntas,* meaning will or desire. No other human political act creates a stronger sense of community and belonging than volunteerism.

What is it that makes volunteering so rewarding? Certainly, we can see and take pleasure in the tangible results of our actions—a food drive, helping to clean up a park, building a stage set for a school play. But the real reward is intangible. It exists in the camaraderie of fellow volunteers, in the humble manner of work freely given, in the satisfaction of doing good, and in the recognition that we all have benefitted from the volunteerism of others in our own lives. A kind word from a friend, an act of chivalry from a stranger, a cup of coffee paid for by an anonymous benefactor—volunteerism happens all the time through groups and by individuals. Volunteerism is an essential political act because it is done solely out of a desire to benefit others. By reaching out a helping hand we maintain and strengthen the polis.

Although some volunteerism is issue oriented such as protecting animal rights, working to reduce climate change, or working on a political campaign, the vast majority of volunteerism lacks any ideological basis. Similarly, most volunteerism is not contentious but is focused simply on trying to help others or to give back to the community. This kind of altruistic approach runs contrary to the self-centered, every-person-for-themselves individualism that infects so much of modern politics and society. It is exactly that kind of individualism that aesthetic citizenship rejects, and volunteerism exposes such selfishness for its corrupting influence on the polis. Laid alongside the noble beauty of volunteerism, ruthless individualism can be seen in all of its hollow ugliness.

Volunteerism, then, is a perfect model for aesthetic citizenship. Taking care of others, attending to those in need, and working together in common cause for a greater good are all ways by which we can strengthen the polis. A single, small act of kindness can have immeasurable impact that reverberates throughout the polis in ways beyond our imagining. The desire to serve the well-being of others releases us from our self-centeredness and returns us to our proper place in the polis.

FOUR

The Body Politic

Over time people have used different metaphors to talk about politics and political institutions and organizations. Perhaps the oldest metaphor is the "body" as in "the body politic." This metaphor in Western usage goes way back to at least the sixth century BCE. An early formulation was in Aesop's tale of "The Belly and its Members." In the fable, the hands, mouth, teeth, and legs decide to go on strike because they think the belly is doing none of the work while getting all of the food. But after a few days the hands could hardly move, the mouth was parched, and the legs were unable to support the rest. The body's members thus learned that even the belly was doing important work and that cooperation between all members of the body was necessary for the body's health.

The analogy of the human body to the body politic continues through Plato and Aristotle, and the ancient poets often referred to the state organically and to threats to the state as diseases or illness. Livy cited Aesop's tale of the belly and its members in his *History of Rome.* With the Christianization of the Roman Empire, the metaphor persisted and became applied to Christ and the Church. St. Paul repeats a variation of Aesop's fable in 1 Corinthians 12:12–27, and declares the church the "body of Christ," and in Colossians 1:18, Christ is referred to as "the head of the body, the church."

In the Middle Ages, John of Salisbury assigned distinct roles within the polis to various body parts:

> The position of the head in the republic is...by a prince subject only to God and to those who act in His place on earth...The place of the heart is occupied by the senate...The duties of the ears, eyes and mouth are claimed by the judges and governors of provinces. The hands coincide with officials and soldiers. Those who always

assist the prince are comparable to the flanks. Treasurers and record keepers...resemble the shape of the stomach and intestines... Furthermore, the feet coincide with peasants perpetually bound to the soil.[1]

According to John of Salisbury, just like each part of the body had its role, so, too, each member of the body politic had its role and was obligated to do its part for the benefit of the whole. At about the same time, the concept of a "corporation" as a "legal person" arose. The idea of the body politic in corporation theory was soon allied to the idea of the *corpus mysticum* or the mystical church of Christ.

Just as Christ was the head of the church, to the medieval mind the king was the head of the body politic. Echoing John of Salisbury, France's first professional woman writer, Christine de Pizan, in her *The Book of the Body Politic* (c. 1407) assigned different responsibilities to different classes of people within the body politic. She recounts the Aesop fable, and attributes the analogy of the body given by John of Salisbury to Plutarch before concluding that each person should do "his own part in the order that God has established," such that "nobles do as nobles should" and "the populace does as is appropriate for them."[2]

The use of "body politic" to justify unitary leadership by Christ or King, and to divide the polity into a hierarchy where each group had their assigned place continued throughout the sixteenth century, perhaps culminating in Henry VIII who took absolute rule one step further by making himself the head of the Church of England in 1531. So, for over 2,000 years the metaphor of the body as the body politic was used to support claims for unitary, absolute leadership, and to keep the lower classes in line. Moreover, this took place solidly within a patriarchal system that restricted rule to men and their male heirs.

---

1. John of Salisbury, *Policraticus: Of the Frivolities of Courtiers and the Footprints of Philosophers,* edited and translated by Cary Nederman (Cambridge: Cambridge University Press, 1990), 66–7.

2. Christine de Pizan, *The Book of the Body Politic,* edited and translated by Kate Langdon Forhan (Cambridge: Cambridge University Press, 2007). Reference to Plutarch, 4; telling of Aesop's fable (without reference to Aesop), 91; remaining quotes, 59.

The idea of the body politic as natural and biological weakened substantially from the mid-seventeenth and into the eighteenth centuries when Hobbes, Locke, and Rousseau developed the idea of a social contract whereby the sovereign gained its authority from the willing consent of the populace. According to this view, the body politic was an artificial construction, not a natural one. Like the idea of a corporation being a legal person. the body politic was an abstraction, an artificial person capable of making contracts and the like but having no natural or biological foundation. This view of the body politic became the more or less accepted view thereafter. The United States Supreme Court summarized the view in *Cotton vs. United States* 52 U.S. 229 (1851), writing that "Every sovereign State is of necessity a body politic, or artificial person, and as such capable of making contracts and holding property, both real and personal."

Although we still refer to political bodies and the body politic, the metaphors have lost their natural and biological connotations. With the growing acceptance of the social contract theory, whereby governments are understood to derive their power and authority from the consent of the governed, a different metaphor began to shape the modern view of political institutions. After the Industrial Revolution, the body politic was no longer corporeal or natural but began to be conceived of as a machine. Beginning in the seventeenth century, the machine metaphor slowly replaced the older, organic view and society, nature, and indeed the human being were all understood in terms of machines. As Carolyn Merchant put it in her book *The Death of Nature,* "as the unifying model for science and society, the machine has permeated and reconstructed human consciousness so totally that today we scarcely question its validity."[3] The terms "machine politicians," and "political machines" come into vogue in the 1870s, and "political science" as a distinct field of study first appeared in the 1880s.

Part of the problem with the metaphor of the body as analogous to the body politic is that it forgets it is a metaphor and hardens into literalism. Although in its earliest usage, the metaphor emphasized the

---

3. Carolyn Merchant, *The Death of Nature: Women, Ecology, and the Scientific Revolution* (San Francisco: Harper, 1989), 277.

natural, organic processes of politics, after it passed through Roman and Christian hands it became a symbol for unitary, absolute rule. The "head" was always at the top and all various parts of the body politic were subsumed under one body. The metaphor was thus used to relegate, and thereby subjugate, the other parts of the body politic to clearly defined and mostly lesser roles. If the peasants were the feet of the body politic, that is all they could ever be. Once a person had been given the place and role that God had ordained for them, it was their duty to remain defined and confined by that role. The feet could never deign to be the head and the hands could not migrate to the heart.

It is the monotheistic cast of mind that wants to reduce the many to the one, to instill hierarchy, and maintain a static political order with clearly defined roles and responsibilities. A different perspective, more animistic or polytheistic, might imagine in terms of the bodies politic, whereby a natural, organic impetus for politics is retained but the subjugation of the many to the one is discarded. It is possible to consider humans to be by nature political animals, and that politics is a natural process, without taking the step of declaring that politics is analogous to a single body.

When we hear people declare that all immigrants should be forced to learn English, or that English should be legally enshrined as the official language of the United States, or that Christianity is integral and essential to so-called American values, or that the United States should have uniform customs and traditions, or that there are clear-cut gender roles (two only), we are listening to a monotheistic cast of mind. Those who wax nostalgically for earlier times when things were simpler are whitewashing the patriarchy, racism, misogyny, violence, and bigotry that was part and parcel of those times. The fear of diversity, complexity, ambiguity, and difference is reflected in a desire for authoritarianism and enforced order. It is no accident that the same cast of mind that favors authoritarian rule also embraces conspiracy theories and fundamentalism. Monotheism easily becomes paranoid because it posits enforced and artificial oneness in the face of natural diversity. Politics fails when it goes against its nature which is inherently diverse and polytheistic.

The machine metaphor for politics does not fare any better. The mechanistic worldview of Descartes and Newton leads to the same fallacy as the body politic by positing clearly defined "parts" working together like cogs in the name of efficiency and productivity. Indeed, the machine metaphor is worse in many ways because it loses the natural, organic origins of the body politic. The machine metaphor has at its base Descartes's separation of mind and body, leaving the greater world beyond human introspection a dead wasteland of *res extensa*. The world is a great watch according to Newton, running according to divine law. And so, the goal of politics is to mimic this machinery. Society becomes a "construct" to be managed and manipulated. Citizens are fungible, replaceable, interchangeable parts to be polled and placated by pandering to their self(ish)-interest. And, just as with the body politic, the machine metaphor encourages authoritarian experts and bosses to run the machine, which in the end is dedicated to power and self-perpetuation.

What if instead of the body or a machine we imagined politics as an aesthetic practice? If we are by nature aesthetic and political animals, then politics is inherently aesthetic, and aesthetics is inherently political. Instead of metaphors and symbols we could view politics in terms of images. Instead of parts we could imagine in terms of particulars. Instead of reducing the many to the one in the name of productivity we could retain the many as many, each citizen contributing their own creativity to a living, constantly changing and fluid mosaic. The polis would still share common goals and strive for shared ideals, but these goals and ideals would be aesthetic in nature instead of ideological, imagined instead of defined.

In his criticism of the social contract theory espoused by Hobbes and Rousseau (who, despite their theory favored absolute monarchies) David Hume wrote of the unlikely forging of an "original contract" as the basis for government. He acknowledged that consent of the people might be one foundation for government, but that it had rarely actually occurred historically. Instead, said Hume, "some other foundation of government must also be admitted."[4] I am suggesting that this other foundation for government, and politics, is beauty. It is beauty that gives rise to the sensate world of things and their relationships, and it is beauty

---

4. "Of the Original Contract," in David Hume, *Essays, Moral, Political, and Literary, Part 2* (1752) (online at *https://davidhume.org/texts/empl2/oc*).

that ignites the desire among political animals to come together. Beauty inspires the erotic longing for community, a mutual yearning for the polis whereby individuals are not parts but particulars, and where each citizen can display and contribute their talents and skills.

An aesthetic approach to politics and government avoids the old dualism about whether beauty is subjective (in the eye of the beholder) or objective (belonging to formal qualities of an object) in favor of third view that would eliminate the need for such a polarizing perspective. By imagining beauty in terms of images, we can appreciate the integrity of each image in itself while not losing sight of the broader ecology of imagination that the image inhabits within the polis. Hillman once referred to an image as the complete "how" of a presentation, such that an image is not only *what* is presented but *how* it is presented.[5] Applied to politics, this would mean we that we would view issues and debates as both possessing specific content (policy decisions, economic impacts, environmental concerns) while also existing within a broader, deeper, and more prismatic aesthetic display (how the content relates to and reflects the community, displays its diversity, and actualizes its multiple voices). Aesthetic politics is attuned to mannerisms, how things are said and presented, and how various aspects of the polis relate and communicate. There is a direct, practical connection to things when they are aesthetically grasped, bodily felt, and tacitly understood. This is a politics of animal faith, sure-footed, alert to the complexity of the greater world in all of its wonder and danger. Aesthetic politics replaces ideology with ideas, avoids polarization through its preference and appreciation for polysemous images, and counters authoritarian control through its dedication to a polytheistic pantheon of equals. All things full of gods.

When things are viewed aesthetically, no one thing is allowed to run roughshod over the rest. Instead, each aspect of an image is recognized, and appreciated, as existing within a specific context, mood, and scene. The "how" of an image's presentation includes the other things that contribute to its ecology of imagination. This is different from a symbolic approach that elevates some images over others because of an assigned

---

5. Hillman, *The Soul's Code,* 123.

meaning (e.g., a dove in a religious painting becomes the Holy Spirit). As soon as an image is assigned a symbolic meaning or interpreted into a concept, we have lost the image. This happens in politics all of the time when a practical concern, say the need for vaccinations during a pandemic, gets turned into a symbol for government overreach. Once that happens the practical concern is lost in the fog of ideology. An aesthetic approach would maintain the integrity of each thing within the context of the polis, a perspective that the psychologist Patricia Berry calls "the full democracy of the image."[6]

To practice politics aesthetically requires careful attention to one's own views because our beliefs and perspectives are so often under the influence of unconscious mental habits and assumptions. When we feel our views hardening into a "position" it is time for caution. Appreciation is all about constantly looking again at things and feeling their deeper significance. There is a natural tension to politics that cannot be resolved. Even as one decision is made, others become possible. That is why politics needs to be adaptive and flexible, open minded and receptive. The polis is constantly changing and so a politics founded on beauty would accept that policies need to be adaptable and flexible so they can change with the times. Heraclitus wrote that "you cannot step twice into the same river," which is an apt analogy to political life.[7] New ideas and perspectives are constantly flowing into and through the polis and we come and go through its eddies and currents.

The metaphor of the body politic, and the metaphor of the machine both give rise to authoritarianism because of their elevation of the one over the many. As evidenced by Hobbes and Rousseau, the social contract theory is not immune from the political aberration of authoritarianism that runs contrary to the human's nature as a political animal. Distilling political power to one person, be they the boss of a political machine or a dictator, violates the essential diversity of the polis. But perhaps here a refinement is in order. The defining characteristic of authoritarian rule

---

6. Patricia Berry, "An Approach to the Dream," *Spring: An Annual of Archetypal Psychology and Jungian Thought* (1974): 64. Reprinted in Patricia Berry, *Echo's Subtle Body: Contributions to an Archetypal Psychology* (Thompson, Conn.: Spring Publications, 2017 [1982]).

7. Wheelwright, *Heraclitus*, 29.

is that it is absolute. Authoritarian regimes need not be led by a single person, but they do require a "singleness of mind," a bending of knee to doctrine, pledged allegiance to proscribed values, sticking to the party line.[8] This singleness of mind, what I have called the monotheistic cast of mind, lies at the heart of authoritarianism. As Hillman points out, we too often focus on the human figures that we identify with authoritarianism, and this literalization protects "us from the absolutism that can rule the psyche in the guise of fundamentalism in religion, bottom-lineism in business and progress in science."[9]

But where does authority actually come from? Does is exist within family lineage the way the royals say? Is it acquired and sustained through force, fear, and violence like in a dictatorship? Is it bestowed by the populace through elections and upheld through laws and constitutions? All of these can be sources of authority but there is something more here. When I was village president, I had certain powers granted by state statutes and local ordinances that gave me the authority to make certain decisions. The office itself granted me a different standing within the village as its titular leader, but whatever authority attached to my office was clearly on loan from the citizens. Whatever authority I had were transient trappings of the office that would eventually be passed on to the next village president.

But there is another kind of authority, another kind of power, that we feel when we are in the presence of an authoritative person. Authoritative, not authoritarian. The latter we know can oftentimes coalesce in brutish, arrogant, and small-minded individuals. But the former presents itself differently. An authoritative person seems to have a kind of radiant authority, as if it is something intrinsic to them, given with their very presence. Sometimes this can be because of education or experience, the way a professor can speak with authority within their field of expertise. Other times, authority can simply be felt as an aspect of the

---

8. James Hillman, *Kinds of Power: A Guide to Its Intelligent Uses* (New York: Doubleday, 1995), 189–90: "Tyranny does not so much require a single monarch or dictator as a singleness of mind literalized as a single ruler. Tyranny can rule by a group...so long as the members do not differ in principle or the in the implementation of principle...Absolutism is not a ruthless ruler, but a ruthless rule."

9. Ibid. 190.

person, part of their character, written in the elder's face, or displayed in the restrained yet fearsome courage of a Mandela or a Tutu. This authority brings weight, gravitas, to a situation and by so doing provides depth and grounding. "Perhaps," says Hillman, "authority rises as the soul sinks gravely—graveward—as one becomes an ancestor, a figure who represents the stored wisdom of the community, a representation rather than a personality."[10] This kind of authority is connected to the ancestors, to a kind of authority that is partly or mostly *impersonal* in terms of not belonging to a single person but to the constituting power of the polis with its innumerous influences both visible and invisible, human and inhuman.

Politics based in beauty avoids the usurpation of authority by authoritarianism by consciously keeping in mind the necessity of the many gods that are always present in any political act or decision. In the Greek pantheon, Zeus was first among equals, and not even he was allowed to interfere in the domains of the other Olympians. This kind of respect and reticence is based on a deference to the ordering power of beauty that adorns each thing with its own intrinsic authority and sphere of influence.

---

10. Ibid., 165.

FIVE

Aesthetic Leadership

The year 2020 was a difficult one as the United States faced the outbreak of the coronavirus pandemic and protests against systemic racism sparked by the murder of George Floyd by police officers. Riverside was not isolated from these events but also faced yet another challenge from a historic flood that impacted hundreds of our residents. In this chapter I want to use those three events, and the village's political responses to them, as examples of how leadership based in beauty works in practice through the aesthetic use of power.

The word "coronavirus" first appeared in our local newspaper on March 4, 2020. The all-caps headline in the paper on March 13 was "LIFE GRINDING TO A HALT," and was accompanied by photos showing long lines outside of grocery stores as shelves quickly became empty. Riverside's first resident died of Covid-19 on April 11. As everyone knows who lived through those times, the following months were full of fear, uncertainty, and a desperate desire for facts and guidance from health professionals and political leaders.

A four-day rain event deluged the village from May 14 to 17, dumping seven inches of rain into an already swollen Des Plaines River. This led to the second highest ever river crests in Riverside's recorded history, sending flood waters into upwards of 200 households. Not only did this devastate residents, it also severely taxed local first responders who were already reeling from the exploding Covid-19 cases associated with the pandemic.

Then, on May 25, came the horrifying video showing the callous murder of George Floyd. Public outrage was swift. On May 31, looters, using the Floyd murder as a pretext, launched a coordinated attack on a shopping mall and stores in our neighboring community of North Riverside. One person was killed and there was widespread property damage and theft. Riverside braced for an overflow of violence from this outbreak, and tensions were high as both residents and first responders waited for what was to come.

Coming in such rapid succession, the village felt under siege by social upheaval, a natural disaster, and a terrifying, invisible presence that seemed to turn every touch or breath into a possible death sentence. It was an unprecedented series of events that called for a varied and sophisticated response by local village government and staff. Blessed with an excellent village manager and chiefs of police and fire, village government went to work.

As I hope I have already made clear, every political response is both practical and aesthetic at the same time, the two can be distinguished but not separated. On the practical side, in response to Covid-19, protocols had to be put into place; in response to the flood, pumps had to be installed to empty basements and streets of water once the river finally receded back into it banks; and in response to the civil unrest following Floyd's murder, police had to prepare for possible violence. Given the team we had in place, I was confident that all of those practical responses would happen in due course. But a populace needs more than procedures and protocols when it feels under attack. It needs clear and honest communication, compassionate leaders, and reassurance that the grounding values of the polis are intact. That job fell to village government in general and to me in particular as the village president.

Just as the practical responses to the various crises had to be coordinated, especially given the limited staff available to a small village, so, too, the psychological response, which is another way of saying the aesthetic or political response, had to be crafted and composed to address the village's fears and concerns. A political leader has two main tools for this—language and personal example. Communication could not be curt, simplistic, or pollyannish. Residents deserved language that accepted the realities we faced without false assurances or avoidance. They needed language of sufficient power to match the challenges we faced as a community. And they needed to see their leaders in action, taking calm and coordinated steps to respond to the matters at hand.

And so, on March 23, I began what would be an extensive public conversation with the community about the pandemic, the flood, and the civil unrest. I used every tool we had available to us—social media, e-mail flashes, communication with the local press, and televised village board meetings—to keep up a constant dialogue with residents. The first message addressed the pandemic, and I share it below because I want to point out certain aspects of it after you read it:

Our lives these days are far from normal. But there are messages in the void. The disruption we feel in our everyday lives is also an opportunity to recognize things we too often take for granted. The unnatural efforts we must take to keep our distance from our fellow humans highlight that our natural state is one of mutual dependence, cooperation, and camaraderie. We are by nature social creatures that need and depend on one another to establish communities bound together by shared ideals and values. When we are disturbed by our eerily empty city streets it is because at some deep level we know that the soul is not the private possession of isolated individuals but rather extends beyond individuals to embrace the greater world.

We have been told to stay at home. Notice how that feels like a confinement. This feeling tells us that home is more than that place populated by our families, animal companions, and possessions, more than the place we lay our heads down to sleep. We are all creatures of the greater world, and when we are confined away from it we long for it. Goethe said "tell me what you long for and I'll tell you who you are." When we long to get outside, back to our forests and our streets, back to the pleasures of social closeness, we are reminded that we require those things to be who we are. Our souls are not limited to the private words we think we hear within our own heads. Without the greater world our souls grow lonely and stifled, and we feel that loss in our longing for beauty, love, and affection.

Perhaps when this crisis finally fades, we will see our responsibility to that greater world more clearly. The many threats to our planet are not external to us. Humans did not create the novel coronavirus, but denial and neglect aided its spread and severity of impact. Like the virus, the degradation of nature, the exponential loss of species diversity, and the deadly warming and acidification of air, earth, and water are not only objective realities. They are also embodied and reflected in our personal and psychological lives. This pandemic, which literally means "all people," shows us that we are inexorably connected to one another and to the many things of the world.

As we persevere through these difficult times, we would do well to also fully feel and appreciate their difficulty. Take some time away from distractions and diversions to reflect on this moment of forced solitude. It is a frightening time, but it is also a time when we can reground ourselves in a fuller understanding of the world and our place within it. We don't know how long we will be kept away from the beckoning world, but eventually this quiet moment will pass and the noise will begin again. When that time comes, we will be better as individuals and as a people if we keep a little piece of disturbing quiet with us. There are other voices straining to be heard, voices that we need to hear.

As you can see, this was not a sound bite. It was intentionally complex because what our village was enduring was complex. What was needed were ideas and images of sufficient depth and power to provide ways to bring order to what we were experiencing. Not the kind of order that seeks to control things, but order as pattern, composition, and arrangement. My job was to acknowledge the full emotional and psychological impact of the pandemic. I was decisively *not* trying to pat residents on the head to tell them everything was going to be okay, because at that time we had no idea how things were going to be. I wanted to offer neither hope nor avoidance. I wanted us as a community to reach for the deeper significance of what we were going through together. The emotional impact of empty streets, the feelings of isolation and confinement, the longing for friends and family—these were hard and bitter, but they also were revelatory images pointing out things that we had taken for granted.

Instead of hope, I asked for perseverance, which etymologically means "to persist in a thing thoroughly." That word was chosen precisely because of that etymology. Words are myths hiding in plain sight as language, *mythos* as *logos,* and by using language mythically, poetically, we can reach more than the mind. At that point in time, our minds were all clouded from uncertainty, looking for a way out or beyond. What I was trying to do was to speak to the soul, encouraging it not to seek a way out but a way down from heightened fear and anxiety, a way to find some coherence and sensibility to what we were all experiencing. My emphasis on the shared experiences we were all having was a reminder of a deeper community that persisted despite our literal individual isolation.

The last paragraph was especially important. I was trying to say that the things that frighten or disturb us are important and need to be held close and respected. I knew even then that those who survived the pandemic were going to be given an opportunity to engage with the greater world in a new way. And because what we all feared at that time was an invisible presence, I called on our village to attend to other invisibles, invisibles that did not intend us harm, invisibles that might emerge from the silence that we were all enduring.

I offer this statement as an example of aesthetic leadership. Whether or not I achieved it, I was striving for eloquence, for language of gravitas and inherent power that was appropriate and offered in service to the pain and fear that I knew we all felt. Crisis does not need boosterism or deflection; it needs to be fully and deeply engaged. Notice, too, that there were no heroic flourishes or promises that "we'll beat this thing." At that point such language would have been dishonest. I had a great trust in the strength and resiliency of my fellow citizens. My goal was not to foster heroics but to encourage and nurture the deep love that sustains any community. This kind of eloquence shines forth darkly in Lincoln's Gettysburg Address, a short speech of just 272 words and ten sentences. The words themselves were simple, but the composition, arrangement, and rhythm gave them extraordinary power. Their intelligence and mood matched the wisdom and melancholy of their presenter and were perfectly appropriate to the somber occasion. Such is the power of words.

The next hardship to fall upon Riverside was its record-breaking flood. This event was unlike the pandemic in many ways, and as a different kind of event it called for a different style of response. This is a core idea of leadership based in beauty. There is no one size fits all response. Each event, each decision must be attended to in its own way. The goal is to allow the event to guide us in our response through a careful, and caring, appreciation of its unique circumstances and characteristics.

The flood did not lend itself to verbal rhetoric in the way the pandemic did. Unlike the hovering, invisible presence of the pandemic, the flood was fully physical and visible and so therefore more susceptible to heartfelt action. I, along with other members of the village board, made it a point to be at the scene of our neighbors' losses. We met them on the streets, rubber boots all, and talked with them about their situations.

We informed them of the village's plans to assist with the flood waters once the river receded back within its banks. But more than anything, we listened, and cried, with them. The polis as a household means that we share familial bonds even if we are not literally related. As president I was also a leading elder within the imaginal family that was our village. These people who were suffering were not just residents, many of them were my friends, and all of them were the people I represented as their elected president. I wanted them to see me, to talk to me, to share with me. I wanted them to know that I, and their government, were there for them and would do whatever possible to lessen their burden.

To my mind, this physical presence of the village board was aesthetic in at least two ways. The first has to do with empathy, a word that comes from the German word *Einfühlung,* which literally means "feeling into." In the first decade of the twentieth century, Edward Titchener and James Ward translated the German word into English as "empathy."[1] *In its original meaning, empathy referred to an aesthetic appreciation of art and nature and did not apply to feelings between humans.* It was not until the middle of the twentieth century that the word took on its interpersonal meaning. Despite being infected by the idea of the interpersonal "self," empathy retains its aesthetic roots. Even today when we talk about having empathy for someone, with someone, we are referring to a kind of deep appreciation of another person that is accomplished through a deep imagining of their situation and circumstance. So, when village leaders engaged empathetically with the residents affected by the flood that was an aesthetic engagement.

Secondly, the physical presence of the village leaders signified the symbolic power of being a public official. When a person becomes a trustee or a president, they take on a quasi-symbolic significance. They are no longer only the citizen they were before. The title bestowed by the electorate anoints the official with a special importance, an inherent emphasis that says they are no longer an ordinary citizen. They represent the

---

1. See Joanna Ganczarek, Thomas Hünefeldt, and Marta Olivetti Belardinelli, "From 'Einfühlung' to Empathy: Exploring the Relationship between Aesthetic and Interpersonal Experience," *Cognitive Processing* 19, no. 2 (2018): 141–45.

polis, and representation is precisely what symbols do, they stand for something else, refer to something else. In the case of a public official that something else is the polis. The word "office" itself means originally "service." And so, as a representative the elected official is in service to the polis. The first definition of "office" in the *Oxford English Dictionary* is "something done toward anyone; a service, kindness, attention." Another meaning is "Duty towards others, a moral obligation. Duty attaching to one's station, position." In its essence, "office" implies a service, kindness, and attention to something greater than oneself, something worthy of moral obligation and duty. To hold office is to be in service to invisible powers capable of bestowing earthly powers, a capability typically associated with the gods.

When I and the trustees showed up on those gray, wet days following the flood to be with our fellow residents, we were showing them the reflection of their own power. We were there for them because they had given us the opportunity to be there for them, to represent them, and it was our duty, a welcomed duty, to be able to embody the greater community that also cared about them and wanted to help them. We were symbolically the face of their community, and in our official service we represented the kindness and attention of their fellow residents. This imaginative, aesthetic connection held together both the empathy we displayed and the symbolic power of the offices we held. We could not replace the photo albums and lost memories that the flood had washed away, but we could represent the beauty of communal kindness and the promise of renewal. Their loss was personal, but the support they experienced was communal, telling them that although they might have lost possessions, their home, in its fullest sense, remained.

George Floyd was murdered on May 25th. Six days later an organized group of looters descended on a shopping mall and businesses in our neighboring community of North Riverside. This was not a protest. There were no speeches, no megaphones, no marches, just mayhem. The police showed great restraint and the only violence was perpetrated by the looters. One person was killed in a gang-related shooting. The riot, which was barely a mile away, created great fear in Riverside. Shops and restaurants in our business district closed in anticipation of the violence spreading. I talked to residents on the street who were unaware of what was happening and encouraged them to return home until things quieted down. Fortunately, nothing ever materialized in Riverside, but the following days were tense ones as we all wondered what would come next.

Working with village staff, we all decided that the social upheaval following the murder of George Floyd required a response from the village based both in language and in action. Floyd's death had demonstrated in the most graphic way imaginable the ugly persistence of racism. On June 4th I released a statement on behalf of the entire village board that read as follows:

> The Village of Riverside is saddened and angered by the horrific death of George Floyd in Minneapolis. We extend our deepest condolences to his family and to those in the Minneapolis community struggling to deal with its aftermath.
>
> This heartbreaking act has rightly sparked legitimate protests across our nation about the need to address systemic racism and the historic vestiges of inequality and racial injustice. We support the fight against racism and the peaceful protests striving to bring awareness to this critical issue. The tragic list of names to which Mr. Floyd now belongs must end.
>
> In the midst of this tragedy, we must seize the opportunity for constructive dialogue to assure that Mr. Floyd did not die in vain. We will not be able to heal the wounds to our national spirit until we put an end to the cause of our suffering—unconscionable acts born of ignorance and hate and sustained by apathy and indifference.
>
> The Village of Riverside works tirelessly to build trust and respectful relationships within our village. Our police department receives constant training on de-escalation, mental health, social justice issues, and other issues around restorative justice. The actions of the officers involved in Mr. Floyd's death are anathema to the noble call to protect and serve.
>
> The Village of Riverside is committed to cultural outreach and transparency. We strive to be a community of diversity, welcoming all who want to be part of our community. And we will steadfastly reject calls that would divide us or breathe clouds of hate into our village.
>
> As we struggle to respond to the enormous losses suffered in Minneapolis and other cities across the country, we must rededicate ourselves to answering the call of our better angels. We will only

heal when we have a nation where all people are duly blessed with the opportunities and protections of justice and equality.

You will notice that this language is quite different from the language concerning the pandemic. The Covid-19 pandemic, in March of 2020, was an unknown, invisible, worldwide threat. The murder of George Floyd was the result of an all too well-known historical presence of systemic racism and bigotry. The purpose of the Floyd statement was to place Riverside squarely on the side of the protesters in rejecting systemic racism and calling for societal reform. Racism exists because of ignorance and hate by those who practice it, and by apathy and indifference by those who don't. What I wanted to do in this statement was to appeal to the latter. In my view, we needed more protests, not fewer, and we needed them both collectively and on the level of individual interactions. I wanted each citizen to be an activist in the name of justice and equality. The visceral reaction to the sickening video of Floyd's death felt by so many was an aesthetic outrage against its manifest ugliness. The casual indifference and smug coldness shown in the slow killing of a human being outraged many, but not enough. That other people remained unmoved by the act pointed to the depth of our societal anesthesia when it came to racial inequality. I was trying to use language to awaken them.

After publishing the statement, I read it at the next village board meeting and announced that the chief of police was going to update the board and the public about the police department's procedures concerning use of force. Riverside had not had a complaint about undue force in over thirty years, and I knew that our police department had already enacted almost all of the police reforms being called for by the protestors. Our chief of police was a person of great integrity and there was no question by anybody in the police department that racism or excessive force would not be tolerated. What was needed was an opportunity to communicate that to our residents. The protests provided an opportunity to do that. I also announced that there would be a town hall with me and the leaders of our police department to discuss issues about police conduct with the public. I talked with our police chief prior to the meeting about this announcement and he readily agreed that it was the right thing to do.

At the same time, a group of young people, barely out of high school, began to organize protest marches in Riverside—an unprecedented event. After one impromptu march, they set about organizing a larger march. I contacted the people organizing the march and asked for a meeting between them, me, the police and fire chiefs, and the village manager. They were surprised, and suspicious. I was a sixty-five-year-old white man, and on that basis alone they found it difficult to trust me. The police and fire chiefs represented exactly what they believed to be the problem. Still, they agreed to meet with us, so we set a time and met in the front yard of one of the organizers so that we could stay socially distanced in accord with the Covid-19 protocols.

I made it clear from the beginning that we were there to support their right to protest, not curtail it. I also told them that I personally agreed with what they were saying and doing. But, I added, my first responsibility to them and the greater community was public safety. After that icebreaking, the meeting went very well as the chiefs and village manager offered ways to facilitate the march. You could see suspicion turn to surprise in the faces of the organizers. This was not what they had expected. I mentioned that they had the four highest ranking officials in the village sitting there, and that all of us were sincere in our desire to protect their right to protest. I didn't say it out loud, but in my heart I was very proud of them. In them I saw our best hope as a village and as a nation.

On the day of the march, my wife and I were there at the park where the protesters had gathered to listen to speakers before the march. I wanted to be seen there, by the protesters, by people driving by, by the press. I wanted to embody the government's support for what they were doing, and to hopefully erode some of the distrust that people felt toward government. I had heard from a small minority of residents who didn't like what I was doing or that the village was supporting the protest. They wanted to know if they could march, too, and I said yes, that the village would allow any lawful protest. But I was also unequivocal that I did not support their views and would oppose them at every opportunity.

The march was peaceful and moving. Another march was planned and carried out later in the month, again with the full support of the village. After that event, one of the organizers publicly thanked the village, and several of the organizers reached out to me personally to thank me for my participation in the protests. It was immensely gratifying to watch their initial suspicion turn to trust, and to have a chance to show them that government, and even older white men, could be allies in what they were trying to accomplish.

The governmental responses to the pandemic, flood, and protests were all based in a style of leadership dedicated to beauty and in the aesthetic use of power. Politics and government are often talked about in terms of power and the machinations of power—how to get power, how to wield power, and how to keep it. James Hillman wrote a remarkable book called *Kinds of Power: A Guide to its Intelligent Use,* that should be required reading for anyone interested in public service or leadership. He teases out the many ideas hidden within "power," and in so doing he disturbs our habitual ways of looking at power, differentiates the idea of power by exploring its many subtle facets, and extends the idea of power beyond individual acts of human will. I will not attempt to define power in these pages, because a call for definition is itself a power move, an attempt to control the spontaneous creativity of the mind and soul. So, for our purposes I ask that you consider whatever ideas or meanings about power that you might have in your own mind as we proceed.

Every person knows the power of beauty. Perhaps more than any other experience, the encounter of beauty has a power over the human soul like no other. Beauty arrests motion—it stops us dead in our tracks. Beauty can sweep us up, give us wings, take our breaths away, and it can also terrify us with its sublime magnificence. It is through beauty that we fall in love, and although love ignites us, it also shows us how powerlessness we become when pierced by love's arrows.

Odd, then, that politicians who are supposedly preoccupied with power give so little attention to beauty. Here I do not mean the manipulation of beauty as propaganda, or of using art and architecture to fulfill and represent ideologies. We have quite enough cathedrals and tall towers with people's names on them. I mean attending to the power inherent in beauty, its ability to open our eyes to possibilities, to stir our hearts, and lead us into action.

An example. We are faced with a cataclysmic threat of climate change. Some think that we are already beyond the tipping point and that all that is left to do is manage the impending disasters to come. There is much talk about what we need to do if we are to back away from the precipice. Much of this talk is of duty, obligation, and responsibility. One view is that humans have so irreversibly changed the environment that we now live in the Anthropocene, a new age where only human action can avert catastrophe. We made the mess and now we are responsible for cleaning it up.

Duty, obligation, and responsibility are all legitimate and necessary responses to climate change. But they are not sufficient. What is needed is a deeper appreciation for the beauty of nature, and to embrace the natural world through love. Only love has the power to inspire us to make the sacrifices that must be made. If you love something you want to protect it, take care of it, and to support it so that it might be more fully realized because of your love. To respond to a crisis of global proportions we must engage the divine power of love.

Our usual ideas of political power belong mostly to the mythic stances of the hero and the warrior. Hercules and Ares guide our politics and styles of governing. Conflict, heated thrusts and parries, red-faced debates, adversarial choices between opposing viewpoints (and views are pointed, like the tip of a spear which "belonged" to Ares), warring partisanship, struggling and wrestling with issues, winning and losing, elections as races, bombastic rhetoric—all of these characteristics influence how we think, and, more importantly, imagine politics.

If we were instead to adopt an aesthetic style of politics, we would restore the full range of mythical powers to the polis. Appreciating beauty requires discernment, careful attention, and the embrace of ambiguity. Aesthetic leadership does not posit choices among competing sides but instead appreciates the necessity of diversity. Leadership in service to beauty requires a deftness of imagination that avoids being caught or dominated by any singular viewpoint. It attempts to maintain the entire pantheon as altogether necessary. Certainly, each situation, each decision, might manifest the influence of one or another god more than others, but all of the rest are always there by implication.

Hillman offers three suggestions about how to discern what mythical influences might be present in a given situation: watch your language, feel your mood, and sense how the world responds. All three rules ask for an aesthetic awareness that every event, every decision has a mythical context that "affects the rhetoric of your thinking, the inwardness of your feeling and the effects you have on others."[2] From this perspective, a political leader needs an educated, sophisticated, and differentiated imagination, an honest sensitivity to one's own feelings, and an active awareness of the responses of the greater world. Beauty provides those gifts by refining our senses, deepening our sensuality, and educating us in the ways of the world. To receive these gifts, however, we need to give up the habitual heroic stance that too often dominates our political thinking and action. The lone hero on his horse has no community and cannot create community. Leadership based in beauty, and the aesthetic use of power offer a far richer range of possibilities. It comes down off its high horse and plants its feet firmly on the street.

One final consideration. We noted in Chapter Three that there were two statues erected in Athens in connection with its founding. Aphrodite was one, and Persuasion was the other. The Greek god of persuasion was Peitho, and she is repeatedly paired with Aphrodite.[3] Peitho had erotic connotations with persuasion as seduction, but equally important was her essential role in democratic states, where persuasion, rather than violence, was the ideal. Political oratory depended on Peitho, as did the harmonious working of society in all of its aspects. Peitho, in part because of her close association with Aphrodite, was also connected with Eros. Her other two most common godly associations were with Hermes, the trickster god who was also the patron god of oratory (*Hermes Logios*), and Athene as the patron goddess of the democratic polis. Athene was the protecting goddess of the city, and it was through Peitho that Athene gained her powers of persuasion and her ability to reconcile competing interests.

Can we imagine a style of politics based on the divine pairing of beauty and persuasion? Peitho was contrasted specifically with Bia (force). So here we are considering a form of political power quite removed from the heroic, warring ideas of command and control. Athene, although having aspects as a war goddess, became patron goddess of Athens by

---

2. Hillman, *Kinds of Power*, 225.
3. Helen F. North, "Emblems of Eloquence," *Proceedings of the American Philosophical Society* 137, no. 3 (September 1993): 406–30.

planting an olive tree. She was also a master artisan, especially of weaving. Could these godly associations suggest that political power in service to the polis requires eloquence of speech, beauty of conduct, artistic interlacing of views, clever responses to tricky problems, and a preference for peaceful, deep-rooted reconciliation? This does not mean that other kinds of power are not also present, but when guided by beauty and persuasion we might find ways to use power with more intelligence (Athene was the goddess of reason and wisdom) and appreciation. Then political power would be directed toward fanning the erotic pulse that gives rise to and sustains the polis.

Aesthetic leadership delights in complexity. It welcomes tightly woven, knotty issues, seemingly intractable problems, and things that disturb habitual thought. The pandemic, flood, and social unrest of 2020 were only three events that occurred during my final year as village president. The ongoing flow of the polis continued despite the rocks thrown into the stream. It was by far the most challenging year of my fifteen years of public service. And despite the fear, sadness, loss, and difficulty that these events entailed—no, not that—*because* of the fear, sadness, loss, and difficulty, it was the year I most enjoyed being in office. It was because things were hard that my service to my community was most gratifying. It is when your talents and skills, experience and education, intelligence and emotion are put to the test, when the stakes are raised and the outcomes unsure, that leadership matters the most. I never felt overwhelmed because "I" was never alone. My hand was on the tiller, but the ship of state had a full crew. The seas were rough, but our vessel was strong (Athene was goddess of ship building). The winds blew hard, but the rigging held fast (Hephaestus was the god of metal-working and husband to Aphrodite). We were no longer on the course that we had planned, but we could still hold a heading despite the waves of fear and the currents of conflict (Hermes protected the wandering, often lost, traveler). It was this trust in one another, in the presence of invisibles, and in the integrity of our craft that created a calm within the storm. We persevered by never seeking to avoid where we were or what was happening. We simply persisted, and slowly a thin horizon reappeared, a sliver of blue separating the grays of the roiled sea and clouded sky, and we knew that the worst had passed.

PART II

Beauty and Ethics

SIX

The Moral Imagination

In the *Protagoras,* Plato tells a story about how humans came by their moral sense.[1] In it, two gods, the brothers Prometheus ("forethought") and Epimetheus ("afterthought") are given the task of distributing to the newly formed animals, including humans, their proper traits and qualities. Epimetheus volunteers to make the distribution, with Prometheus to inspect afterwards. Epimetheus proceeds to give out the traits and qualities to the animals, giving some strength without swiftness and others swiftness without strength. Some he armed, and others he left unarmed. Of the latter, some he made large such that their size would protect them, and others he made small such that they could fly or burrow into the ground. All of these things were done so the animals would have the natural attributes they needed to survive. Next, he distributed ways of protecting them against the seasons, clothing them with fur and thick skins to defend against cold and heat and providing them a natural bed of their own when it was time to rest. They were given hooves and hard, callous skin on their feet. Some would eat herbs, others fruit or roots, and some were made to eat other animals. Some were made to have few offspring, while those who were prey were made prolific.

After he had distributed all of the traits and qualities, Epimetheus, true to his name, realized that he had forgotten the humans. When Prometheus came to inspect, he found that "man was naked, unshod, unembedded, unarmed."[2] Prometheus recognized that humans could not survive among the other animals that had superior qualities, so he improvised by stealing fire and the mechanical arts from Hephaestus

---

1. The story is found in *Plato,* vol. 2: *Laches, Protagoras, Meno, Euthydemus,* translated by W. R. M. Lamb, Loeb Classical Library 165 (Cambridge, Mass.: Harvard University Press, 1924), 320c-323a.

2. Ibid., 321c.

and Athene and giving them to the humans. He hoped that this technical ability would be enough to allow humans to survive. At first these gifts seemed to work. Humans, with their forethought and technical wisdom, developed speech and the ability to give things names. They also learned how to construct houses, make clothes and shoes and beds, and how to draw sustenance from the earth. But they were still at the mercy of the stronger, more well-equipped animals.

Although humans had technical wisdom and other intellectual skills, in the beginning they remained scattered in splintered groups. As the onslaught of the other animals intensified, humans finally tried to come together in cities, but they lacked political wisdom, the "art of politics" (*politiké techné*), and so treated one another badly and were unable to form and sustain a community. Finally, Zeus, seeing that humans would surely go extinct without further help, decided to send Hermes to "bring respect and right among men, to the end that there should be regulation of cities and friendly ties to draw them together."[3] Hermes asked Zeus if these qualities should be distributed like those of the arts, where only favored ones received them, or given instead to all. "To all," said Zeus, "let all have their share for cities cannot be formed if only a few have a share of these as of other arts."[4]

And so, then as now, it was not fire that saved us, or our gifts of speech and rational intellect, or even our cleverness with tools. It was our moral sense, our divinely given nature as political animals that allowed us to form and sustain community. According to Plato's story, the moral sense lies at the heart of the art of politics. *Techné* means art or craft in the sense of shaping or constructing something artistically. It comes from a Proto-Indo-European root, *teks* meaning "to weave" (Athene again). The art of politics, then, requires both aesthetics and ethics. Even more, humans need both aesthetics and ethics to be fully realized, and this fullness can only be achieved through the polis. It is community, not individualistic introspection, that constitutes a person.

---

3. Ibid., 323*a*.
4. Ibid.

During the Enlightenment and Romantic periods, philosophers and poets began to speak of a "moral imagination."[5] They argued that imagination was essential to ethics because imagination is necessary for empathy. How else do we put ourselves into another person's shoes, or share their thoughts and feelings? Shelley, in *A Defence of Poetry*, recognized this ethical basis in imagination:

> The great secret of morals is love; or a going out of our own nature, and an identification of ourselves with the beautiful which exists in thought, action, or person, not our own. A man, to be greatly good, must imagine intensely and comprehensively; he must put himself in the place of another and of many others; the pains and pleasures of his species must become his own. The great instrument of moral good is the imagination.[6]

Shelley considered poetry to be necessary to strengthen imagination as "the faculty which is the organ of the moral nature," because "it awakens and enlarges the mind" by opening it to previously unapprehended thoughts. "Poetry lifts the veil from the hidden beauty of the world, and makes familiar objects be as if they were not familiar."[7] Although some of our enlightened and romantic forbears believed that the moral imagination was important because it led to moral action, Shelley disagreed. He believed that "enlarging the circumference of the imagination" could itself affect moral change. Here Shelley rejects the tired dichotomy between the imagination as a subjective, purely personal act, and objective, physical action. Imagination cannot be separated from the greater world beyond the person, and what occurs in imagination reverberates throughout that greater world.

Plato and Socrates thought of ethics as "care of the soul," and that to care for the soul one had to become a thoroughly ethical human being. Compare this to how we usually think about ethics as choices between

---

5. Mary Watkins, "In Dreams Begin Responsibilities: Moral Imagination and Peace," in *Facing Apocalypse,* edited by Valerie Andrews, Robert Bosnak, and Karen Walter Goodman (Thompson, Conn.: Spring Publications, 2021 [1987]), 78.

6. Percy Bysshe Shelley, *Selected Poems, Essays, and Letters,* edited by Ellsworth Barnard (New York: Odyssey Press, 1944), 540.

7. Ibid.

right and wrong, good and evil, just and unjust. Ethics, especially in the political sphere, is usually governed by codes and regulations. To be ethical is to follow the rules and check the boxes. Either the letter of the law has been followed or it hasn't, and if it has then ethics is satisfied.

The oppositional thinking that so often accompanies ethical discourse perhaps crystallizes most clearly in an "ethical dilemma." Just see how easily in our habitual minds these two words slide together. Indeed, it is difficult for us to imagine one without the other, one horn seems to beget the other. This affinity suggests that ethical dilemmas imply dilemma ethics, a manner of imagining ethics that sees in terms of dilemmas, in the style of dilemmas. If so, then "dilemma" connotes a psychological perspective, a genre of imagination.

"Dilemma" comes from Greek meaning "a double proposition, or argument in which one is caught between two difficulties." The Latin root *lemma* means "assumption," and refers back to the Greek "a thing taken; in logic a premise taken for granted." The dictionary defines "dilemma" as "a situation requiring a choice between equally undesirable alternatives." Under this definition we are caught on the horns before we even get started. There are only two choices and *by definition there are no good answers.* Dilemma ethics posits ethical choices in a manner where there are nothing but bad options, and even compromise is largely a matter of cutting losses. "Nobody is going to be satisfied with this solution," says the politician, as if that is a sign of a good solution.

But wait. Must we think of ethics this way? Must ethics be cast in the manner of dilemmas? Don't we have a choice? Just as soul has traditionally been imagined as a middle and mediating ground holding together spirit and body, ethics as care of the soul looks for alternatives beyond either/or choices.

The word as myth has a clue. "Dilemma" as a double proposition or assumption of things taken for granted, especially in logic, suggests that perhaps the difficult problem we find in dilemmas is a result of us imagining them in terms of assumptions and logical choice. Perhaps what is more important are the pre-logical assumptions on which we rest our propositions and arguments. Assumptions point to where we are unconscious. An assumption is not arrived at through contemplation or thought, it is a premise taken for granted. But who grants its authority?

What mythical perspective is speaking in an assumption? One tradition in psychotherapy, by which I mean caring for the soul, is to make the unconscious conscious. If Plato and Socrates are correct that one way to care for the soul is through ethics, then perhaps we need to encourage our unspoken ideas to find their voices so that we might be able to discern the gods that are at work in our assumptions.

I am suggesting here an aesthetic approach to ethics that is embodied in our nature as political animals. Instead of wrestling heroically with the hard and pointed-horned beast we could instead approach it as an ethologist approaches a new species. We watch and observe its behaviors, how it inhabits its ecological niche, how it relates to others, both of its own and different kinds. This observation must be done without projection or interpretation, both of which cloud our observations with assumptions. In other words, we do not allow symbolic understanding to replace imagistic precision, we don't postulate intent or ask "why" questions. We stick with what, when, and how, letting the animal beneath the horns show itself more fully in its living, breathing, pawing presence. After all, horns are not only weapons, they are also adornments. Their power comes not only from their use in war but in the beauty of their display.

If we look back to Plato's story, technical ability was insufficient to create or sustain community. The moral sense, the ability to discern ethically, was needed, and so Zeus sent "right and respect" to humans (Jowett's translation of Plato says "reverence and justice"). I take this to mean that to achieve community humans had to be given the natural ability to see beyond narrow, individual self-interest. Reverence for the gods, respect, humility, and a sense of justice and rightness are what allow humans to act on behalf of something larger than themselves. Remember that Shelley said the moral sense required love as a means of "going out of our own nature." Note that Zeus sent two gifts to humans. The first were respect and right, which were to be the regulating principles of the polis. The second was friendship to draw people together. "Friendship" comes from roots meaning "love," and is allied to "free." So, it is through the ability to love others that we become free, and the polis becomes possible.

To be a friend, or to love someone means that we want to do right by them, to treat them with respect, to put aside selfish concerns so that we may better attend to their concerns. We cannot achieve this through technical means, through reliance on codes and rules and regulations. Instead, we must turn to that great instrument of moral good, the organ of moral nature, the imagination. If ethics is given to us as part of our nature, then in the first instance we will *feel* ethics. Conceptualizing ethics in terms of choices will always be an afterthought (Epimetheus) that leaves out our animal nature. The deeper, precognitive appreciation of ethics will appear through our animal responses, in our being drawn to the beautiful and repelled by the ugly. As political animals we innately sense that community depends on authenticity, sincerity, fairness (in both its ethical and aesthetic connotations), friendship, love, and freedom. And we recognize, resist, and are repelled by fakery, deceit, hypocrisy, inequity, selfishness, hate, and tyranny. Our ethical sense is bred in our bones and received through our aesthetic sensibilities.

Plotinus wrote that for the soul "the Good is its own natural act" (1.7.1). If so, then we care for the soul when we facilitate its natural goodness. Instead of speaking in terms of choices that necessarily limits our options, we approach each situation as an opportunity to craft appropriate responses that are in accord with its particular and peculiar circumstances. Equality does not mean treating everyone the same, it means treating everyone fairly, and that requires an empathetic eye capable of perceiving uniqueness and context, foreground and background. Ethics is art in political dress, a way of honoring the gods through friendship and just behavior. The more beautifully we design, craft, articulate, compose, and arrange the polis in ways that further reverence, justice, friendship, love, and freedom, the more we fulfill the soul's natural propensity to act in the name of the good and the just. "Beauty and Justice are alike in that humans do not make them; they make us human."[8]

Riverside has several locations in the village for the posting of banners either by the village or local organizations to publicize events such as the village's annual July 4th celebrations or a Boy Scout Pancake Breakfast at a local church. In 2017 a local organization asked to put up a banner for Gay Pride Week. It was simply a rainbow, but at the bottom it said

---

8. James Hillman, *La Giustizia di Afrodite/Aphrodite's Justice* (Capri: Edizioni La Conchiglia, 2017), 34.

"in solidarity" and "Action for a Better Tomorrow." The village manager was on vacation when the application came in, and the acting village manager approved the application.

As soon as the banner went up the complaints started coming in. The phone calls were extreme, belligerent, and hateful. People demanded the banner be taken down because it did not represent their values. When staff looked more closely at the application, it turned out that the banner should not have been hung because "Action for a Better Tomorrow" was actually a political activism group, which the village's banner policy did not allow. So, the question was whether to take the banner down, and appear to bow to the vocal minority who were so loudly objecting or leave it up in accord with the application that had already, though wrongly, been approved. We decided to leave it up because it was only a few days until the next banner was due to go up. Later that year, the village board revised the banner policy so that it was clear that banners that "advocate, promote, debate, discuss or relate to any social issue, cause or event" were prohibited.

That same year, I decided to write a resolution specifically stating that one of Riverside's founding ideals was "to create a beautiful environment that encourages civic interaction and social discourse among residents and visitors alike." The resolution stated that people from varying backgrounds, perspectives, ideas, and cultures were what made Riverside a desirable place to live and concluded that the village "celebrates and encourages diversity and a spirit of inclusion among its residents and visitors, and will continue to advance the principles of freedom, equality, and justice for all." I thought it worthwhile to publicly state these values.

It was a simple, straight-forward resolution that stated what I believed to be in line with the vast majority of our residents. But when the resolution came before the village board, three trustees objected to it. Two trustees, who in the past had clearly shown their right-leaning ideologies, found technical reasons for opposing the resolution. One said that it should have been reviewed by an advisory commission before coming to the board. The other said the resolution wasn't needed because by law the village was not allowed to discriminate. He also questioned how much attorney time and expense had been incurred by the resolution

(I pointed out none because I had written the resolution). The third trustee had an unusual objection. He didn't think that Riverside was diverse enough and that more diversity was needed. I never really understood how that was a basis for opposing a resolution supporting diversity, but people's minds work differently. In the end, three trustees supported the resolution and three abstained. Because abstentions are counted with the prevailing side, the resolution passed.

It was a disheartening victory because I knew that the views of the first two trustees were not majority views within the village. But the optics was of an evenly split board on the question of supporting and encouraging diversity. It was also telling that instead of actually stating their ideological objections to the resolution that two of the trustees decided to deflect the discussion by claiming that correct procedures were not followed, and that existing law already forbade discrimination. The former was not true because resolutions were never submitted to commissions for prior review, and the latter missed the point. The resolution was not about legal obligations, it was about values.

A couple of years later, the question of diversity was back. Another political advocacy group gave the village a Pride flag and asked that it be flown during June, which is Pride month. The village didn't have a flag policy, so village staff brought the request to the village board. Unfortunately, the village did not receive the request until early June and the next village board meeting wasn't until June 20. When the flag was not immediately flown, the village began receiving complaints by phone, email, and social media accusing the village board of bigotry even though the village board had not even had an opportunity to discuss the matter.

What should the village do? Should it fly the flag or not? It soon became clear that the village could not fly donated flags because that would convert the flagpole into a limited public forum and open the door for any and all groups to demand certain flags be flown. To confuse matters further, the American Legion had also donated a flag to the village asking it to be flown in September in honor of the American Legion's 100th anniversary. Again, we knew we couldn't fly a donated flag, but how to distinguish between the two requests? If we decided to fly the Pride flag, then didn't we also have to allow other flags? The questions seemed to present a dilemma.

When the village board was finally able to meet on June 20, it quickly became clear that there was unanimous support for flying the Pride flag, not only that year but in ensuing years (the two trustees who had opposed the diversity resolution were no longer on the board). But the board refused to be caught by the purported dilemma that if it flew the Pride flag it would be required to fly other flags. Instead, the board made clear that as a governmental entity it had the right to free speech that included flying flags that the board decided expressed the values of the community. I stated that the Pride flag at issue was not associated with any group or organization but rather had a widely accepted status that transcended organizational flags. It was a symbol of equal protection under the law, fairness, and decency, all of which were ideals embraced by the great majority of Riverside residents. I also asked that the motion to fly the flag specifically refer to the diversity resolution the board had passed in 2017. That wording reinforced the village board's position that flying the Pride flag was an expression of civic values and could not be used as a precedent requiring other flags be flown. The trustees also took the opportunity to respond to the unfair criticism they had received by explaining how the request to fly the flag had come in late and that this was the board's first opportunity to discuss it.

After the vote, several residents who had been among those criticizing the board on social media apologized for their comments and admitted they had jumped to the wrong conclusions by assuming (there's that word again) that because the flag was not being flown the village had decided not to fly the flag. Other residents persisted in their objections to the flag because it did not represent their personal values, but they did so in a more muted, respectful manner than the objectors to the Pride banner. Perhaps this was because it is easier to be strident on the phone or social media than in person, but I also thought that perhaps the unanimity of the village board and its eloquent support of the flag as a symbol of inclusion and diversity had somewhat deflated the extremity of their objections. Perhaps their ideological stance had received a seed of doubt from the manner in which the village board had made and articulated its position.

The board later found a compromise on the American Legion flag by agreeing to fly it on the day of the Legion's 100th anniversary. Because the American Legion was chartered by Congress and was a tax-exempt and non-political organization, the board felt comfortable with allowing the flag to be flown to commemorate the Legion's anniversary without opening the door generally to other organizations.

What was interesting about how the board handled these controversies was how it avoided being drawn into simplistic either/or choices. It also rejected appeals to technicalities and subterfuges to remain focused on the deeper issues at hand. By keeping its discussion and decision within the realm of ethical values instead of forced choices, the board illuminated the ugly assumptions that were hidden in objections to the Pride flag. By firmly standing its ground on behalf of inclusion and diversity, and strongly advocating for equality and justice, the board was able to implicitly reject the bigotry lurking in the opposition. This was an exercise of aesthetic power in the service of beauty that furthered the purpose and potential of the polis. Exclusion cannot create community. Cliques and cults are not communities, they are by nature insular and isolating and are inherently tyrannical and hierarchical. That is why they are so fragile and volatile—they lack the natural strength and integrity of a polis inspired by love.

We have wandered widely in this chapter, which is perhaps appropriate given the presence and influence of Hermes in Plato's tale. Gathering the many threads, though, we can come to some preliminary findings. First is that ethics, which is necessary for the art of politics, is an aesthetic practice. It cannot be confined in codes or limited by regulations. It is better imagined as an emotion, a disturbance of mind and feeling. Emotion is intimately felt and at the same time moves us out and away (the etymological meaning of "emotion") into the greater world, as Shelley put it, "out of our own nature." It is telling in Plato's story that before Protagoras tells his tale he asks Socrates whether he should proceed by telling a fable or through more rational exposition. The gathering encourages Protagoras to proceed however he wishes, and he responds "Well then...I fancy the more agreeable way is for me to tell you a fable."[9] I take this to mean that ethics and politics best proceed through the persuasive powers of imagination, story, fiction, and myth.

---

9. Plato, *Protagoras*, 320d.

Ethics as emotion arises from the heart and gut, which are always more susceptible to being moved by story than by reasons and explanations.

A second strand is that ethics necessarily puts us in relation to invisible powers greater than ourselves. I have used "moral imagination," "moral sense," "morals," "ethics," and "values" interchangeably, probably to the chagrin of my more philosophically inclined readers. The usage, however, is intentional. Morals resonate to the Western mind more in the realm of religion, while ethics feels more secular and at home in law and business. By blurring these lines, I think we are closer to the spirit of Plato's tale. Reverence is one of the pillars of the polis. That does not mean that the polis is a religious entity, or that one religion or the other is necessary to the polis. Reverence here is not a literal belief in a god or gods. Rather it is a *reverential and appreciative attitude* toward life in all of its aspects that is essential to the polis. "Reverence" comes from the Latin *revereri,* meaning "to stand in awe of, respect, honor, fear, be afraid of." Its Proto-Indo-European root is *wer-* meaning to "perceive, watch out for." The same root appears in the words "aware" and "regard." A reverential attitude, then, is one that appreciates the presence and importance of things beyond self-interest and self-centeredness. Reverence draws us beyond the self by asking us to be more perceptive and aware, to regard, honor, and respect the presence and power of other things, beings, and invisibles. And lest we miss its finer point, reverence suggests that we would do well to watch out for the fearful consequences of self-importance and selfishness.

Third is that humans are constituted by the polis and are bound to it through their moral sense. Every person will possess their own unique aesthetic and ethical sense, their own eccentric way of relating to their community. The diversity of perspectives that are inherent in community is one source of its beauty and strength. Each person will honor the gods in their own way, and each person will have their own sense of justice. But the ideals of reverence and justice are held in common by the polis. Part of the art of politics is articulating various ways in which reverence and justice might be served.

Fourth, ethics is best modeled through friendship and freedom. Both inspire and rely upon love and selflessness. A good friend is a true friend, someone we can rely upon to relate to us without deception or manipulation. Freedom requires faith in a greater world that is inherently supportive and trustworthy. Friendship and freedom then become baselines for ethical, civic-minded discourse.

Lastly, the technological arts that Prometheus stole from Hephaestus and Athene were not sufficient to sustain a community. Even the human advances of speech and the rational intellect were not enough. Community needed another kind of *techné*, the artistic weaving of reverence and justice, friendship and freedom. Community is not a weaving in the sense of a final product but rather is the act of weaving, the ongoing intertwining of perspectives and ideas, stories and myths. Community thus is lost when it becomes hardened into single-mindedness and ideology. Fascism can never lead to real community. The art of politics becomes malformed when it is imagined and practiced as hard-knuckled and heroic. At its essence, the art of politics is a soft art of fabric, texture, warp and woof. It proceeds through subtle seductions, relying on persuasion more than force. This aesthetic style of politics rejects simpleminded oppositions and instead relies on deeply felt and imagined ethical responses. If Shelley is correct that the great instrument of moral good is the imagination, then the ultimate goal of ethics is not to determine good or bad, just or unjust, or even right or wrong, it is the "identification of ourselves with the beautiful."

SEVEN

To Have and to Hold

The idea of "order" plays a big role in how we think about governing. Order can refer to arranging things, or to giving a command. Order can also mean maintaining stability or control. We can order a meal, or be a person of first order, or belong to a fraternal or religious order. Perhaps most habitually in our Western minds we pair order with law. Without order we tend to think things will get messy and out of control, become chaotic, maybe even dangerous. Little wonder then that one of government's central duties is imagined as maintaining control, of policing the polis.

We will look first at order as arranging things and as maintaining stability or control. To my mind these two meanings are far more important to politics, ethics, and governing than giving orders as commands. The latter once again ensnares us in hierarchy, order as command structure. The first two are more overtly aesthetic, requiring us to pay attention to how things go together, and how maintenance is an integral aspect of order.

The ancient Greek word *kosmos,* from which we get our *cosmos,* was for the Greeks an aesthetic term that meant "fitting order." It was also an ethical term, meaning "good order, good behavior, decency." Other meanings are becomingly, duly, decently, form, fashion, ornament, decoration, embellishment, and dress. *Kosmos* was also "descriptive of sweet songs and ways of speech." The verb *kosmos* meant "to arrange, adorn, furnish."[1] *Kosmos* was also used to describe governmental order and could refer to a ruler or magistrate. Thus "*kosmos* connotes both aesthetic and ethical order, both adornment and decency."[2] Notably, none

---

1. James Hillman, "Cosmology for Soul: From Universe to Cosmos," *Sphinx: A Journal for Archetypal Psychology and the Arts* 2 (1989): 21.
2. Hillman, *Aphrodite's Justice,* 50.

of these meanings have the all-enveloping connotation of our "cosmos." Instead, the word *kosmos* referred to the "general arrangement of things."[3] The particularity inherent in the early Greek usage of *kosmos* can be contrasted with the later Roman translation of *kosmos* into *universum,* meaning "the whole world turning around one (*unus—verto*)."[4] As an aesthetic term, "cosmetics" is far more in keeping with the original meaning of *kosmos* than the vastness of "cosmos."

When I would call a village board meeting "to order" I often had *kosmos* in mind. I liked thinking that proper decorum, setting an example of good and respectful behavior, appropriate attire, and a touch of formality were influential in setting the tone of our meetings. An atmosphere of civility and respect led to better ideas and more varied debates and discussions. This was a different kind of order than order as control or command. We would also sometimes literally rearrange ourselves, moving trustees around so that they could get to know one another better while also changing the order of voting. Who votes first is a responsibility that should be shared, because voting first can sometimes be difficult, just as being the last vote called can sometimes be the deciding vote. Order mattered.

Ordering principles are best achieved through principled ordering. By that I mean attending to order through ethical conduct, displaying reverence for the invisibles, and striving for small-j justice in your everyday affairs. When it came to our board meetings, I saw my job as doing right by the trustees. I was there to serve their needs, to help them more fully realize the potentials of their office, and to better and more beautifully fulfill their duties. And so, I made sure that everyone had an opportunity to voice their views, that we kept our discussions civil and never resorted to innuendo or a questioning of motives. Another critical part of maintaining order was making sure that the trustees had the information and background they needed to have informed discussions. Knowledge itself

---

3. Aryeh Finkelberg, "On the History of the Greek κοσμοσ," *Harvard Studies in Classical Philology* 98 (1998): 119. Finkelberg is compelling in his argument that the imposition of "world" onto *kosmos* is a later occurrence and that there was no such correlation among the early Greeks.

4. James Hillman, "The Practice of Beauty," *Sphinx: A Journal for Archetypal Psychology and the Arts* 3 (1992): 21.

has an ordering power by providing not only information but patterns that hold the information and make it sensible. The more the trustees understood the broader context of the issues before them the better they could discern the nuances, pitfalls, and complexity that exist in even the most apparently simple decision.

As presiding officer, I sat in the middle of the board alongside the village manager, with three trustees on either side. The manager and I were the middle ground, representing the necessity of both political guidance and expert management. The soul as mediatrix is often seen as being in the middle of things, finding imaginative connections between conflicting or contrasting ideas. As the middleman, it was my job to help convey ideas and thoughts, to be an intermediary, a facilitator. Operating from the middle also meant trying to help the trustees reach a consensus, which originally meant "feel together." And when discussions became heated, as they inevitably do from time to time, being in the middle of things was the perfect place to be if things started to get out of hand because the middle ground provides a buffer, a kind of open space where tempers can cools and hardlines can soften.

If we imagine civic order aesthetically, we might try to incorporate more artistic ideas into public service. Read the following list of words against a backdrop of politics and government, trying to feel and imagine them in terms of political and governmental action and discourse: composition, perspective, collage, expression, harmony, contrast, foreground, background, middle ground, canvas, setting, pose, sketch, architecture, narrative, design, shape, choreography, scale, proportion, form, symbolism, framing, texture, contour, palette, value, pattern, theme. Each of these words has to do in one way or another with "fitting order," of arranging and presenting things appropriately. Instead of thinking of order as rigid, hierarchical, and bossy, it can become an opportunity for delight, order as arranging a bouquet of flowers, setting the table, composing a song. Trying to cram all of the many aesthetic facets of order into one narrow, control-minded perspective is the surest route to disorder. When the ever-flowing waters of the polis are blocked and unduly restrained it is just a matter of time before the dam breaks.

By viewing order through aesthetics, we are better able to match the diversity and vitality of the polis, like treating like. After calling a meeting to order, a presiding officer could then conduct the meeting as a musical event, keeping time, pacing the discussion, minding the rhythm of debate. Policies would not just be analyzed in terms of bureaucratic necessities and economic burdens but rather seen as opportunities to give values compositional form. We would shape and frame our civic discourse around themes that were "descriptive of sweet songs and ways of speech." Order would be freed from its confines in the court and restored to its natural place within the polis where it would thrive as the general arrangement of things presented becomingly, duly, and decently.

One of the primary ways of keeping things in good order is maintenance. We have lightly touched on maintenance already, but its relationship to order requires a closer look. Maintenance (literally "hand-holding") is a major aspect of many governmental decisions because of the resources it requires in terms of time and personnel and its ongoing costs. Maintenance costs can sometimes be a deciding factor in policy decisions. When talking about public facilities, maintenance can sometimes even outweigh construction costs. And the cost of upkeep seems to keep going up.

Despite its importance, maintenance is often granted low status. Maids, janitors, and maintenance men and women tend to be lower paid and given far less respect than their essential services deserve. One positive aspect of the Covid-19 pandemic was that the people who take care of daily maintenance were specifically recognized as "essential workers."

The lack of attention at every level of government to our infrastructure of roads, sewers, and bridges similarly reflects an ignoring ignorance of their critical importance. When we do agree to pony up to pay the costs of maintenance we often do so begrudgingly, treating maintenance as a burden or an unwelcomed obligation. And so, we search for low maintenance solutions, things that won't require too much attention, or so much investment of time and capital.

The more we imagine maintenance as a burden, and treat it with reluctance, the more we constellate its shadows—breakdown, collapse, interruptions. The more we put off maintenance the more rundown and worn-out things become, the more their condition deteriorates. When we just try to maintain, to get it all together, to keep it together, we become fatigued, we burnout.

You surely hear the psychological dimensions of these words. But it is neither maintenance nor its absence that leads to breakdowns, it is our way of imagining maintenance as a burden, of maintenance as a chore taken under duress. When we seek ways to have hands-off maintenance and management, we trap ourselves in a paradox because the hand is right there in the words themselves. To restore dignity to maintenance we need to revalue the hands and their work. Then we would see that it is precisely the people who work with their hands that are essential to maintaining the polis.

Another demon lurking in our usual way of looking at maintenance, especially of material things like buildings or cars or sewers, is our denigration of matter. Here we tend to be thoroughly Cartesian in imagining matter as inanimate, inert, and dead—just stuff. With this attitude in mind, maintenance is merely mechanical, tinkering with the watch to keep it ticking away time in the name of efficiency and productivity. If we perceive a building to be imposing, or a boat graceful, we attribute these feelings to us and say that they are our projections. We don't consider that things themselves have their own power, their own presence and importance. Although we might have an emotional relationship with our cars, even giving them names, we still assume that we are projecting our feelings onto them. We usually don't imagine that the car is capable of having a relationship with us.

When we deny the things of the world soul, when we reject the imaginal power of *anima mundi,* then maintenance becomes a purely secular act. We take care of things without caring about them, and in so doing we deprive them of their intrinsic integrity, worth, and value. The mind wanders when maintenance is just repetitious, we forget to put the oil cap back on, or to put detergent in the washer. Our caring is careless because we are not paying attention to that which we are attending. When we don't care about things, they become fungible, disposable possessions. And when we deny things their inherent value, we have to have more and more things, our consumerism becomes rapacious, out of control.

Another way of imagining maintenance is as service to an ensouled world. In some religious practices, the laying on of hands is believed to confer a blessing or authority. So, we might imagine maintenance as a manner of spiritual practice. When we respect the things of the world and embrace all things as animated then our care for them takes on new meaning and significance. The necessity of returning to things over and over to attend to them is then felt less as repetitious boredom and more as ritualistic attending. Things want and need us to care for them, they delight in our touch, take pride in a fresh coat of paint, and pleasure in a well-oiled hum. Think how we have a special cup for our morning coffee, the one that feels right in our hand, our own chalice. Might we imagine, too, that the cup likes being singled out, enjoys being taken up and held by our particular hands, being made to feel special.

When we value things for their intrinsic worth, we don't need as many things, and the fewer things we have the easier they are to maintain in good order. Instead of cheap, disposable, throwaway materials we are willing to invest in quality "goods" that will endure, providing years of service. For the ancient Greeks, "good" referred to the usefulness and functionality of things in service to a virtuous life. From this perspective, we begin to establish relationships with things, no longer seen as mere possessions but as partners, members of the household. Just think how we come to trust things that we hold over time, how we learn and appreciate their idiosyncrasies and take pleasure in our shared experiences.

When maintenance is handled in this manner it changes, too, how we think about the time and cost associated with maintenance. Instead of quick fixes we seek long-term solutions that mirror the value of long-term relationships, we look for things that will stand the test of time, long lasting and trustworthy, like old friends. Instead of seeking the least expensive alternative we seek the ones that provide the greatest value, where value is not reduced to dollars and cents.

This latter point is important. Both maintenance and a sense of order are largely dominated in modern political and governmental thought by economics. Policy discussions almost always end up being cast in the mode of costs and benefits, placed on a balancing scale of pros and cons, and trying to get the biggest bang for the buck. But if we shift maintenance and order into the fields of service and value then our attitude about economics would also change.

Economics and ecology share common roots with *oikos,* our "eco," at their heart. *Oikos* means "home," and "economics" combines *oikos* and *nomos,* home and management. From the perspective of service, economics ordered by beauty refers to household management. A properly managed and maintained household takes care of all of its inhabitants, visible and otherwise. It is frugal and careful with its resources. And because economics and ecology share a common origin in the home, economics would be naturally sensitive to protecting habitats and the broader environment. It would be bad economic policy to place profit over preservation and protection because to do otherwise would be hubristic and disrespectful. Instead, economics would rely on one of its favorite terms—appreciation—to restore economics to an aesthetic base. Appreciating value would mean not only monetary increase but also an increase in that which matters to us, what we care for, esteem, and treasure. Here again we find so many soul words embedded in our economic thinking—bond, yield, safe, credit, duty, interest, share, debt, trust, save. Freed from the domination of predatory capitalism and its pseudo-Darwinian belief in the survival of the fittest, economics would return to home base, regaining its familial connections to what it really takes to maintain a household, the ordering powers of love, attention, caring, and gratitude. Imagine a polis in which essential workers were compensated in keeping with their value. The growing income inequality in the United States is an aesthetic and ethical disorder that points to the need of getting our house in order.

Riverside has several commuter parking lots. The largest one sets beside a large park that is adjacent to our central business district. The parking lot is on one of the busiest streets in town and is used both by residents and by folks who drive through the village as a short-cut to get from a major road, 1st Avenue, to another major road, Ogden Avenue. The parking lot also is right beside a private swim club. For all of the above reasons, the parking lot is seen by a lot of eyes.

The existing asphalt of the parking lot had reached its end. There were cracks and potholes that were beyond patching, so it was time to redo the lot. The village board initially considered replacing the old with the new and installing another asphalt lot. That was the cheapest alternative in the short term, and also the easiest and least expensive to maintain. I suggested a different approach. Years earlier I had written a referendum question in favor of sustainable practices and green infrastructure. It had passed with 80% support by our residents. A major aspect of the village's sustainability efforts has to do with stormwater management. Most of the village still has a combined sewer system, meaning that both water runoff and sewage are carried in the same sewer lines. In major rain events the combined sewers can become overloaded, leading to backups in basement—a most unpleasant occurrence. So, keeping storm water out of the sewer system is important.

I suggested that we convert the commuter lot into an example of cutting-edge stormwater management. It would incorporate permeable pavers, a rain garden, and natural swales with native plants where overflow could be held naturally until absorbed by the soil and taken up by the plants. Not only would it be vastly more attractive than asphalt, it would help keep storm water out of our sewers and out of people's basements.

The estimated cost for an asphalt surface was $400,000 with an estimated life of fifteen years. The lot I was suggesting would cost $1.2 million and have a life of fifty years. The village board was open to the idea of a "green" solution, especially given the significantly longer lifespan of the permeable pavers. It asked staff to see if grant funding was available to off-set some of the costs, and over the next few years staff was able to obtain almost $900,000 in grant funding from local agencies that were themselves urging innovative solutions to stormwater management. It took years to accomplish, but at the end of the project Riverside ended up paying about $315,000 for the lot—less than the cost of an asphalt lot. The new parking lot is able to retain about 224,000 gallons of storm water, which is filtered into the ground slowly instead of sheet draining into the village's sewer system.

The lot, with its rain garden and natural swales was designed by the village's engineer with specific instructions to make it beautiful. The resulting design is so attractive and innovative that the village put up informational signs describing how the stormwater management aspect of the project works. What was a plain, asphalt parking lot became a beautiful source of civic pride, all because the village board had the will and patience to give it a chance and village staff was so creative in finding grant funding.

The lot became a foundation for future projects, and the village continues to use permeable pavers and other green technology in other parking lots and alleys. The residents support these efforts with their tax dollars, understanding that Riverside has a special connection to its environment and that such efforts also help to keep the smelly stuff out of basements!

At about the same time that the parking lot was under consideration, the village board approved moving forward with repairing the roof on the village's iconic train station, which stands right beside the commuter parking lot just described. The roof is made of ceramic tiles and it was to be a labor intensive and expensive project—about $1.3 million. Some of the tiles were broken and unusable, but the contractor who received the project proposed a novel solution. The tiles that could be saved would be reinstalled in their original places with new tiles interspersed with the old. The result was a mosaic-like look of contrasting colors that was more beautiful than the original. When the roof was finished the village then restored the platforms and hand railings. Once again, staff rose to occasion and obtained grant funding for all except $100,000 of the project. Once the exterior was complete, the local historical commission paid to have an installation put inside the station outlining Riverside's history. The train station was more beautiful than ever before.

The crowning piece of the commuter lot and train station renovations once again combined practicality with beauty. As an active commuter stop, commuters were walking across one of Riverside's busiest streets at a location that put them at risk. The village once again turned to its engineers who designed a new layout that incorporated the recent changes to the train station while also re-routing pedestrians to a safer crossing. Raised planters and bike racks were installed and the entire area was tied together with uniform brickwork. This project had a price tag of $540,000. The village was able to obtain $378,000 in grant funding, leaving the village to pay only $162,000 for the project.

Over a five-year period, the village was able to transform a degrading parking lot, a historic train station with a leaky roof, and an unsafe pedestrian crossing into an architectural gem. Each project brought together technical expertise, creative and innovative design, overwhelming public support, a village board dedicated to providing the best value and service to the village, and a committed village staff that embraced the economic challenges. Also, in each project, beauty was an essential component. Instead of being an afterthought or considered mere window dressing, the projects had beauty as their driving force. The political will and technical skill involved were guided by and directed toward finding beautiful solutions that answered practical needs. In fact, practicality and beauty were considered two sides of the same coin. It was the beauty of the projects that created public and political support for the projects and that aided staff in finding grant funding. Beauty was the ordering principle that turned what could have been rote maintenance into public art.

I was proud of the village board, our engineers, our staff, and the civic partners who made these projects possible. They were big projects for a small village, and they required all hands on deck. The trustees refused to reduce the economics of the projects to just money and rejected the easiest, quickest, and cheapest way out. They instead appreciated the impact these projects would have on the community, not just its current residents, but generations to come. They took the long view, seeing the value in creativity and innovation and the deeper benefits that these projects provided. At the heart of these projects were noble ideals— honor for nature, history, and the well-being of the polis. By restoring maintenance to its foundation in service, and by respecting the things and materials being maintained as having intrinsic value, these public works projects became opportunities for soul-making. They were tangible expressions of communal values, of civic pride. And none of it would have happened without beauty.

We return now to the other main meaning of order as command. This can mean assertive as when someone who is imbued with authority by the government, a police or military officer, for example, uses that authority to compel action or obedience—hands in the air, take that hill. Or it can be more amenable and polite, as in ordering a meal or a delivery of flowers. All along that spectrum, however, order retains its meaning as a command from one person who is given authority to direct the actions of another. Even the server who comes to take our dinner order is not empowered to reject it or insist that we order something else.

When we look closer at order in terms of command, we find that we are on familiar ground. "Command" is another hand word. It comes from Latin roots meaning "together" (*com-*) and "to put in the hands of, entrust to" (*mandare*). In its most appealing sense, then, order as command would be based on a coming together based on trust, on putting ourselves in the hands of another. The citizen obeys the police, and the private obeys the captain, not out of fear but out of mutual trust. At the same time, the ones giving the orders owe due respect to those they seek to command; the trust and loyalty upon which order as command rests must be a two-way street. To expect obedience in the absence of trust is tyranny. Only when order is a joining together of hands can true order be maintained. Otherwise, it is only enforced order, compliance in the face of punishment or coercion. Certainly that, too, is a necessary aspect of order as command. The hand can be a fist or an open palm, something that strikes with force or reaches out to calm and pacify. Both are necessary for politics, ethics, and government, but surely the latter is the ideal we seek.

The trust that is necessary for command binds people together in common service to a greater ideal or power. We might usually imagine the chain of command as vertical and top-down, but a chain also links us horizontally, commands passed from hand to hand, order ultimately based upon everyone along the chain depending upon one another, the chain only as strong as its weakest link. Benjamin Franklin wrote in his *Poor Richard's Almanack* that "He that cannot obey, cannot command," and I take this to mean that all order in the manner of command is derivative. It derives always from greater powers beyond the organization or the polis. When I was village president, I knew that I had the authority to command, but I never considered myself a higher authority. Whatever authority I had came from the trust of the people who had elected me and from the other public officials with whom I served in common purpose.

If we are to maintain good order in the polis through ethical and respectful arrangement and through commands based in mutual trust, then we must also maintain our connections with the invisibles that nurture and make possible the polis. Thomas Moore points out that another word for city life that is closely associated to politics is "civil." Civil refers to the concerns of citizens and also to a style of courteous and respectful interaction as "civility." Moore reminds us that the root of "civil" is the Indo-European *kei,* which means "bed, rest, endearment, and is related to 'cemetery.' "[5] He takes this to suggest that the role of politics and civil,

---

5. Thomas Moore, *The Re-Enchantment of Everyday Life* (New York: HarperCollins, 1996), 116.

civic life and behavior "is to make a home for the dead, give us all a place where we can sleep, and foster a sense of mutual endearment."[6] This move downward into the grounding presence of the ancestors, to providing a bed where we might both rest and also receive dreams, and to expressing through act and word feelings of gratitude and love provide a deeper basis for the ordering powers of politics and civic life. Remember that *kosmos* was "descriptive of sweet songs and ways of speech." Could this mean that one way of creating and maintaining the life of the polis is through terms of endearment? When we listen to the etymology of a word with an ear to imagination we are not trapped in its literal meaning. Bed, rest, endearment, and cemetery are not just literal things and acts, they are images that resonate in the soul. Moore goes on to make a useful distinction. As we have seen, our usual idea of politics stress administration, bureaucracy, and lawmaking, all of which rely on "thought, judgement, and heroics." An alternative, which is what this book is about, is a politics that puts an "emphasis on imagination, caretaking, and depth of vision."[7] In Jungian psychology the former style is associated with the *animus,* or spirit. The latter belongs to *anima,* or soul. Although we go astray when we conceive of these ideas as opposites, their different styles can help us gain insight into our styles of political practice. They are both necessary but neither alone is sufficient for civic life.

The hands that arrange, maintain, and command order also have other gifts. Hands can beckon, confer greetings and farewells, lift us up and press us down, they can point the way or point blame, they can wave on action or stop it with raised palms. Hands can massage, caress, stroke, and sooth. And they can slap and clap. They are holders of tools and can practice techniques of all manner (another word with hand in it) of arts. They fashion, craft, and mold. Machiavelli would doubtless add that they can also manipulate (yet another hand word). The gifts of the hands provide the talents and skill necessary to political leadership based in beauty and ethics. How we handle things shows far more about our politics than the rules we establish or the procedures we ordain. Creating

---

6. Ibid.
7. Ibid., 117.

and maintaining order requires the full ranges of the hands' abilities to manage and interact with the many things of the polis. In marriage we vow to have and to hold, and adorn the hands with golden rings. So, too, we honor a polis that is founded in the bonds of love and revealed through the grace of the hands.

EIGHT

And Juſtice for Eaċh

According to Plato one of the main ordering principles for the polis is justice. There are many religious, philosophical, and jurisprudential theories about justice. For our purposes, I am not interested so much in what justice means in conceptual terms as in how it is felt and experienced. Our appreciation of an act of kindness and our visceral reaction to rudeness are both examples of how we have aesthetic responses to things we perceive as good or bad, just or unjust.

Two related words bring together beauty and justice—fair and fairness. They derive from the Gothic *fagrs,* meaning pleasing to behold, beautiful, attractive, and fit, both in the sense of "pleasing to the eye" and as "firmly placed."[1] "Fair" is connected to the Dutch *vegen* and German *fegen* meaning to make clean, pure, or beautiful. *Fegen* is in turn related to the verb "fay," meaning to join, to fit, to unite, to pact. "Pact" comes from the same root as *pax, pacis,* the word for peace. "Fair" possibly comes from a Proto-Indo-European root that meant to fasten or fit together. Another view connects "fair" with a Proto-Indo-European root meaning to be content.[2] The earliest uses of "fair" were strictly aesthetic. One meaning was blonde or beautiful or both, such as in "fair skin" or "fair hair." In another sense it meant favorable, helpful, and good, such as "fair wind," "fair weather," and "fair tide." In the mid-fifteenth century, "fair" came to mean right conduct in competitions such as in fair play, fair game, fair race, and fair chance. This is about the same time that "fair" and

---

1. This etymology is taken from Elaine Scarry, *On Beauty and Being Just* (Princeton, N.J.: Princeton University Press, 1999), 91–92.

2. This is the view of David Hackett Fischer, *Fairness and Freedom: A History of Two Open Societies—New Zealand and the United States* (New York: Oxford University Press, 2012), 15.

"fairness" acquired their meanings as ethical terms such as fair price, fair judgment, fair footing, and fair and square. Sometimes "fair" also meant a disposition to act fairly, such as fair-minded, fair-natured, and fair-handed. Through all of their ethical applications, "fair" and "fairness" are basically about not taking undue advantage of other people.[3]

Although fairness is just as difficult to define as justice, it has a less abstract feel to it. Fairness seems more immediate, more like a felt response than a conceptual ideal. Research suggests that children as young as four-months old have a sense of fairness at least in the sense of unequal distribution of resources.[4] In one study, infants sat on a parent's lap and watched as two identical penguin puppets (operated by a hidden assistant) came from behind openings in the back wall of a small stage. There was a small place mat in front of each puppet. During the introductory part of the experiment, the penguins "danced" by tilting from side to side every second and then paused while the infant watched. This phase was to familiarize the infant with the scene. During the test trial, the penguins danced until a female experimenter opened a curtained window in the right wall of the stage. The penguins turned toward her and watched as she brought in a plate with two identical cookies and announced, "I have cookies!," to which the penguins responded, "Yay, yay!" in two distinct female voices. Next, the experimenter placed a cookie on the place mat in front of one penguin and then either placed the other cookie in front of the same penguin (unequal event) or the other penguin (equal event). Finally, the experimenter left with her empty plate, closing the curtain at her window, and the penguins looked down at their place mats and paused. The infants watched this paused scene until the trial ended.

By timing how long the infants looked at the penguins in both the unequal and equal events, the researchers found that even a four-month-old infant looked longer at the penguin that received an unequal share of

3. Ibid., 15–16.

4. Melody Buyukozer Dawkins, Stephanie Sloane, and Renée Baillargeon, "Do Infants in the First Year of Life Expect Equal Resource Allocations?," *Frontiers in Psychology* (19 February 2019): 1–19 (online at *https://www.ncbi.nlm.nih.gov/pmc/articles/PMC6389704/*).

the cookies. Fascinating enough, but even more interesting is that when "inanimate" objects replaced the dancing penguins the infants did not look longer at the unequal share. The recognition of the unequal distribution appears to matter only in regard to animated entities. Another interesting variable was that if, instead of having the cookies distributed by an experimenter, they instead were revealed on the place mats by removing covers, the infants did not distinguish between the unequal and equal shares. Apparently, the infants were reacting to the unequal distribution by a third-party to animate entities in recognizing inequity and unfairness.

As noted in Chapter One, there is also a growing body of research that a sense of fairness extends beyond the human and also appears in other species. So far researchers have found what appears to be a recognition of inequitable distribution in monkeys, apes, dogs, cleaner fish, and corvids. One interesting aspect of this research is that a task is required for non-human animals to react to inequities. If unequal rewards are freely given, non-human animals don't react but if unequal rewards are given in response to an effort by the animal the inequity is noticed and objected to. The level of effort performed does not appear to matter, merely the act itself. In addition, research indicates that some non-human animals respond negatively to receiving too much or better rewards than their research partner. That is, they react negatively to inequity even if it benefits them.[5] In one experiment, two capuchin monkeys were given the task of handing a rock to a researcher, who then gave them a food reward. The first monkey gave the rock and received a piece of cucumber, which monkeys will eat but it is not a favored food. The first monkey then watched as the second monkey gave the researcher a rock and was in turn given a grape—a much preferred food. When the researcher returned to the first monkey, it presented a rock and was again given cucumber, which he promptly threw at the researcher!

The presence of at least a rudimentary sense of fairness in infants and some non-human animals perhaps suggests that fairness belongs to the nature of political animals, and that they are innately able to recognize

5. Sarah F. Brosnan and Frans B.M. de Waal, "Fairness in Animals: Where to from Here?," *Social Justice Research* 25, no. 3 (2012): 336–351.

acts that disrupt good or appropriate order. The notion of fairness as good or appropriate order connects beauty and justice. The etymology of "fair" and "fairness" shows that the ethical meanings of the words came later and that they derive from their earlier aesthetic connotations. The recognizing gaze of the infant and the irritation of the monkey who received the cucumber both displayed innate aesthetic discernments of unfairness. Political animals seem to have an instinctual aversion to injustice.

The idea of justice, of course, existed long before "fair" and "fairness" appeared as words. Still, beauty, order, good, and love appear together from the early days of our Western tradition. Plato's *Symposium* is but one example where Diotima speaks of beauty, good, and *eros*. According to Socrates she says that we first associate beauty with physical beauty, then learn to see beauty of the soul. After that, a person who is devoted to beauty and love will eventually be "compelled to view the beauty in pursuits and laws, and perceive that all [beauty] is interrelated."[6] Similarly, Plotinus wrote that "minds that lift themselves above the realm of sense to a higher order are aware of beauty in the conduct of life, in actions, in character, in the pursuits of the intellect; and there is the beauty of the virtues" (1.6.1). The continuing theme is that beauty leads to an appreciation of the good and virtuous.

The connection between beauty and justice is also found in the very words themselves. "Beauty" comes from the Latin *bellus,* meaning fair, which is a variant of *bonus,* meaning good. The ancient Greek word that comes closest to our meaning of beauty was *kalos,* which meant beauty and also good or noble. For its part, "justice" derives from roots meaning "that which is fitting." Here again is the idea that justice is revealed by beauty as that which is appropriate and fitting, which also ties justice to *kosmos* as "fitting order."

The philosopher Elaine Scarry points to symmetry as holding together beauty and justice. She mentions Aristotle's statement that justice is a perfect cube, and to the scales of justice that balance and weigh both sides of an issue. She concludes that the symmetry and balance that are often

---

6. *Plato,* vol. 3: *Symposium,* edited and translated by Chris Emlyn-Jones and William Preddy, Loeb Classical Library 166 (Cambridge, Mass.: Harvard University Press, 2022), 210*b–c.*

ascribed to beautiful things give rise to the notion of fair distribution and equality. She quotes a phrase from John Rawls that fairness is "a symmetry of everyone's relation to one another."[7]

Philosophical speculation aside, I am suggesting that beauty reveals justice as part of the cosmos of each thing that is innately fittingly ordered and coherent, that particularity comes complete with integrity, and that appreciation is inherently respectful. In infants, inequity was recognized only when animated entities were involved and when the inequity was the result of third-party action. In at least some non-human animals, inequity is objected to only when effort is unevenly rewarded. Both instances implicate an innate sense of unfairness as being disrespectful. If justice is grounded in respectful appreciation of each thing just as it is, then fairness as equality naturally arises as part of our natures as political animals. This is not the same thing as "natural law," which from Cicero onward has implied eternal, immutable, and unchanging law. An aesthetic approach to justice is multiple and varied, adapting to each thing and circumstance in the most appropriate manner possible. Although justice can be contemplated and codified through reason, its immediate presence or absence is grasped through aesthetic responses.

In Greek mythology, four goddesses are particularly important for our consideration of beauty and justice: Themis and her daughters Dike (justice), Eunomia (good order), and Eirene (peace). Themis was a bride of Zeus and was responsible for divine order. It was Themis who called the gods to counsel, and who gave natural divine law, as distinct from the laws made by mortals which were overseen by Eunomia. Themis is the model for our Lady Justice and was depicted as holding a balance scale. But the blindfold we see on Lady Justice was a later addition and did not belong to Themis, rather Themis was a seer, and according to Aeschylus was the second prophetess at the Oracle of Delphi (the first being her mother, Gaia).[8] Themis represented the divine order which

---

7. Scarry, *On Beauty*, 95.

8. Aeschylus, *Oresteia: Agamemnon, Libation-Bearers, Eumenides,* translated by Alan H. Sommerstein, Loeb Classical Library 146 (Cambridge, Mass.: Harvard University Press, 2009), 355.

gods and humans alike were expected to follow. The etymology of her name means "that which is put in place," and so it was through Themis that humans learned the laws of justice and morality, rules of hospitality, good governance, how to conduct an assembly, and how to make reverential offerings to the gods. To defy or ignore Themis was a transgression against the gods, an act of cosmic disorderliness, and such transgressions were responded to by Nemesis, another goddess who meted out "revenge for the violation of [Themis's] Order."[9]

Themis's daughters—Dike, Eunomia, and Eirene—were called the Horai and were the goddesses of the seasons, protectors of the gates of heaven, and presided over the revolutions of the constellations. Themis also bore the Moirae, the goddesses of fate and the destiny of humans. Together, the Horai were especially important for the polis and civil order. Dike was referred to in classical literature as an unsullied fountain and a sure supporter of cities. She is called unswerving and bright-throned, depicted as walking in wide streets, and a helper in fine deeds. She is responsible for guiding all things to their proper end. Elsewhere she is referred to as voiceless, unseen, hallowed, and inexorable. Aeschylus wrote that "the anvil of Dike is planted firm."[10] (This last statement harkens back to the etymology of "fair" as firmly placed.) Dike was the mother of Hesychia, goddess of tranquility of mind.

Eunomia was responsible for the internal stability of the polis and oversaw good laws and the maintenance of civil order. She was referred to as rose-bloomed and revealed all what was orderly and fitting. She was often depicted in the company of Aphrodite. Solon said of her that "she makes the rough smooth, puts a stop to excess, weakens insolence, dries up the blooming of ruin, straightens out crooked judgements, tames deeds of pride, and puts an end to acts of sedition and to the anger of grievous strife. Under her all things among men are fitting and rational."[11]

---

9. Karl Kerényi, *The Religion of the Greeks and Romans,* translated by Christopher Holme (New York: E. P. Dutton, 1962), 121. Also see Kerényi's discussion of Themis, 116–18, and Hybris, 118.

10. All references to classical literature are from the entry for Dike at *https:// www.theoi.com/Ouranios/HoraDike.html*

11. Entry for Eunomia at *https://www.theoi.com/Ouranios/HoraEunomia.html*

Lastly come Eirene, whose name is closely related to the Greek word for spring. Late spring was the political campaign season in ancient Greece, a time when Eirene's oversight was particularly needed. She was the goddess of wealth, protector of children and families, and was referred to as blooming, garland-wearing, fair, and gentle. Aeschylus wrote that "she honours a city that reposes in a life of quiet, and augments the admired beauty of its houses."[12] Pindar called her "the city's friend."[13] In Eirene we see another connection to the etymology of "fair" as related to *pax* or peace.

Taken together, the Horai were responsible for the ordering and adornment of human life. As divine sisters they inform one another, each a facet of the others and of their parents, Themis and Zeus. The recurring idea of proper, good, appropriate, and fitting order goes hand in hand with aesthetic epithets such as bright-throned, rose-bloomed, and garland wearing. All are associated with the gentle, fair season of spring and the cyclical rotations of the heavens that marked the passage of time.

In the classical literature, Dike and Eunomia are specifically opposed to what for the Greeks was perhaps the greatest human transgression—*hybris,* from which we get "hubris." In the tragedies, hubris was excessive pride toward or defiance of the gods, acts that were contrary to the divine laws of Themis and that led to the revenge of Nemesis. Dike and Eunomia, justice and proper order, stand against and negate the arrogance and inflation of hubris. Indeed, it might be that hubris lies at the heart of all injustice. Acts of violence against another person, the excesses of greed, or the frauds of deceit and deception all require that one person assumes a superiority over another, a self-importance that underpins the disorderly conduct. Hubris is the greatest threat to justice, order, and peace because it replaces reverence with pretensions of godliness. Hubris belongs to those who, to recall Aristotle, consider themselves "self-sufficing" and independent from the polis.

Beauty, and the appreciation it engenders, is an antidote to hubris. Scarry says that beauty leads to a "radical decentering" that reminds

---

12. Entry for Eirene at *https://www.theoi.com/Ouranios/HoraEirene.html*
13. Ibid.

a person that not only are they not the center of the world, they are not even the center of their own world.[14] Beauty overcomes self-centeredness and selfishness, which are necessary for hubris, by eviscerating the very idea of the self. Scarry quotes two lovely passages in the regard. Simone Weil writes that beauty requires us "to give up our imaginary position as the center...A transformation then takes place at the very roots of our sensibility, in our immediate reception of sense impressions and psychological impressions."[15] Iris Murdoch writes that "anything which alters consciousness in the direction of unselfishness, objectivity and realism is to be connected with virtue." She then specifies that the most "obvious thing in our surroundings which is an occasion for 'unselfing'...is what is popularly called beauty."[16] Another passage from Murdoch strengthens her point:

> Beauty is the convenient and traditional name of something which art and nature share, and which gives a fairly clear sense to the idea of quality of experience and change of consciousness. I am looking out of my window in an anxious and resentful state of mind, oblivious of my surroundings, brooding perhaps on some damage done to my prestige. Then suddenly I observe a hovering kestrel. In a moment everything is altered. The brooding self with its hurt vanity has disappeared. There is nothing now but kestrel. And when I return to thinking of the other matter it seems less important. And of course this is something which we may also do deliberately: give attention to nature in order to clear our minds of selfish care.[17]

Weil suggests that beauty alters our self-centeredness and opens the soul to the inherent multiplicity of the *anima mundi*. Murdoch shows how beauty frees us from the self-interest of "brooding self with its hurt vanity," and releases us back to our natural place as political animals.

14. Scarry, *On Beauty*, 110.

15. "Love of the Order of the World," in Simone Weil, *Waiting for God,* translated by Emman Craufurd (New York: Harper and Row, 1951), 159. Quoted in Scarry, *On Beauty*, 111.

16. Iris Murdoch, *The Sovereignty of Good over Other Concepts: The Leslie Stephen Lecture* (Cambridge: Cambridge University Press, 1967), 2. Quoted in Scarry, *On Beauty*, 113.

17. Iris Murdoch, *Sovereignty of Good* (London: Routledge, 1999), 84.

Scarry concludes that through beauty "all the space formerly in service of protecting, guarding, advancing the self (or its 'prestige') *is now free to be in the service of something else*" (emphasis added).[18]

This last point shines the brightest light on the connection between beauty and justice. Beauty redirects our gaze outward through a reverential appreciation of other people and things. It overcomes self-centeredness and selfishness by revealing the divine luminosity in all things that calls us to service beyond ourselves, to the polis that allows our fullest realization. By its example it encourages us to act more beautifully and even to create beautiful things, including institutions, laws, and ideals of good relations. Just as with the old idea of *kosmos,* beauty and justice both seek the proper ordering and adornment of life. Beauty draws the eyes and heart to how harmonious relationships benefit the general arrangement of things and reveals how balance and equality can create a polis where people don't just live but live well.

Appreciation of beauty teaches us about appropriateness, about how things fit together, how good and proper order can create compositions of elegance and power whether it be in music or governance, and how arrangement as bricolage can hold diverse things together while revealing new aspects of their uniqueness whether on a canvas or in a democracy. Beauty humbles us and instills a deep and abiding respect, which in turn benefits justice, order, and peace. How impossible it is to puff ourselves up with hubris when we turn our eyes to the starry night sky and the quiet, majestic procession of the constellations.

All of this suggests that the order of *kosmos* and rose-bloomed Eunomia does not lend itself to rigidity, hierarchy, linear progress, or one-size-fits-all solutions. Dike seeks to guide all things to their proper end, Eunomia reveals all that is orderly and fitting, and Eirene augments the beauty of homes in peaceful cities. Justice, Order, and Peace are aesthetic endeavors at once divine and organic that call upon the best of our creative natures as political animals. Jurisprudence and governance, institutions and organizations, households and cities cannot flourish, thrive, and bloom without the generative powers of beauty, justice, order, and peace.

---

18. Scarry, *On Beauty*, 113.

Like the constellations that circle overhead, Plotinus wrote that "The Soul exists in revolution around God to whom it clings in love, holding itself to the utmost of its power near to Him as the Being on which all depends; and since it cannot coincide with God it circles about Him." (2.2.2). He contrasted this with the forward path that is characteristic of the body. This is an apt metaphor to hold close when we are confronted with matters of justice, order, and peace. Instead of a head-long rush to judgment, we can revolve around the matter, observing it lovingly from all sides, re-specting (looking again and again) the divine mystery within all things. Instead of a strident forward march, we can be more willing to retreat, fall back, maybe take a different road. Instead of reducing things to simple choices between opposites, we can be aware that sometimes justice is voiceless and unseen, requiring different senses beyond the preferred rational methods of hearing and seeing. In the underworld, wrote Heraclitus, "souls perceive by smelling."[19]

To find just and good responses to the complexities of political life, then, we need to rely on all of our senses to tease out the aesthetic challenges and opportunities they present. Our search is for appropriate responses that are adapted to, indeed derived from, the complexities themselves, responses that are apt, fitting, well-suited, and proper to the situation at hand. We already have a term for this kind of blending of the aesthetic and ethical in the name of justice. We call it poetic justice. We find poetic justice especially satisfying and pleasing precisely because it is so apropos. Like poetry itself, poetic justice operates with precision; just as a poem finds the right words to spark the imagination, so, too, poetic justice finds a right response that answers the injustice to which it responds. Poetic justice offers a closure and completeness that rote application of generalized laws and procedure cannot attain. Perhaps that is because poetic justice takes us back the Horai and their other sisters, the Moiria, or fates. It fell to the Moiria to allot each human their share (Moira means "share") or proper allotment of life and destiny. When we say of poetic justice that someone "got what was coming to them" or "what they deserved" we invoke the invisible hands of the fates.

---

19. Wheelwright, *Heraclitus*, 59.

Justice for all means that we approach all things fairly, but that does not mean that all things are treated the same. Similarly, equal treatment under the law does not mean that everyone receives the same result. Justice in the service to beauty is always particular, always striving to find an appropriate response to each situation or circumstance. Instead of justice for all, beauty gives us justice for each that recognizes and appreciates the integrity, context, and uniqueness of each event and then responds aesthetically, like treating like to craft an equitable response. When young people in Riverside marched in opposition to systemic racism, they received the same police protection that would have been afforded people who wanted to march in support of the status quo. Procedurally they were treated the same because the right to peaceful protest extends to everyone, but the village also made clear in the manner of its response that it supported the first group and opposed the latter.

Politicians could learn a great deal about individualized justice from teachers. Great teachers excel at being able to educate both the class as a whole and students as individuals. They flow seamlessly from generalized language to language specially tailored for the ears of one student. They know that there are countless ways to express an idea and are constantly experimenting with new approaches and new styles of presentation. For a teacher, few things are more gratifying than seeing the light flicker in the eyes of a student when the right words get through. And for a student, few things are more gratifying than being singled out by a teacher, attended to as special, not just looked at but seen.

When I was in graduate school at Southern Methodist University, I was fortunate to take a theology course taught by Schubert Ogden. He was an amazing, and demanding, teacher. He expected students to be fully prepared for class and he held class discussion firmly on point for that week's topic. He had specific knowledge he wanted to impart and would not let students stray away from a difficult concept or idea. But he paired his class material with an extraordinary personal touch. Every week, every student in the class was allowed to write him three questions about any theological or philosophical idea they wanted. And he would then handwrite extended responses to your questions. His only requirement was that they had to be good questions, meaningful and well-thought out. Throughout that semester I and every other student in class was privileged to have a one-on-one conversation with a great intellectual. Even at the time I knew I was experiencing something special, and fifty years later I still have a folder with our conversation, all written in cursive!

In the end, it is love that makes the difference. To craft poetic justice, to bring good order to the polis, and to sustain peace all require that we first find ways to connect with one another. Remember that while reverence and justice were the ordering principles of the polis, it also required the bonds of friendship. I remember like it was yesterday another experience from school. Benjamin Ladner, who first opened my eyes to philosophy, was talking to me during a class. I was struggling with some idea now long forgotten, but he had his eyes latched on me and an expression of recognition crossed his face. As we talked, he came out from behind the lectern and slowly walked toward me, locked intently on our conversation. I remember how the rest of the class disappeared from my view. It was like we were in a tunnel, just Ladner and me. It was a life-changing moment. We both saw something in one another, something familiar and kindred, even though he was far more knowledgeable and gifted than I. And in the intimacy of that engagement, he showed me things about myself that I had never seen. It was as if I could see myself through his eyes. There is no other word for that moment than love.

We know Eros, the Greek god of love, mostly from the depictions of him in the later poets where he is usually described as a young boy and one of the youngest of the gods. There are multiple versions of his parentage, and he is sometimes referred to as a son of Aphrodite and other times as her companion. But there is an earlier version of Eros that places him among the oldest of the gods. In these tellings, Eros has a cosmogonic significance.[20] Quite apart from the later stories where he instills

---

20. "In truth, first of all Chasm came to be, and then broad-breasted Earth, the ever immovable seat of all the immortals who possess snowy Olympus's peak and murky Tartarus in the depths of the broad-pathed earth, and Eros, who is the most beautiful among the immortal gods, the limb-melter—he overpowers the mind and the thoughtful counsel of all the gods and of all human beings in their breasts." Hesiod, *Theogony, Works and Days, Testimonia,* edited and translated by Glenn W. Most, Loeb Classical Library 57 (Cambridge, Mass.: Harvard University Press, 2018), 116. See also references gathered at entry for Eros at *https://www.theoi.com/ Protogenos/Eros.html*

desire and love in gods and humans alike, in the earliest stories it is Eros that brings order and harmony to the world, reconciling the conflicting natures of Chaos. The stories also say that he ruled over the minds and the council of both gods and humans. According to this tradition, Eros is an ontological and epistemological necessity. Plato even says he was the oldest of gods, precursor of the pantheon.[21] All of this suggests that love must be the foundation of all mortal attempts at justice, order, and peace. Revenge and retribution are unworthy foundations for civic life and betray the call of justice. Even punishment and penalty must rest on the pillars of Aphrodite and Eros, Beauty and Love. They are the powers that present the world to our senses and allow us to connect with it, including connecting to one another. Without beauty, justice cannot appear, and without love, there can be no bonds of friendship. The life of the polis, which is to say the lives of us all, are held in divine hands.

---

21. "Thus I declare that Love is the oldest and most honored and most powerful of the gods." Plato, *Symposium*, 180*b*.

NINE

The Way of Integrity

Early in Chapter Three I wrote that we are by nature aesthetic animals and that we exist to appreciate beauty, to create beauty, and to be beautiful. And I added that this is all the world asks of us. If so, then these three aspects of human life can be seen as opportunities of service to the greater world, including the polis. To appreciate beauty requires a reverential attitude of respect to the inherent integrity of all things. To create beauty extends to how we relate to others through proper and good order, the creation and crafting of fair and just institutions and manners of governance, and the reconciling bonds of friendship. Lastly, to be beautiful is to strive to answer the call of our daimon, that informing spirit that is revealed in our styles, characters, and reputations. As we have seen repeatedly, this last opportunity for service depends upon the first two, because it is through reverence, justice, and friendship that the polis is able to afford our fullest realization.

Another story from Riverside can help to illustrate how these ideas and ideals appear in everyday, practical political life. This story is one of how disagreement can boil to conflict and how the above three ideas can respond to conflict through respect and appeals to the common good.

In March 2018 there was a county-wide referendum on whether cannabis should be legalized for recreational use. Two-thirds of Riverside voters said that it should be, mirroring the county-wide vote. In June 2019 Illinois passed a law that made recreational cannabis legal. As part of that law, local municipalities were empowered to "opt out" of allowing recreational cannabis to be sold within their jurisdictions. Possession and use of recreational cannabis would remain legal under state law, but municipalities could refuse to allow dispensaries within their borders. Municipalities had until January 1, 2020 to decide whether to opt out. After that date they would no longer be able to opt out and dispensaries would be permitted.

Almost immediately, Riverside was approached by companies interested in opening a dispensary in Riverside. They were especially interested in properties on two of the roads that formed Riverside's borders. These roads were main thoroughfares that would offer easy access to a dispensary, and the demographics of Riverside and its neighboring communities were very favorable in the eyes of the cannabis companies.

This issue had a larger economic backdrop. Riverside is a non-home rule community. In Illinois, that means that property taxes, which pay for the major part of Riverside's governmental services, can only be increased annually by the rise in the consumer price index or five percent, whichever is less. In practice, the tax cap results in Riverside being able to increase property taxes by less than two percent annually. On the other side of the ledger, village costs, especially driven by pensions and health care, typically increase from ten to twelve percent annually. This matter is made worse because one of Riverside's biggest financial problems is that it doesn't have a large business base and so Riverside businesses don't generate significant tax dollars. That's why the financial burden falls largely on property taxes. Moreover, the village's portion of the annual property tax bills is only fifteen percent. These factors create a structural deficit that has been looming over Riverside for decades, and by the mid-2000s it became apparent that the village would either have to significantly increase fees, which the village could control, or it would have to reduce services to residents. Capital needs were especially threatened as the village struggled to find resources to maintain infrastructure and public safety. The possibility of a cannabis dispensary, which could generate tens of thousands of dollars in revenue annually offered at least a partial solution to this problem.

Immediately after the law was passed containing the "opt out" option, I met with village staff to plan a way forward. Given the strong support for legalizing cannabis by the village's voters, I suspected that the village board would not want to opt out. I knew that there was likely to be a very vocal minority that was opposed to having a dispensary in Riverside. I also knew that municipalities all around us were already looking at the issue. Some of our neighboring communities had sufficient revenues that they could likely offer financial incentives to cannabis dispensaries that

Riverside could not, so the question was how to position Riverside favorably in the event that the village board decided to allow dispensaries. We determined that the best way forward was to move quickly to draft a clearly worded village ordinance that would be welcoming to a cannabis dispensary. If we couldn't offer financial incentives, we could find ways to make it easier and more cost-effective for a dispensary to choose Riverside as a location.

In early July, the village began providing information to residents on how recreational cannabis dispensaries were going to work, and that Riverside needed to make a decision on whether or not to opt out. We had our village attorneys draft a list of Frequently Asked Questions and distributed them to the village board and the residents. The FAQ was a thirty-page document that clearly described how the various aspects of the state law applied to municipalities. It was factual and in no way advocated for or against allowing a dispensary. I was adamant, and all agreed, that the time for debate would come at the village board and other public meetings. Our initial duty was to fairly inform both the board and the residents of the facts and the process. I also began talking with the trustees individually to gauge their interests and concerns. I publicly announced that the board would begin the discussion about whether to allow a cannabis dispensary in Riverside at its July 18 meeting.

Given the experience of the video gambling discussion, I anticipated that the minority opposition to a cannabis dispensary would be loud and the majority support would be quiet. I saw this dynamic over and over during my service as a public official. Opponents were always the ones who were the most vocal while proponents remained more muted in public. The village board would hear from supporters in person or by email, but they rarely came to village board meetings. Most people don't relish the idea of being attacked by their louder neighbors. This always put the village board in a quandary. The trustees *were* trustees because they were deeply involved in and cared about their community. They had a wide range of friends and family, and so overall the village board had a good sense of what the majority view was on things. The trustees were also more educated on the facts and nuances of public policy than the average resident, who rightly expected their elected officials to make reasoned choices for the good of the village. But publicly, the village board meetings were dominated by the vocal minority. And this vocal minority tended to be driven more by knee-jerk, personal responses than by facts and evidence.

Given this prior experience, I was surprised when not a single resident showed up to comment at the July meeting. Among the trustees, there was a consensus to further explore the idea of having a dispensary and to not opt out at the time. Only one trustee opposed the idea of having a dispensary in Riverside outright. She opposed it on moral grounds, saying that a cannabis dispensary was not in keeping with Riverside's values and brand. That trustee was the former chair of the village's Economic Development Commission (EDC), and she asked that if the board was going to consider a cannabis dispensary further that the EDC be allowed to discuss the idea and provide an advisory opinion. This request would come back to haunt her. Other trustees were more favorably inclined to at least have further discussions on the issue. One trustee made a point that would gain strength over time—because it was likely that a cannabis dispensary would be established somewhere in proximity to Riverside, it was better for Riverside residents for our police department to have jurisdiction over such a dispensary and for the village to receive the tax revenue such a dispensary would provide.

Our chief of police, who I knew was personally and professionally opposed to the legalization of recreational cannabis, nonetheless informed the board that the police could work with a dispensary to address traffic and safety concerns. He also noted that security cameras were required by state law. His even-handed remarks and assurances that the village was ready and able to make a dispensary safe made a big impact on the board.

After all of the trustees had weighed in, I suggested that we continue the discussion at our next meeting and consider having the issue discussed by our Preservation, Economic Development, and Planning and Zoning Commissions. I did this to agree with the trustee who had asked for EDC consideration, and also to increase the number of opportunities for public discussion and input. My goal was to make the process as transparent and inclusive as possible, one because that is what the village deserved, but also to forestall what I knew would be inevitable claims that the process lacked transparency and that residents had not been properly informed. This was a typical charge from minority opposition who, regardless of the efforts made by the village, always fell back on cynical claims that the process was rigged. At the end of the meeting, I again asked that all residents who had an opinion on the matter contact the village board with their views.

Between the July meeting and the board's first meeting in August, staff and the village attorneys worked diligently to prepare a draft ordinance for consideration by the commissions and the village board. The proposed ordinance would limit the location of a dispensary to the two roads that formed our eastern and southern border. These locations eliminated the possibility of having a dispensary in our central business district, most of which was too close to schools anyway for a dispensary to be allowed under state law. The locations also would keep traffic concerns on the periphery of the village. The draft ordinance also called for a cooperative policing agreement whereby our police department could proactively enforce traffic and safety laws without having to be called to the site by the owner of the dispensary. These two items directly addressed main concerns that had been raised by the trustees. Other provisions were that no signage could depict any image of a cannabis plant or refer to cannabis, that no odors could be detectible outside the dispensary, that it would have to have one parking space for every 300 square feet, and that the dispensary would work proactively with Riverside police in designing the security for the site. The ordinance provided only for a dispensary, no growing or cultivation of cannabis would be allowed. The state restrictions already included provisions that no on-site consumption would be allowed, that no cannabis or related items could be visible from outside the facility, and that no appeals to minors could be made in any way. Between the July and August meeting, I continued to ask for public input on social media, and the trustees all did their part in reaching out to residents to gauge public sentiment.

At its first meeting in August, the board continued the discussion with one more trustee now saying he favored opting out because he had safety concerns, he believed that cannabis use led to addiction, and that a dispensary was "off brand" for Riverside. That left the board split with four trustees in favor of continuing the discussion and two being ready to opt out. Two residents attended this meeting, both saying they were opposed to cannabis use generally and did not want a dispensary in Riverside.

One trustee said he was receiving largely positive emails in support of a dispensary while another trustee said the opposite. I knew that the comments on social media were heavily in support of allowing a dispensary. I had been talking with numerous people every day since our July meeting, and my impression was that a majority of the residents were in favor of allowing a dispensary. But I also knew we had only had two opportunities for public discussion. I asked the board to send the issue to our commissions for advisory opinions and everyone agreed. We were lucky because the Preservation and Planning and Zoning Commissions already had meetings scheduled for August. Upon the board's direction, the EDC added a special meeting for August. That meant that there would be three more noticed, public meetings for welcoming public input.

What happened next was unexpected. All three commissions reviewed the cannabis issue during August and all three unanimously supported having a dispensary in Riverside. The commissions reached their decision without having any contact with me or any of the trustees—no lobbying had been involved. Their discussions were all independent and transparent and the conclusions they reached were on the basis of their public consideration of the issue. The Preservation Commission said that a dispensary at the locations described in the draft ordinance would not negatively impact Riverside's national landmark status. The EDC was strongly in favor of a dispensary and specifically stated that it would not hurt the village's brand and may indeed benefit the brand by bringing more visitors to the village. The EDC also pushed back on what would become an especially contentious issue within the draft ordinance. The draft ordinance included a 1000-foot "buffer zone" between any cannabis dispensary and any pre-existing private or public school. One of the most likely locations for a dispensary was just barely within 1000 feet of a high school in a neighboring community. However, this was true only if you measured to the property line of a huge athletic field that stood between the potential location and the actual school buildings. Moreover, the school was on a corner on the other side of a major thoroughfare. In fact, from the potential dispensary location you could not even see the school, only the very top edge of a sign that sat in the corner of the athletic field. The EDC felt this was an unnecessary and overly restrictive requirement, and unanimously recommended that no buffer zone should be required. No residents attended the Preservation Commission meeting and only one attended the Economic Development Commission meeting to say he was opposed to allowing a dispensary in Riverside because there were too many "negative effects" from dispensaries (he did not say what these negative effects were).

The Planning and Zoning Commission was the last advisory commission to review the draft ordinance. Seven residents attended this meeting, three supporting a dispensary and four opposing it. One resident, who would become the very vocal leader of those opposed to a dispensary spoke several times, and between her comments and the other residents who were opposed the lines of argument quickly became clear. Opponents would fixate on an amorphous perceived danger to children who lived in the vicinity of the possible dispensary, even though the most likely location for a dispensary fronted a very busy street where it was highly unlikely young children would be playing. They also asserted that a cannabis dispensary was contrary to the village's family values, and that traffic would be negatively affected. To a person, they endorsed a 1,000-foot buffer, knowing of course that this would make the most likely dispensary location unavailable. One resident, who disrupted the meeting after the time for public comment was over, specifically said she did not want it in her back yard. We would hear this again and again, a singularly self-centered and anti-community sentiment. It seemed like NIMBYism was the perennial snake in the grassroots. In another attempt to circumvent the draft ordinance, opponents wanted to add libraries to pre-the buffer because there was a public library across the thoroughfare from the most likely dispensary location. One proponent for a dispensary countered by saying that when he was growing up there had been a number of strip clubs near his neighborhood. He said that as a child he never even knew what they were and didn't care.

For its part, the Planning and Zoning Commission was not swayed by the bald and unsupported assertions of the opponents. Instead, it made a methodical review of the draft ordinance, questioning the chief of police and village attorney in detail. The chief of police reiterated the fact that there was no evidence to support a claim that a dispensary would increase crime and that he was not concerned about any potential traffic or parking issues. He said that no additional policing resources would be needed if a dispensary were to locate in Riverside, and that in his opinion people would simply come to the dispensary and buy legal cannabis for home use. All of this from a man who was well-known to be opposed to legalized recreational cannabis.

Over the course of a three-hour meeting, the Planning and Zoning Commission revised the draft ordinance, making is less cumbersome and more straight-forward. The village attorney readily said that the draft ordinance was overly inclusive in terms of restrictions because it was easier to have all of the potential restrictions included so the commission could remove what it didn't want. The commission talked at length about whether a dispensary should be a permitted or special use. If it was a permitted use, then a dispensary would simply have to comply with the restrictions contained within the village code to open up shop. If it was a special use, a dispensary would be subject to public hearings to determine if additional restrictions were necessary given the location of the dispensary. The commission noted that package liquor stores, tattoo parlors, tobacco shops, restaurants, brew pubs, distilleries, and microbreweries were all permitted uses. It failed to see how a cannabis dispensary was qualitatively different from these other businesses. The commissioners unanimously recommended that a dispensary be a permitted use. This would turn out to be a big deal.

The commission then turned its attention to the issue of the buffer zone. It noted that package liquor stores, two of which sat right across the street from the high school property that opponents were trying to use to exclude one potential dispensary location, only had a 100-foot buffer zone. After much discussion, the commission reached a compromise by recommending a 500-foot buffer zone. The commission also recommended adding a lighting plan to the materials that a potential dispensary would have to submit to the village in addition to the existing requirements in the draft ordinance for security, parking, and traffic plans. And the commission changed the 6:00 a.m. to 10:00 p.m. hours of operation proposed in the draft ordinance to 9:00 p.m. to 10:00 p.m. By the time it was finished, the commission had crafted a draft ordinance that was both responsive to resident concerns while still being a viable ordinance that could serve the business needs of a cannabis dispensary. It was exemplary work and provided a template for the upcoming discussion by the village board.

In the six weeks since the village board's initial discussion there had now been five opportunities for resident input at public meetings. All of the meetings had been noticed through emails and on social media. There had also been two front-page articles about the issue in the local newspaper. I and the trustees were all getting emails, although not that many given the village's population. Most of the emails I received were supportive of having a dispensary. The tone of these emails was more pragmatic—the village had voted overwhelming to make cannabis legal, there were plenty of regulations in place to answer any concerns that might come up, we had an exemplary police department, and the village could make good use of increased revenue. The emails against dispensaries were more strident and personal—we were not listening to the residents, were destroying the village, would never be re-elected, were harming children, not upholding family values, encouraging addiction, were unconcerned about the increase in crime that they promised would come if a dispensary came to town, all we cared about was money, etc. It sometimes amazed me when I read emails like this that the people writing them seemed to have forgotten that the village board were all Riverside residents, too. Nobody was more concerned about the safety and well-being of our village than the village board. But, because we did not accept their unequivocal demands that things had to go their way, we were villains.

All of this set the stage for the village board's first meeting in September. At each of the three the commission meetings in August, in the coverage by the local press, and through every media and communication tool the village board had at its disposal, we had made clear that the village board would be voting on an ordinance allowing cannabis dispensaries in Riverside at its first meeting in September. That meeting turned out to be a doozy.

Before we get to that meeting, though, let's review how the process had been handled by the village board, staff, and the advisory commissions. The first step was to provide plenty of factual information as a background for the discussion. The next step was to methodically ensure that there would be plenty of opportunities for public input, both through direct communication with the village board, on social media, and in public forums. Then came the critical, pivotal step of drafting an ordinance that would provide specific form to how a cannabis dispensary in Riverside would be conceived, built, and regulated. The Illinois state law legalizing recreational cannabis was unusual in the degree to which it granted power to municipalities to regulate cannabis dispensaries, and through the work of our village attorneys, chief of police, and the EDC and Planning and Zoning Commission they had crafted an ordinance specifically tailored to Riverside's particular concerns and circumstances.

This process and run-up to the September meeting, especially the careful drafting and revising of the draft ordinance, were to my mind thoroughly aesthetic. Every step of the way the process was both respectful to and encouraging of the widest possible range of viewpoints, including those of residents who gave diverse input, the practical needs of the village, the ideas and concerns of the various commissioners, and the legitimate business needs of the cannabis dispensaries themselves. The approach was multi-faceted and fully embraced the complexity of the issue. The early village board discussions, and the independent discussions of the commissions were all examples of good order and fair consideration carried out in a spirit of camaraderie and civility. Even when opponents tried to disrupt the Planning and Zoning Commission meeting, the village attorney calmly explained that when the public comment section of the meeting was closed, some residents who had spoken had left, and that it would not be fair to allow others to speak out of turn in their absence. That simple statement quelled the dissent, and the meeting was able to continue in an orderly fashion. In all of the meetings, the character and integrity of the trustees, commissioners, and staff were fully on display. I felt that anyone who looked at the process in a balanced way would see that the village was striving for the best response to a complex issue. And then there was the tangible result of the draft ordinance, particularly crafted to respond to Riverside's needs and concerns, indeed derived from those needs and concerns. It might have been styled in the language of the law, but it resonated with the language of the soul, precise, nuanced, poetic.

By immediately agreeing to the request of the trustee who opposed dispensaries from the start that the matter be referred to the EDC, I showed deference and respect for her position, and demonstrated by example that the matter was going to get a full and open consideration. When the EDC unanimously favored a dispensary, specifically saying that it not only would not hurt but could benefit Riverside's brand, and recommended that the ordinance be made more amenable to the business interests of potential cannabis dispensaries, the arguments of the two trustees who favored opting out were considerably weakened. My goal all along was to do everything possible to inform the board and the residents and to trust the process of education, review, and discussion that we had put in place. There is a saying from the *Tao Te Ching* (sometimes translated as "the way of integrity") that a person should "prevent trouble before it arises [and] put things in order before they exist."[1] This kind of deep preparation, respect for multiple perspectives, willingness to yield to requests for further consideration, and of making every attempt to ensure the issue was fairly and fully considered is an example of aesthetic leadership. Having done all I could to prepare the board for what I assumed would be a tumultuous meeting, it was now time to let the process play out. In the *Tao,* there is one idea that is repeated three times throughout the book: "Do your work, then step back;" "Just do your job, then let go;" and "The Master does her job and then stops."[2] Just like in creating art, it is important in politics and governing to know when you have done all that needs doing. Over-reaching and pushing too hard are not part of the way of integrity.

We had an overflow crowd for the board's September meeting. Nineteen residents would speak, some many times, over the coming hours, and in addition the board had received dozens of emails, most of which supported a dispensary. That view would be reversed at the meeting where eighteen people would speak against a dispensary and only one in favor. The resident who had self-appointed herself as leader of the opposition, almost all of whom lived on two streets that were in

---

1. Lao-tzu, *Tao Te Ching,* translated by Stephen Mitchell (New York: Harper Perennial, 2006), 64.
2. Ibid., 9, 24, 30.

the vicinity of one of the potential dispensary locations, led the charge. She returned again and again to the podium, each time growing more strident, until she finally was pounding on the podium and yelling at the board that the people there were not going to allow the board to vote because they "could make some noise." A few people tried to claim that the process had not been transparent, even accusing the village of trying to hide the issue because the Economic Development Commission meeting had not been televised. I had to correct them by noting that the only commission meetings that were ever televised were the Planning and Zoning Commission meetings. Others said the board was rushing to judgment (after six weeks and six public meetings). Then came the usual claim about harming children, including the high schoolers in our neighboring community that could not even see where the one possible dispensary might be. More unsubstantiated claims were made about an inevitable increase in crime, and excess traffic and parking problems. But the main claim was that cannabis was bad and a dispensary was not in keeping with Riverside's values and brand. This would go on for three hours. Except for the outburst by opposition "leader," and a few inappropriate remarks by one of the trustees opposed to dispensaries, things remained mostly orderly and respectful. The same trustee, and one resident, tried to compare the debate on a cannabis dispensary to the debate about video gambling. That went nowhere with the majority of the board, perhaps because roughly the same margin of voters that had opposed video gambling had also supported legalizing recreational cannabis. I kept a light hand on the gavel, only stepping in if things started getting out of hand. I knew that the residents who were speaking were sincere, and I intended to let them talk until they had no more to say.

Public comment was always the first item on our village board agendas. After all of the residents had spoken, it was time to return to the agenda. At the request of one of the trustees we took an agenda item out of order. This agenda item specifically addressed the traffic and safety concerns of the people who lived in the vicinity of one of the possible locations for a dispensary, the residents who were most vocally opposed to a dispensary "in their backyard." After discussing several options, the trustees voted to have the village engineer do a traffic study of the area and recommend alternative solutions. I thought that asking to consider this issue before we got to the cannabis issue was an especially astute and respectful act. The board showed that it took the residents' concerns seriously, and it also undercut claims that the village could not adequately address issues of traffic and parking.

When the trustees began their discussion on the cannabis issue it quickly became obvious that it was still a four to two split. The trustee who had asked for the issue to be considered by the Economic Development Commission said she disagreed with the commission and insisted that a dispensary was contrary to Riverside's brand and values. She claimed that to approve the draft ordinance would be a dereliction of duty because the board was not listening to resident input. She also argued that at a minimum the 1,000-foot buffer zone be kept in the ordinance and that libraries be added to pre-existing schools. We had already seen those gambits at the Planning and Zoning Commission, but it was fully within her right to try it again with the village board. The other trustee who opposed having a dispensary unfortunately impugned the reputation of the trustees who were in favor, saying he was "embarrassed" by their position. He probably did more harm to his position with that language than with any of his other arguments, none of which went much beyond that he thought a dispensary violated Riverside's values and brand. This despite the fact that the EDC, the commission directly responsible for informing the village board on branding efforts (and which in the past few years had done remarkable work in updating and beautifying the village's brand), had flatly contradicted him with a unanimous vote. He also tried to claim that a dispensary would lead to addiction and crime despite the repeated statements by our chief of police to the contrary. And despite six public meetings, copious posts on social media, and two front page stories in the local paper, he argued that the process had not been transparent enough. I kept waiting for one fact, one shred of evidence to support such claims but none were forthcoming.

The four trustees who supported allowing a dispensary in Riverside methodically knocked down every argument that had been made against a dispensary. One thing that became apparent was that those opposed to a dispensary were simply unwilling to accept factual evidence that went against their views. Their minds were made up and closed. The furious outburst from the self-appointed leader of the opposition showed the ugly fundamentalism at the base of many of their arguments, which basically boiled down to a personal disapproval of cannabis. They simply did not care that the vast majority of residents were in favor of allowing a cannabis dispensary in Riverside. What the four trustees did was to return to the factual record before us that consistently showed that the fears that they raised were unfounded. One trustee forcefully rejected any sense of "embarrassment," noting that twenty commissioners had unanimously found in favor of allowing a dispensary, that there was strong support for a dispensary on social media, and the emails that we had all received were similarly mostly in favor.

I should probably note here that I had been having repeated conversations with the trustees individually about the pros and cons of having a cannabis dispensary. I thought it was a significant opportunity for the village and could help address the village's structural deficit. I told the trustees that I believed we had a good chance of getting a dispensary if we moved quickly and came up with an ordinance that addressed legitimate concerns while also being welcoming to the dispensary companies. That included not having a buffer zone and making a dispensary a permitted use. My view was that the cannabis dispensary debate was unlike the one over video gambling because a dispensary was not predatory in the way the gambling machines were. The state laws regarding video gambling provided none of the regulatory power to municipalities as did the cannabis legislation. If the village had allowed video gambling the machines could have gone anywhere and would be beyond local regulations. The cannabis dispensary law was night and day from the video gambling law. The entire attempt to conflate the two issues was a red herring. Meanwhile, all around us, other villages were working toward trying to get a dispensary. If we approved the draft ordinance, especially with the provision that a dispensary was a permitted use, Riverside would immediately surpass their efforts, giving us the best shot we had of getting a dispensary.

So, the trustees had these thoughts in mind as they carefully went through the draft ordinance. On the other hand, the trustees were extremely independent, and I knew that they would each make up their own minds regardless of what I might say. The board was so fortunate to have the draft ordinance that had been revised by the Planning and Zoning Board. Because of the work that commission had done, the village board was able to immediately go to the central issues at hand. Despite attempts to disrupt the meeting by the same angry resident who kept insisting that there should be a referendum on the issue, the trustees kept focused on the ordinance and doing their jobs as elected officials.

Several trustees reiterated the Planning and Zoning Commission point that almost all local businesses, including package liquor stores that in addition to liquor sold cigarettes, tobacco products, and rolling papers, were all operating as permitted uses. The four trustees who favored allowing a dispensary argued that it would be unfair to put heavier restrictions on a cannabis dispensary. When it came to the question of a 1,000-foot buffer zone that would exclude one of the most likely locations for a dispensary, the trustees were evenly split on whether to have a 1,000-foot buffer or the 500-foot buffer recommended by the commission. I cast the tie-breaking vote in favor of 500 feet.

After all of the trustees had a chance to speak and interact, I decided that I should make my personal view known. It was evident to me that the ordinance was going to pass, but on an issue of this magnitude I thought that residents deserved to know where their president stood. I also saw this as an opportunity to further my governing ideals of beauty and soul by focusing on the two central claims that I found most troubling. One was that a cannabis dispensary was contrary to Riverside's values. Two was the claim that the board was not listening to residents. Values and respect were central to aesthetic leadership, so this was a good time to address both. I spoke directly to the residents who were there because I wanted them to know that I had listened to them and now wanted to respond to them. I knew that I would change no minds, but that wasn't my goal. All I wanted to do was sow seeds of doubt in the hardened fields of their obstinate certainty. I pointed out that the stigma that they attached to cannabis was a self-imposed stigma. The stigma did not belong to cannabis but to their view of cannabis. Similarly, when they said that a cannabis dispensary violated Riverside's values, I asked "according to whom?" The majority of residents I had spoken to didn't agree with that statement, and I didn't agree with that statement. So, again, we had an assumption masquerading as a fact that was based solely on individual opinions. But there remained that pesky vote where two-thirds of Riverside voters had voted to legalize cannabis. My last point was the one I suspected would fall on mostly deaf ears. I challenged the assertion that the board was not listening to them by saying that listening to someone didn't mean you had to agree with what they were saying. Hidden in their charge against the majority view was the voice of tyranny—to listen to me means that you must obey me. What I didn't say was that the singularity of their perspective, the lock-step repetition of the same unfounded claims, the glib moralism, the strident rejection of facts, and the demonization of those who had differing views revealed the suffocating fundamentalism that too often accompanies a monotheistic cast of mind.

In the end, the trustees voted four to two to approve an ordinance that included cooperative policing, addressed traffic and safety concerns, and in general ensured that a dispensary would not adversely affect the community. By making a dispensary a permitted use, the ordinance was also a very attractive ordinance to cannabis dispensaries because they knew exactly what was expected of them by the village. At the board's next meeting it voted to impose a three percent cannabis tax in addition to the one percent sales tax, one percent non-home rule sales tax, and one percent business district tax. That meant that if the village ever got a dispensary, it would receive a six percent tax on all sales.

The village was now well-situated to attract a cannabis dispensary. Several companies were interested, and then, unexpectedly, the state changed the way it was issuing licenses for dispensaries and things came to a screeching halt. As I write this, two years have passed since that tumultuous meeting. Several companies have come close to buying the property that was the main focus of the meeting, and they all said they were especially interested in the Riverside location because of the permitted use provision in the village's ordinance. One deal came very close to closing, only to again be thwarted by the state's permitting process. When that potential deal was announced in the local newspaper, it received nothing but positive responses. Not a single person who had railed against the board two years earlier said a word. It still seems likely that a dispensary will open in Riverside in the future.

It has been gratifying to watch the hard work of the village board, commissions, and staff pay off. They did their village proud through their commitment to fairness and the way of integrity. Throughout the process, the three aspects of appreciating beauty, creating beauty, and being beautiful held sway. Despite disagreements, all residents were listened to and their viewpoints were give due appreciation. The various meetings of the commissions and the village board, along with the crafting of the ordinance, were carried out carefully and in a well-ordered manner. And, in the end, all of the board members remained true to themselves and reached informed decisions in line with their views of what was right and good for Riverside.

TEN

In Dependence

The United States of America began with a declaration of independence. Even before that declaration, people came here to escape oppression or discrimination based largely on religion. From the beginning there was a mythic aspect to America, a calling that beckoned others to a new, unencumbered way of life. Our founding document explicitly says that America was established on the basis of ideas, on the assertion of self-evident truths, including that all people were created equal and endowed with the God-given unalienable rights of life, liberty, and the pursuit of happiness.

Also from the beginning, the ideas of individualism and self-reliance have held sway. Before the young nation declared its independence, the colonists had embraced the idea that each person was a sovereign, independent being that was constituted by personal introspection (the "self" we addressed in Chapter Two). Tocqueville famously pointed out that Americans were Cartesian even though they never read Descartes because of their belief that each person was an independent monad, essentially disconnected from all other people and indeed the greater world itself. Tocqueville also correctly recognized that America was so thoroughly infused with Christian doctrines that they were no longer even questioned. "The Americans," he wrote, "having admitted the principal doctrines of the Christian religion without inquiry, are obliged to accept in like manner a great number of moral truths originating in it and connected with it."[1] As we noted in Chapter One, one does not have to read Descartes to be Cartesian, nor profess to be a Christian to nonetheless embody Christianity's monotheistic cast of mind and its fallout.

---

1. Alexis de Tocqueville, *Democracy in America,* translated by Henry Reeve, 2 vols. (New York: Vintage Books, 1990), 2: 6.

Americans have also long harbored a belief that America is exceptional, the last great hope, a shining city on the hill, the beacon of freedom, etc. This belief has led to a proselytizing impetus in the American spirit, a belief that the rest of the world would be better if only they adopted the American way of life. Indeed, many Americans believe it is anti-American to deny that America is the world's best, brightest, and most virtuous country. According to this view, America is not America if it is just one among others. It must be exceptional, the most powerful, the most feared, the richest, the driver of the world's economy, and the leader of the free world if it is to live up to its founding ideals.

All of this suggests that "America" is a belief system.[2] The "America" that draws immigrants from all over the world is a fantasy, a dream—and don't we repeatedly talk about the American Dream?—that enlivens the imaginations of others who are seeking a better, freer, more just life. Equality, liberty, freedom, and justice for all are indeed beautiful and compelling ideas and ideals. I have long thought that immigrants who come to America are more truly American than those of us who were born here because they come seeking what we take for granted. The desire for freedom and equal opportunity burns brighter and hotter for those who cross borders and leave homelands to achieve them. Native-born Americans for the most part accept the fundaments of American thought just as they did in Tocqueville's day—without inquiry. We are born into a belief system already underway and the ideas and ideals that so spark the imaginations of immigrants are simply taken by us as rote, just as we habitually believe in ourselves as self-actualizing individuals. In terms of what it means to be an American, then, it is not citizenship that matters, it is belief in the dream. I suspect that those to seek to restrict and ostracize immigration know this even if they cannot acknowledge it. The American dream is weak in them, as shown by their affection for authoritarianism and voter repression, both of which are antithetical to American ideals.

---

2. This idea of America as a belief system comes from a conversation that I had with James Hillman in 1997 on America. The one-hour conversation was recorded and is available as *America: A Conversation with James Hillman and Ben Sells.*

The deeper political and ethical question is what lies in the shadow of belief? If America is a belief system, and if to be American means to be a true believer in ideas claimed to be self-evident, then what is the fallout from such belief? Every idea or ideal, no matter how bright and enticing, is accompanied by fellow travelers. Indeed, it sometimes seems that the brighter the idea or ideal the longer the shadows they cast.

Inherent in the idea of belief is doubt. Belief always begs a question, and even if those questions are repressed and denied they nonetheless persist. One need only look at American literature from the earliest settlers onward to see the persistent theme of doubt—what is America, what does it mean to be American, what is the American dream and how does one attain it? America has always been in a perpetual identity crisis, trying to figure out who and what it is. Tocqueville pointed to how Americans always had to be busy and to our inability to be satisfied in the midst of plenty. The constant drive for more—more wealth, more things, more success, more fame—is given with the American penchant for belief because it seeks to distract attention from the disquiet and unease that simmers within the American mind. Little wonder anxiety disorders are the most prevalent mental illnesses in contemporary America. Something in the manner of American belief seems to necessitate anxiety (fear without an object), depression, and obsessive-compulsive behavior. And this was true long before the DSM assigned them names. My sense is that the manic drive to stay busy, the constant search for identity, and the gluttonous desire for more of everything are defenses against the repressed existential doubt that accompanies all belief. What belief cannot bring itself to admit is that perhaps it is wrong.

Another shadow cast by belief and closely related to doubt is literalism. Because it cannot free itself from doubt, belief longs for firm declarations of self-evident truths. One way it attempts to satisfy this longing is through literalism, whereby belief is expressed through singleness of meaning, everything by the letter. One dictionary defines literalism as "unimaginative exactness." If something is literally true it exists "beyond a shadow of doubt" and goes without question. There is a fragility and brittleness that attaches to literalism that can be seen in the myopic fervor of true believers. Literalism by its very nature seeks to limit the spontaneous creativity of the imagination by insisting on single-minded definitions.

The American craving for personal identity and the equating of success with wealth are examples of how belief ascends into literalism. The first seeks to define a person in concrete terms of "what I am," while the second posits success as the accumulation of literal things. The person with the most toys wins. Similarly, the American preference for plain speaking and straight talk, and our suspicion of fancy talk and eloquence shows how our beliefs repress and resist the nuance and complexity of the actual polis where one finds many ways of talking. Belief tries to impose a literal, linear narrative on America and resists alternative narratives that challenge the status quo. Witness the fundamentalist rage against feminism, LGBTQ+ human rights, non-white immigration, and critical race theory. Such perspectives must be both denied *and demonized* because they call into question the literalism inherent in the single-minded narrative of the status quo. Literalism cannot tolerate tolerance because tolerance accepts that our natures as aesthetic and political animals are wandering, circuitous, eccentric—in a word, free. And it is that freedom that is revealed in the inherently poetic and imaginative polis.

Literalism begets fundamentalism. Here the literal truth of one's beliefs becomes set in stone. Fundamentalism has a specific relevance for America as an historic creation of the American Protestant mind that fuels much of America's proselytizing ways.[3] Because Americans believe that America is fundamentally better than other countries, indeed the greatest country in the world, it only makes sense that other countries should (and note the moral imperative in that "should") become like America. The evangelical and hubristic tone of American exceptionalism is broadly recognized, and found offensive, by other countries and is epitomized in "the ugly American."

Doubt, literalism, and fundamentalism come together in denial. Belief lives in a state of denial that represses the generative power of beauty that is revealed in the natural diversity of the polis. Denial turns a blind eye to the daily atrocities of American life committed through hate and bigotry, and unconsciously erodes the very ideals to which it nominally

---

3. For more on the peculiar American style of fundamentalism, see my "Answers and Explanations: Fundamentalism as a Variety of Rational Experience," *Spring: An Annual of Archetypal Psychology and Jungian Thought* 68 (2001): 1–16.

pledges allegiance. The ugliness of the anti-vaxxer minority puts this on full display. The refusal to accept scientific fact, the persistence in believing objectively false claims, the embracing and glorification of ignorance, the vilification of long-serving public servants and medical workers, and the sheer selfishness of their actions all manifest the power of denial and its devastating effect on the polis. Their defense to such charges is as American as you can get—I am a free individual and have the unalienable, God-given right to do as I damn well please. I owe no obligation to you, to other people, or to society. My personal belief is all that matters to me because I am all that matters to me.

The effects of American denial can be seen in the ugly perversions of actual American history and life. The indefensibly cruel treatment of indigenous people, the horrors of slavery and its still-present aftermath, the shame and tragedy of the Civil War, the denigration of women as less than full partners in the American experiment, the mistreatment of immigrants, the championing of greed and predatory capitalism, and the rapacious mistreatment of America's earth, air, and water barely scratch the surface of the long shadow of America's belief system. Many Americans, of course, do know and accept these realities and work diligently to respond to them. My point is that these kinds of atrocities are psychologically linked and made possible by the degree to which we are unconscious to the beliefs that exist within and motivate our habitual minds and actions. We cannot separate the bright ideals and their shadowy partners, but we can turn our aesthetic sensibilities to the task of discerning where and how they appear. Aesthetic appreciation is not only positive, but also embraces those aspects of our ideals that repulse us. That is why aesthetic citizenship and leadership require imaginal courage, a willingness to enter into the shades and shadows, the alleys and the "bad parts of town," and to engage with others perhaps radically different than ourselves.

Beauty, and the appreciation of beauty, do not require belief and so offer ways to be free from the constraints of belief. We can perceive beauty, feel its sensual reality, and be supported by its innate sensibility without need of belief. Other political animals do fine without any apparent need to believe in abstracted ideals. The baby's recognition of acts of inequity and the monkey throwing cucumber at the researcher were immediate, instinctual responses that required no belief in the idea of fairness. Beauty presents itself without doubt, effortlessly resists literalism, cannot be constrained by fundamentalism, and exposes denial by irrepressibly showing things as they are.

I am not so naïve as to think that native-born Americans can cease to believe in the belief system that is "America." That is another reason we so desperately need the perspectives of immigrants and of other nations. Just as a person is more fully known through the imaginations of others, so, too, a city, state, or nation depends on the imaginations of others to be fully realized. American isolationism is an extension of the crippling concept of the self as isolated and self-sufficient. To retreat to nativism and "America First" is the most certain way to perpetuate the malaise that is endemic to America's spirit. When we refuse to *really* experiment with America, we lose the mythical essence that others see and feel so deeply about America. It is telling that at the same time so much of the world fears America because of its blindness about itself, people are still drawn to America's enduring mythical calling.

The usual American view of independence is premised on and in service to the fundamental(ist) American idea of individualism. We saw in Chapter Two how individualism appears in the concept of the self and how that concept works against community. What would happen to our American ideals if we were to alter how we imagine ourselves as individuals? The current state of affairs cannot be sustained, because, as Robert Bellah and his co-authors saw nearly forty years ago, "what is at issue is not simply whether self-contained individuals might withdraw from the public sphere to pursue purely private ends, but whether such individuals are capable of sustaining either a public *or* private life."[4] When we think of ourselves as isolated individuals we deny the gifts of the polis that are essential to soul-making at the same time that we silence the communities that comprise our own souls. Let me be blunt—American individualism is a pathological idea that perverts the very ideals it proclaims to advance.

---

4. Robert Bellah, Richard Madsen, William Sullivan, Ann Swider, and Steven Tipton, *Habits of the Heart: Middle America Observed* (London: Hutchinson, 1985), 143.

If I am an isolated, essentially secret individual known only to myself, then how can I ever truly relate to others? When people talk about not getting what they need in a relationship, or that they are not satisfied with a relationship, or that they give and give and don't receive what they want in return, they give voice to the perversity of individualism. The notion that relationships are supposed to be reciprocal turns relationships into either economic barters or evolutionary struggles. You exist in relationship to me to either satisfy my needs or perpetuate my selfish genes. And because we assume that this is exactly how other people relate to us, we are perpetually paranoid and suspicious, always alert for clues that other people are trying to use or manipulate us for their personal gain or advantage. American individualism makes betrayal inevitable and leads to a state of constant agitation, a world of knee-jerk responses, hair triggers, and road rage. The distrust that people feel toward government, the media, and each other will only continue to grow the more isolated our view of ourselves becomes.[5]

What if instead of individualism imagined as solitary, we begin from a perspective that all people are intimately connected and that we depend upon one another to realize our own uniqueness? If the soul is at least partly the interiorization of the polis and the *anima mundi,* then we are not isolated individuals. We are born into a welcoming world that offers us support and opportunity with absolutely no expectation of receiving anything in return. We are born equal not because we are all the same but because the world affords each of us the potential of our own destinies. The American ideal of equal protection under the law is one way of trying to ensure that all people share in the opportunities of life, liberty, and the pursuit of happiness.

---

5. A poll in 2019 showed that 75% of Americans believed that distrust in government was growing and 64% said they believed that distrust in one another was growing (online at *https://www.pewresearch.org/politics/2019/07/22/trust-and-distrust-in-america/*). Similarly, seven in ten Americans say that their ethical and moral belief are derived solely from within themselves and do not depend on relations with things greater than themselves. Gerard Robinson and Maury Giles, "America Divided: Why It's Dangerous That Public Distrust in Civic Institutions Is Growing," *USA Today* (15 March 2021, online at *https://www.usatoday.com/story/opinion/2021/03/15/why-americans-growing-distrust-civic-institutions-warning-column/4668616001/*).

If we imagine ourselves in such a manner, the nature of our relations with others radically changes. Instead of looking at you as someone to satisfy my needs, I can see you as a possibility for soul-making, both yours, mine, and the *anima mundi*. Because I can appreciate you in ways that are unattainable to you, I can therefore provide opportunities for your peculiar destiny to unfold. The poet Rainer Maria Rilke wrote that the highest task of a bond between two people was to "stand guard over the solitude of the other."[6] How different this is from the *quid pro quo* and tit-for-tat style of American individualism and relationship. I am suggesting that as political animals our need for one another is ontological, that there is no "I" without "you," and that our souls are inherently communal, intermingling and penetrating one another. We are each an each, but we are not isolated or alone. We all are born with destinies waiting to unfold, and each of us exists in part to aid in the unfolding of the destinies of others. We guard one another's solitude not to receive something in return, but to aid in the fuller blossoming of the polis and the enrichment of an ensouled world.

In such a world, independence no longer means standing alone and apart, but instead means recognizing and appreciating the myriad ways that we are *in* dependence, the ways that we held and supported, loved and encouraged, by the things upon which we depend. I am free only to the extent that I belong to a world upon which I depend, and the more fully I can appreciate my dependence and belonging the more I am free to realize my destiny. We tend to imagine freedom as freedom *from,* the absence or overcoming of encumbrances or obstacles, but freedom is also freedom *to,* the opportunity to contribute to the ongoing life of the polis. If we reflect on our lives, we will see that the world repeatedly comes to us for particular talents, perspectives, and gifts. We each relate to the world in our own unique ways precisely because of our eachness, and it is through the mutuality of our common striving that each of us contributes to the destiny of others and of the polis.

Being in dependence is a difficult idea for the American mind. We treat dependence as meaning weak and vulnerable, we list our dependents

---

6. Rainer Maria Rilke, *Letters of Rainer Maria Rilke 1892–1910,* translated by Jane Bannard Greene and M. D. Herter Norton (New York: W. W. Norton, 1945), 65.

on our tax forms, or we talk of being dependent on alcohol or drugs. Co-dependency is a bad thing, referring to destructive relationships that are one-sided and abusive. To depend on someone or something is a violation of our individualism that is supposed to be strong and self-standing, free from need or reliance on others. This manner of thinking about dependence is thoroughly adolescent. The goal is always to grow up and move out, get your own car, your own place, out from under the roof and dependency on your parents, to become your own person free to do as you please.

A more mature, and realistic, view is that we are all dependent upon countless things and people. The daily round of life immerses us in dependency, on the air we breathe, on the earth upon which we walk, and the food and water that sustain us. We depend on our work for our livelihoods and, one hopes, the opportunity to use our particular talents and skills. We depend on friends and partners who provide the joys of shared life and love. We depend on the polis that provides a broader context through which to realize our souls and our destinies. We depend on the ancestors who came before, literally making us possible. We depend on our bodies through and by which we embrace the world and are held by it. We depend on memories, dreams, reflections, ideas, and fantasies that give testament to an ensouled world of which we are a part. And we depend on the animals, plants, spirits, and invisibles that inspire us with their blessings and power.

To carefully appreciate and differentiate how we are dependent requires an aesthetic sensibility. We saw in Chapter Eight how the things and people that we find beautiful move us beyond our self-centeredness. Wherever we find beauty we can feel the warm embrace of dependency. This kind of dependency engenders freedom because it releases us from our solitary confinement and pulls us into a waiting and supporting world. If freedom is God-given, then that God's name is Aphrodite.

Contrary to our usual American view, where we are dependent is where we are most free. Watch the certainty of an animal in the woods, the sureness of a squirrel's jump or a cat's pounce and you will see the grace of dependency. James Gibson wrote about the idea of affordances, and how animals relate to their environment in part based on what their environment affords them. A branch affords a bird a place to land and a squirrel to jump. The bird lands without doubt nor need for belief because it trusts a trustworthy world. So, too, we humans afford one another the possibilities of our natures as political animals. We naturally depend upon others and the greater world because they are dependable, and through being in dependence we are free to fulfill our destinies.

Plato told a story in the *Republic* that before coming to earth, each soul picks its next life. The lives of every animal, human, and condition were available.[7] Some souls that had been animals before chose to be human and some humans chose animal forms. The only requirement was that the souls had to pick a life different than the ones they had already lived. The life chosen was to be the soul's destiny in its next life. But before coming to earth, the souls are made to forget what they had chosen. Every person, according to this myth, was thus born with a daimon, a tutelary spirit that was seeking to fulfill the destiny chosen by the soul before its arrival on earth. Socrates said that his daimon always cautioned him against things but never provided advice on what to do. In others the daimon is strong and demanding. When we read biographies or reflect on our own lives and the lives of others we will see patterns, a kind of unfolding over time that this myth would attribute to the daimon. What is beautiful about this myth is that it suggests that each of us has the opportunity to aid the daimon in fulfilling its destiny. Central to this myth is that the daimon is not mine, it does not belong to me but rather we accompany one another, partners in destiny. It is through our relationship with the daimon that we are each a chosen one. We are each born in service to fate.

Each person, then, has the opportunity to guard the solitude of the daimon that has chosen them, and to aid in the unfolding of its destiny. But sometimes we try to resist or repress the daimon and our intimate dependence upon one another. When I was a practicing psychotherapist, I saw many people struggling to oppose their calling and attempting to deny their fate. Again and again people would tell me that although they were doing one thing in life they were "really" meant to do some-

---

7. The myth or Er appears in Book 10 of Plato's *Republic*.

thing else. And yet they were not willing to accept the reality of what that "really" entailed. A high-powered lawyer would lament that he was really a poet, and yet he wrote no poetry and found the actual life of a poet unimaginable. This feeling of being divided and conflicted resulted from his unconscious belief in individualism and that he could only be identified in one way. His suffering was not a crisis of identity or thwarted self-realization but a failure of imagination. What he lacked was the courage of his convictions; it was his failure to serve the best interests of his daimon that he felt as personal failure.

Ask any parent if they see something in their grown children that was already there in the cradle and they will almost always say yes. We can all see similar consistencies in old friends, or partners and family of long standing. There is something there in each person, something undefinable yet real, a mannerism, an impetus or reticence of spirit, an intensity of focus or mood. This something that is given with each person from the beginning is the daimon already in play, fate already at hand. Each person experiences the daimon differently. Sometimes it is the gentle voice of caution as in the case of Socrates. Other time it appears with a flash. When the great cellist Jacqueline du Pré was four years old, she was listening to a radio program about orchestral instruments with her parents. When she heard a cello, she immediately said to her parents "I want one of those." What the Greeks called the daimon the Romans called the genius. Often the daimon's call can be felt most strongly in our oddities and eccentricities, and in our longings and infatuations. When we sense an irrepressible urge or push, or a sudden resistance it could be the touch of the daimon's hand.

Because the life we live is shared with the daimon to which we are in service, we owe it respect and appreciation. Similarly, as political animals, we owe respect and appreciation to the budding destinies in each of our fellow citizens. Remember that the daimons we encounter daily all chose to be here, in this place and time, and so our daimons implicate one another. The things and people we encounter in the daily round are all threads of the daimons' communal fate, all belong to the unfolding of their destinies. To elevate our desires over the daimon's call is thus a cosmic breach, a hubristic disordering, an aesthetic affront. To work in concert with the daimon fulfills the soul desire:

148

The daimon then becomes the source of human ethics, and the happy life—what the Greeks called *eudaimonia*—is the life that is good for the daimon. Not only does it bless us with its calling, we bless it with our style of following.[8]

Here is another way of imagining our American ideal of the pursuit of happiness. The unalienable right that each of us enjoys is the opportunity to pursue happiness for the daimon that we accompany through life. Not my happiness, but *its* happiness. It is the *daimon*'s life and liberty that we each must protect, nurture, and ensure. This is the ethics of soul-making, the loving attempt to do right by the daimon that chose us. It is this common fate of service to the daimon that frees us from the binding and blinding coils of individualism and self. And it is through this shared service that we are all created equal.

8. Hillman, *The Soul's Code,* 260.

PART III

Beauty and Nature

ELEVEN

Olmstedian Soul

In 1855, at the age of thirty-three, a decade before he would commit himself fully to his calling as a landscape architect, Frederick Law Olmsted wrote a letter to his half-sister Mary advising her on how to educate herself during her European travels:

> The best thoughts come to us unawares; not by study; that is, not directly by study. But if entirely without study, you will not have knowledge enough or strength enough to pick up the gold you stumble upon. But don't let study or what you have arrived at or hope to arrive at by study be the end, only the means... What you want is unconsciously and incidentally to cultivate your eye and the eye of your mind and heart... It will come when you don't know it—this appreciation of excellency, never fear.[1]

The word "unconscious" as an adjective first appeared in English in 1751 and more frequently after 1800.[2] But in 1855, the idea that the greater world could unconsciously influence the mind and heart was a radical and remarkable claim. Already at this point in his life, Olmsted was aware that nature had the power to influence the soul, an idea that would later find full bloom in his landscape architecture.

Twenty-seven years later, at the full height of his artistry, Olmsted would make the connection between his work and the soul more directly. He wrote that while in conversation we often say that we think something despite the fact that we were unaware of such a thought until we

---

1. Olmsted to Bertha Olmsted, 1855. Frederick Law Olmsted Papers, Manuscript Division, Library of Congress. Quoted in Irving David Fisher, "Frederick Law Olmsted and the Philosophic Background to the City Planning Movement in the United States" (PhD diss., Columbia University, 1976), 190.

2. Lancelot Law Whyte, *The Unconscious before Freud* (New York: Basic Books, 1969), 66.

said it. He concluded that "Much that we call tact, sense, genius, inspiration, instinct, is of the unconscious process:"

> Holding this experience in view, it will seem probable that the mind not only produces thoughts and gives direction to the body without conscious effort, or process to be recalled, but that it *receives* impressions, information, suggestions, the raw material of thought; that it stores and holds them for after use; that it is fed, refreshed, revived and restocked by what it thus receives, all unconscious of the process...I am equally sure that the distinction will be intelligible that I propose to make between what I shall call conscious, or direct recreation, and *unconscious, or indirect recreation.*[3]

In a related idea that would become a recurring theme in his landscape architecture, Olmsted also thought that objects that were addressed to conscious or direct recreation, which caused people to halt and "utter mental exclamations of surprise or admiration," often interrupted or even prevented the processes of indirect or unconscious recreation.[4] It was the latter that Olmsted reached for in his designs. For him, the highest value of a park was in elements and qualities of scenery that were subject to little conscious awareness. Indirect recreation resulted from design elements that "are of too complex, subtle and spiritual a nature" to be consciously grasped.[5]

As an example of the difference between direct and indirect recreation, Olmsted compared a common wildflower "peeping through dead leaves or a bank of mossy turf," and a "hybrid of the same genus, double, of a rare color, just brought from Japan, now first blooming in America, taken from under glass, and shown us in a bunch of twenty, set in an enameled vase against an artfully-managed back-ground." Although the latter was the more decorative, rare, and costly, Olmsted believed that the former, which we had passed by without stopping, and which had not interrupted our conversation, nonetheless "touched us more, may have come home to us more, may have had a more soothing and refresh-

---

3. "Trees in Streets and in Parks" (1882), in *Olmsted: Writings on Landscape, Culture, and Society,* edited by Charles E. Beveridge (New York: Library of America, 2015), 592–93.

4. Ibid., 593.

5. Ibid.

ing sanitary influence." He saw an association between scenes and objects that we are apt to call simple and natural, and their ability to "touch us so quietly that we are hardly conscious of them."[6]

At the heart of Olmsted's artistic work lay a profound psychological idea—that the natural world, both in its raw state and as presented through landscape architecture, unconsciously influences psychic life. This influence operates in the same manner as the arts, the "influence is a poetic one,"[7] and, like the impact of music, it "is of a kind that goes back of thought and cannot be fully given the form of words."[8] For Olmsted, landscape architecture, as an art, was conceived by and directed to the imagination, but the psychological impact *originated in nature*. For Olmsted, nature itself had psychological power.

Olmsted believed that nature's unconscious influence was healing and restorative and that through nature, a psychic "unbending" could take place that relieved the tensions and pressures of city life. He thought that nature's psychic healing occurs through an unconscious process whereby the mind is influenced by the imagination that is subtly and spiritually touched by the charms of nature. Regarding Central Park, Olmsted wrote that its main affect would be found in its ability to produce "certain influences on the imagination of those who visit it, influences which are received and which act, for the most part, unconsciously to those who benefit by them."

Although Olmsted thought of himself primarily as an artist, he explicitly intended his work to be "a prophylactic and therapeutic agent of vital value."[9] Olmsted believed that there was "a sensibility to poetic inspiration" in all people, and that the suppression of our poetic sensibilities

6. Ibid., 593–94.

7. "Superintendent of Central Park to Gardeners," in Frederick Law Olmsted, *Forty Years of Landscape Architecture,* vol. 2: *Central Park,* edited by Frederick Law Olmsted, Jr. and Theodora Kimball (Cambridge, Mass. and London, England: The MIT Press, 1973), 356.

8. "Seventh Annual Report of the Board of Commissioners of the Department of Parks for the City of Boston for the year 1881," in *Civilizing American Cities: A Selection of Frederick Law Olmsted's Writings on City Landscapes,* edited by S.B. Sutton (Cambridge, Mass. and London, England: The MIT Press, 1971), 261.

9. Frederick Law Olmsted, *Mount Royal Montreal* (New York: G.P. Putnam's Sons, 1881), 22.

led to a "sadly morbid condition" that could be attended to through the restorative power of nature. "Poets, we may not be, but a little lifted out of our ordinary prose we may often be to our advantage."[10] For Olmsted, "the charm of natural scenery is an influence of the highest curative value."[11] Olmsted was the father of landscape architecture, but he also was perhaps America's first eco-psychologist. He recognized and appreciated the psychic power of the *anima mundi,* the ensouled world, and through his work he attempted to provide therapy for the urban psyche.

Olmsted's psychological art also included another powerful idea—that the restorative powers of nature and landscape architecture were critical for social reform and the democratic process. He believed that beauty was a moral force. He followed John Ruskin, who Olmsted read and greatly appreciated, in the belief that "impressions of beauty…are neither sensual nor intellectual, but moral."[12] Not only did Olmsted believe that public parks and greenspace provided natural settings for citizens of all races and classes to interact, the more profound impact of nature and landscape architecture was to stimulate the free flow of imagination, thereby providing citizens "a sense of enlarged freedom."[13]

Olmsted's conviction that nature has a healing and restorative influence on the human soul, and that nature is a civilizing force in society were influenced both by his personal history and by his intellectual studies. As an adult, he looked back fondly and with great appreciation at the role his father played in his early appreciation of nature. His father had a high regard for nature and scenery that he shared extensively with Olmsted. But Olmsted's embrace of the power of imagination and of nature's unconscious influence on the human soul also had two main progenitors—the eighteenth-century Swiss physician Johann Georg von Zimmermann and the prominent Congregational theologian of Olmsted's own time, Horace Bushnell.

---

10. Ibid.

11. Ibid., 23.

12. *The Works of John Ruskin,* vol. 4: *Modern Painters II,* edited by E.T. Cook and Alexander Wedderburn (London: George Allen; New York: Longmans, Green, and Co., 1903), 42.

13. Olmsted, Vaux & Co., "Report of the Landscape Architects," Board of Commissioners of Prospect Park, Sixth Annual Report (1866). Quoted in Fisher, "Frederick Law Olmsted," 235.

Olmsted read Zimmermann's book *Solitude Considered, with Respect to Its Influence on the Mind and the Heart* as a boy and then picked it up again in his early twenty's. It had a great impact on Olmsted's thinking, and he wrote to his father in 1845 that he had "sat up with a hot fire reading Zimmermann on Solitude (which will rank next to the Bible and Prayer Book in my Library)." Olmsted effused that "I think it is one of the best books ever written, I wish everybody would read it."[14]

In *Solitude,* Zimmermann described how he had left his mountain canton of Berne to minister to the ailing Frederick the Great. Separated from his home and family, Zimmermann sank into a deep melancholy. He discovered solace by taking daily walks in a garden "cultivated in the English taste" of a friend near Hannover.[15] Zimmermann became interested in how the walks were able to bring relief from his melancholy. After much reflection, he concluded that:

> The heart owes the most agreeable enjoyments which it derives from Solitude, to the IMAGINATION. The touching aspect of delightful nature; the variegated verdure of the forests; the noise of an impetuous torrent; the quivering motion of the foliage; the harmony of the groves, and an extensive prospect, ravish the soul so entirely, and absorb in such a manner all our faculties, that the thoughts of the mind are instantly converted into sensations of the heart. The view of an agreeable landscape excites the softest emotions, and gives birth to pleasing and virtuous sentiments; all this is produced by the charms of imagination.

Zimmermann was especially taken by the power that the small garden he visited had on his thoughts and feelings. He was surprised by the degree to which the garden could "imitate the enchanting variety and the noble simplicity of nature."[16] Zimmermann's deep appreciation of nature, his belief that solitude in nature was the appropriate and neces-

---

14. Olmsted to John Olmsted, 2 February 1845, in *The Papers of Frederick Law Olmsted,* vol. 1: *The Formative Years,* edited by Charles E. Beveridge and Charles Capen McLaughlin (Baltimore: The John Hopkins University Press, 1977), 203.

15. Johann Georg von Zimmermann, *Solitude Considered, with Respect to Its Influence upon the Mind and the Heart,* translated by J.B. Mercier (New London: Cady & Eells, 1807), 174.

16. Ibid., 177.

sary counterpart for human society, and that nature's power could be recreated in smaller, planned gardens made a deep and lasting impression on Olmsted.

Even more than Zimmermann, Horace Bushnell influenced Olmsted across a wide range of topics, all of which would contribute to Olmsted's thinking and art. The Bushnell family were neighbors of the Olmsted family for several years, and Bushnell would eventually become the Olmsted's family pastor. Bushnell had a rebellious and fertile mind, and his 1842 sermon on *Unconscious Influence* was directly responsible for Olmsted's later thoughts on the unconscious influence that nature had on the human psyche and character. Bushnell's ideas on unconscious influence also greatly impacted Olmsted's best friend, Charles Loring Brace, who said that the sermon had affected his whole life.[17] Throughout the 1840s, Olmsted and Brace had long discussions about Bushnell's ideas.

In his sermon, Bushnell starts from the premise that each individual is a "fractional element of a larger and more comprehensive being, called society."[18] This concept would play a major role in Olmsted's life-long quest for social reform. For Bushnell, "all society is organic. A pure separate, individual man, living *wholly* within and from himself, is a fiction."[19] In stark contrast to the excessive individualism of Olmsted's time, Bushnell was seeking to strengthen society, not the individual. Instead of thinking that individuals created society through a social contract, Bushnell believed that it was society that created the individual.[20]

Within society, all humans are "ever touching unconsciously the springs of motion in each other...We overrun the boundaries of our personality—we flow together."[21] For Bushnell, there were two sorts of influence, one that is active and voluntary, and the other that is unconscious and that "flows out from us, unawares to ourselves."[22] This lat-

---

17. *The Papers of Frederick Law Olmsted*, 1: 72.

18. Horace Bushnell, *Unconscious Influence: A Sermon* (London: Partridge and Oakey, 1852), 15.

19. Horace Bushnell, *Christian Nurture* (New York: Charles Scribner, 1861), 31.

20. Daniel Howe, "The Social Science of Horace Bushnell," *The Journal of American History* 70, no. 2 (1983): 310.

21. Bushnell, *Unconscious Influence,* 4.

22. Ibid.

ter influence "flows directly from our character and conduct."[23] This unconscious influence follows character "as the shadow follows the sun," and goes "streaming from us in all directions."[24]

Just as we have two sorts of influence, so, too, we have two ways of receiving the influences of others, again voluntary and involuntary. We can receive influences directly through speech, but the more important influences are received in "the expression of the eye, the face, the look, the gait, the motion, the tone or cadence, which is sometimes called the natural language of the sentiments."[25] For Bushnell, we are endowed "with two inlets of impression; the ear and the understanding for the reception of speech, and the sympathetic powers, the sensibilities or affections, for tinder to those sparks of emotion revealed by looks, tones, manners, and general conduct."[26] These sympathetic powers "catch the meaning of signs," and through them "it is as if one heart were thus going directly into another, and carrying in its feeling with it."[27]

Bushnell thought that our sympathetic powers resulted in an "assimilating power of sensibility and fellow-feeling."[28] Brought together by these powers, "we all adhere together, as parts of a larger nature...one mass, one consolidated social body, animated by one life."[29] Moreover, this involuntary communication and sympathy between the members of a state or family "results in what we call the national or family spirit; for there is a spirit peculiar to every state and family in the world."[30]

We can hear in Bushnell's words the seeds of Olmsted's later thoughts on how we receive unconscious influences not only from other people but from nature. But Bushnell's thoughts on unconscious influence are even more remarkable when we remind ourselves that during his time the idea of the unconscious was still evolving. The word itself was used almost exclusively either as an adjective or as having the general mean-

---

23. Ibid., 6.
24. Ibid.
25. Ibid., 13.
26. Ibid., 13–14.
27. Ibid., 14.
28. Ibid.
29. Ibid., 17.
30. Ibid.

ing of being unaware. This is long before Freud, Jung, and others posited contents for the unconscious. And yet here is Bushnell in 1868:

> Here in the soul's secret chambers are Fausts more subtle than Faust, Hamlets more mysterious than Hamlet, Lears more distracted than Lear; wills that do what they allow not, and what they would not, do; wars in the members; bodies of death to be carried, as in Paul; wild horses of the mind governed by no rein, as in Plato; subtleties of cunning, plausibilities of seeming virtues, memories writ in letters of fire, great thoughts heaving under the brimstone marl of revenges, pains of wrong and of sympathy with suffering wrong, aspirations that have lost courage, hates, loves, beautiful dreams and tears; all these acting at cross purposes and representing as it were to sight the broken order of the mind. Getting into the secret working, and seeing how the drama goes on in so many mystic parts, the wondrous life-scene,—shall we call it poetry?—takes on a look at once brilliant and pitiful and appalling, and what we call the person becomes a world of boundless capacities shaken out of their law, energies in full conflict and without government, passions that are wild, sorrows that are weak. By such explorations, never to be exhausted by discovery, our sense of person or mind or soul is widely opened and may always be kept fresh.[31]

This extraordinary passage, in which Bushnell describes a multifaceted, polysemous, and autonomous soul *that is essentially poetic* presages not only Freud and Jung's work but also Hillman's. Bushnell also had a sophisticated philosophy of language that emphasized the poetic power of words that he believed had a liberating effect on the soul. "Words," wrote Bushnell, "are given, not to imprison souls, but to express them."[32] He believed that the etymologies of words were always a "latent presence," and that even if people did not know these etymologies, they nonetheless affected the use and understanding of the words. (This, too, is similar to

---

31. Horace Bushnell, *Building Eras in Religion* (New York: Charles Scribner's Sons, 1881), 233–34.

32. "Preliminary Dissertation: Language as Related to Thought and Spirit" (1848), in Horace Bushnell, *God in Christ* (New York: Charles Scribner's Sons, 1876), 50.

Hillman's view of a "poetic basis of mind.") For Bushnell, the power of words reaches its fullest form in poetry. "Poets, then are the true metaphysicians, and if there be any complete science of man to come, they must bring it."[33] Olmsted noted in a letter to his brother in 1849 that he was reading Bushnell's philosophy of language.[34]

Another aspect of Bushnell's thought that affected the young Olmsted was his theory of play. Recreation would be a central concept in Olmsted's landscape architecture, and it was Bushnell that loosened the Puritanical grip on both play and art. Bushnell defined work as "activity *for* an end," and play as "activity *as* an end."[35] In terms of language, prose was work because it was meant to communicate a message, but poetry was play because the expression was itself the end. For Bushnell, the true goal of human existence, and the essence of religion itself, was to move beyond work to engage in more creative forms of play. Rejecting Calvin's suspicion of "images," and the restraint he placed on aesthetics, Bushnell exalted poetry and art. Olmsted agreed, writing that:

> the Puritans, whatever their moral elevation, were very low in civilization, and they possessed and bequeathed to their descendants one element of public opinion strongly antagonistic to civilization. Their requirements were meagre. They considered the fine arts for instance as devices of the devil. They strangled or turned into savage directions the natural demands for festive recreations.[36]

The quest for social reform, the power of nature to unconsciously influence the soul, the moral power of beauty, the poetic essence of language, the value of play, and the intrinsic value of natural beauty were all gifts to Olmsted from Bushnell, a man that the young Olmsted had the good fortune to sail with and talk ideas. As one commentator con-

---

33. Ibid., 73.

34. Olmsted to John Hull Olmsted, 24 February 1849, in *The Papers of Frederick Law Olmsted,* 1: 326–27.

35. See Howe, "Social Science," 309.

36. Fragment from a draft of a proposed work by Frederick Law Olmsted titled "Civilization in the Last Fifty Years." Possibly written while Olmsted was in Mariposa Bear Valley, California, around 1863. Quoted in Fisher, "Frederick Law Olmsted," 169–70.

cludes, "Olmsted's eventual formulation of his philosophy of public parks as instruments of moral influence and reform and of the value of passive recreation and unconscious mental and spiritual refreshment are thoroughly Bushnellian ideas."[37] As for Olmsted himself, in a letter to his friend Brace he sums up his respect and admiration for Bushnell by exclaiming "Hurrah for 'unconscious influence' all the world over!"[38]

Apart from his intellectual influence on Olmsted, Bushnell also had a more direct influence on Olmsted's work as a landscape architect. At a time when there was widespread anti-city sentiment, Bushnell celebrated the city. In 1853, the same year that Central Park was proposed in New York, Bushnell proposed a public park for Hartford. In a report of the Hartford Park Committee formed to investigate Bushnell's proposal, and likely written or at least contributed to by Bushnell, special note is made of the park's social context and purpose. The proposed park would be "a social exchange...where high and low, rich and poor will exchange looks and make acquaintance through the eyes." The park would be "an outdoor parlor, open for the cultivation of good manner and a right social feeling...that will make us more completely conscious of being one people."[39] This idea that a park had a social and moral function within civil society was integral to Olmsted's views on the use and function of landscape architecture.

After winning overwhelming voter support for the park in 1854, Bushnell began considering the questions of comprehensive urban design. In autumn of that year, he announced the formation of a local Society for Public Improvement. The society planned to invite prominent citizens to present lectures on such topics as Economy of Taste, Public Parks, Public Architecture, Street Architecture, Color, and Trees

---

37. George Scheper, "The Reformist Vision of Frederick Law Olmsted and the Poetics of Park Design," *The New England Quarterly* 2, no. 3 (1989): 378.

38. Olmsted to Charles Loring Brace, 1851. Quoted in Scheper, "The Reformist Vision," 378.

39. "The Proposed Park," *Hartford Daily Courant,* 16 November 1853. Quoted in Donald J. Poland, *Unconscious Influence: Olmsted's Hartford,* manuscript prepared for the Amistad Committee, New Haven, Connecticut (October 2020), 97 (online at *https://portal.ct.gov/-/media/DECD/Historic-Preservation/03_Technical_Assistance_ Research/Research/Frederick-Law-Olmsteds-Hartford2020.pdf*).

and Shrubbery. Bushnell himself was to present a lecture on the Planning of Cities. Remarkably, Bushnell was the first person to specifically call for a "city-planning profession, as truly as an architectural, house-planning profession."[40] He saw great opportunity in being able to plan cities. "Every new village, town, city," said Bushnell, "ought to be contrived as a work of art, and prepared for the new age of ornament to come."[41]

For an even more striking correlation between Bushnell and Olmsted, here is Bushnell writing about design in city planning fifteen years before Olmsted's design for Riverside:

> Accepting, thus far, the lines of nature, which will commonly be curvilinear, and will make irregular angles with each other, the skeleton of the plan that is to be, is made out, and the filling up only remains. And this will be done to a considerable degree, at least, by a rectangular blockwork, adjusted by some principal straight line, or lines, running up and along the natural summits, or ridges between the low grounds and their avenues. These principal, straight line streets, having position of dignity, will be the Broadways of the plan.

Olmsted wrote in his plan for Riverside, "we should recommend the general adoption, in the design of your roads, of gracefully-curved lines, generous spaces, and the absence of sharp corners, the idea being to suggest and imply leisure, contemplativeness and happy tranquility."[42] (Here Bushnell and Olmsted's ideas on city planning, design, and unconscious influence fuse together.) Also, in his plan for Riverside, Olmsted envisioned a great boulevard connecting the suburb to Chicago. Bushnell's "Broadways" are Olmsted's boulevards, and the curvilinear streets of Riverside are indeed laid out in a rectangular blockwork, a less-ridged grid softened by the absence of right angles. In sum, Bushnell's statement that a new village, town, or city, ought to be "contrived as a work of art" is a fitting description of Olmsted's life work as a landscape architect

---

40. Horace Bushnell, "City Plans" (1854), in Horace Bushnell, *Work and Play: or Literary Varieties* (New York: Charles Scribner, 1864), 336.

41. Ibid.

42. "Preliminary Report upon the Proposed Suburban Village at Riverside, near Chicago" (1868), in *Olmsted: Writings on Landscape, Culture, and Society,* 448.

written a decade before Olmsted even became a landscape architect.[43]

One last story about Bushnell and Olmsted bears telling. In 1846, Bushnell gave the annual address to the Hartford County Agricultural Society. After emphasizing the importance of farming in New England, Bushnell encouraged the society to keep an eye to beauty. He told them to pay more attention to domestic and rural architecture. "Study situation, material, plan, form, color, everything that belongs to picturesque effect."[44] He says that if their local builders can only build them "an oblong clapboarded box, with a gable to the street," then they should become their own architects or go to one who has taste and experience. He says, "Put your style and your barns where they belong." In the context of Olmsted, during his time as a farmer at Staten Island, he endeavored to make the somewhat ramshackle buildings of his farm more appealing. In particular, "he moved the barns to a new location behind a knoll and changed the driveway so it approached the housing in a graceful curve."[45] There is no way to know whether Olmsted was aware of Bushnell's direction to the Agricultural Society, but the episode certainly shows a kindred spirit between the two men.

Olmsted's art was not a dalliance. From his earliest days, Olmsted wanted to make a difference, to advance the social well-being and the springs of democracy. Writing to his friend Frederick Kingsbury in 1846, Olmsted wrote that he wanted to make himself "useful in the world—to make happy—to help advance the condition of Society."[46] A year later he would write to Brace: "Throw your light on the path in Politics and Social Improvement and encourage me to put my foot *down* and *forwards.* There's a great *work* wants doing in this our generation. Charley, let's off our jacket and go about it."[47]

Although he first experimented with being a farmer, Olmsted became

---

43. Poland, *Unconscious Influence,* 106.

44. "Agriculture at the East," in Bushnell, *Work and Play,* 258.

45. *The Papers of Frederick Law Olmsted,* 1: 8.

46. Olmsted to Frederick Kingsbury, 12 June 1846, in *The Papers of Frederick Law Olmsted,* 1: 243.

47. Olmsted to Charles Loring Brace, 26 July 1847, quote in Scheper, "The Reformist Vision," 382.

a champion of the city, considering it to be the seat of civilization. He lived in a time of enormous population growth in American cities, and he believed that despite the value and promise offered by urban life it also came with a psychological price:

> whenever we walk through the denser part of a town, to merely avoid collision with those we meet and pass upon the sidewalks, we have constantly to watch, to foresee, and to guard against their movements... Our minds are thus brought into close dealings with other minds without any friendly flowing toward them, but rather a drawing from them. Much of the intercourse between men when engaged in the pursuits of commerce has the same tendency—a tendency to regard others in a hard if not always hardening way... This is one of the many ways in which it happens that men who have been brought up, as the saying is, in the streets, who have been most directly and completely affected by town influences, so generally show, along with a remarkable quickness of apprehension, a peculiarly hard selfishness. Every day of their lives they have seen thousands of their fellow men, have met them face to face, have brushed against them, and yet have had no experience of anything in common with them. [48]

Olmsted bemoaned the conditions of urban life that "compel us to walk circumspectly, watchfully, jealously, which compel us to look closely upon others without sympathy.[49]

Quite apart from the unpleasantry of such conditions, Olmsted believed that they forced people to deny their very natures. Like Aristotle, Olmsted believed that we are by nature political animals having an instinctive inclination to gregarious and neighborly interaction. When this nature is repressed or thwarted the result is a sense of alienation and fragmentation whereby people become "incapable of creative activity and moral determination." The cause of this discontent was attributable not only to overcrowding but to the design of the city itself with its imposed grid, regimented blocks, straight lines, and right angles.

---

48. "Public Parks and the Enlargement of Towns," in *Olmsted: Writings on Landscape, Culture, and Society,* 470–71.
49. Ibid., 482.

Olmsted believed that poor city design and planning partitioned the social imagination, leading to a breakdown of communication and community that resulted in feelings of isolation and a general debilitation of "the mind and moral strength."[50] With the enlargement of cities, for all of their economic and civilizing benefits, also came "vital exhaustion," "nervous irritation," and "constitutional depression."[51]

It is important to note that for Olmsted these ailments were both psychological and social. Indeed, for Olmsted these two ideas were inseparable—psyche and polis existed as one, and when the soul suffered so, too, the city. His landscape architecture was expressly therapeutic, intended to serve not only the individual psyche but the moral and social underpinnings of democracy. The intent and purpose of his art was to serve society by encouraging the appreciation of beauty, thereby cultivating the imagination and refining the tastes of all people whatever their station in life. The unconscious influence of his art he understood as *poetic,* touching the soul subliminally through natural scenery:

> It is not simply to give the people of the city an opportunity for getting fresh air and exercise…It is not simply to make a place of amusement or for the gratification of curiosity or for gaining knowledge. The main object and justification is simply to produce a certain influence in the minds of people and through this to make life in the city healthier and happier. *The character of this influence is a poetic one and it is to be produced by means of scenes,* through observation of which the mind may be more or less lifted out of moods and habits into which it is, under the ordinary conditions of life in the city, likely to fall. (Emphasis added.)[52]

It was through the common, shared experience of beauty that he hoped to instill and further a sense of community. His goal was to facilitate a move from "a mentality of…an individualistic, alienating, competitive commercial culture—to a mentality of…a tradition-oriented, neighborly, communitarian culture in which things and other people are

---

50. Ibid., 470.

51. Frederick Law Olmsted, *A Consideration of the Justifying Value of a Public Park* (Boston: Tolman and White, Printers, 1881), 19.

52. Olmsted, *Forty Years of Landscape Architecture,* 356.

regarded not as instruments or means but as extensions of one's own sympathies and abilities."[53]

For Olmsted, "service must precede art, since all turf, trees, flowers, fences, walks, water, paint, plaster, posts and pillars in or under which there is not a purpose of direct utility or service are inartistic if not barbarous... So long as considerations of utility are neglected or overridden by considerations of ornament, there will be not true art."[54] But Olmsted's idea of "utility" was not simplistic, short-term practicality. His meaning of utility "always had reference to a long-range vision of civilizing America."[55] Indeed one of the remarkable aspect of Olmsted's genius was his ability to project his designs imaginatively to the future. He recognized the "general townward movement of the civilized world," and was able to adapt his art to needs that would take decades to manifest.[56] Writing of his design for Central Park, he noted that it was "not planned for such use as is now made of it, but with regard to future use, when it will be in the center of a population of two millions."[57]

Olmsted believed that by working sympathetically with nature, landscape architecture, which he considered to stand alongside the other fine arts, could improve upon the unconscious influence that nature had in its raw, unworked state. The art of landscape architecture was to produce a new perception of nature "which will in truth be equally natural in aspect... and far more charming than the best that nature, *unencouraged,* would much more slowly give you."[58] The idea of working in concert with nature in a mutually fulfilling way found expression in the idea of the genius of the place, a phrase from Alexander Pope that Olmsted embraced. The curvilinear roads of Riverside are a good example of how Olmsted

---

53. Scheper, "The Reformist Vision," 386–87.

54. Manuscript fragment, Frederick Law Olmsted Papers, Library of Congress. Quoted in Charles E. Beveridge, "Olmsted—His Essential Theory" (online at *https://www.nps.gov/frla/learn/historyculture/flo.htm*).

55. Carol J. Nicholson, "Elegance and Grass Roots: The Neglected Philosophy of Frederick Law Olmsted," *Transactions of the Charles S. Peirce Society* 40, no. 2 (Spring 2004): 341.

56. "Public Parks," in *Olmsted: Writings on Landscape, Culture, and Society,* 462.

57. Ibid., 492.

58. Olmsted, *Mount Royal Montreal,* 34.

adapted his designs to the topography and spirit of the place.

In each of his designs, Olmsted would begin with a comprehensive study of the place. This Olmsted conceived of as a fully rational, conscious process. The second phase of the design displays Olmsted's philosophical and psychological influences. A design emerges through "a natural, spontaneous, individual action of imagination—of *creative fancy*."[59] "It is a matter of growth; involuntary and unconscious growth. I cannot come to a designing conclusion just when I want to. I must muse upon the conditions to be dealt with, have them upon my mind, and, after a time, I find a conclusion. I do not make it. It has come to be in my mind without my knowing it."[60] Referring to the design for Central Park, Olmsted wrote that "the best conceptions of scenery, the best plans, details of plans—intentions—the best, are not contrived by effort, but are spontaneous and instinctive."[61] He said that the work of design necessarily supposes "a gallery of mental pictures" that he constantly had before him and that he was laboring to realize.[62] The design, said Olmsted "must be almost exclusively in my imagination," and it was the imagination that dictated what was to be done.[63]

A central them of Olmsted's designs and of his art in general is that an artist must educate, civilize, and refine the tastes of the spectator. "A great object of all that is done in a park, of *all* the art of a park, is to influence the mind of men through their imagination."[64] But this influence could not be heavy-handed or flashy. Olmsted's art was meant to touch the psyche by activating the poetic sensibilities he believed possessed by all people. Part of his art was to conceal his art and in so doing enliven the social, democratic, and moral impulse. He intended the influence of his art to be as a "gentle, persuasive dew, falling so softly as to be impercep-

---

59. Olmsted to the Board of Commissioners of the Central Park, 22 January 1861, in Olmsted, *Forty Years of Landscape Architecture*, 309.

60. Olmsted to Dr. Edward Moore, 26 January 1889, in *The Papers of Frederick Law Olmsted*, 8: 573–74.

61. Olmsted, *Forty Years of Landscape Architecture*, 310.

62. Ibid.

63. Ibid.

64. "Public Parks," in *Olmsted: Writings on Landscape, Culture, and Society*, 484.

tible, and yet delightfully reinvigorating in its results."[65] Through art he could negate the harsh realities of the crowded city, restore the sense of community that he believed was essential to our nature at gregarious and neighborly beings, and fan the embers of democracy.

Here we come to the great synthesis that Olmsted accomplished through his work. He understood that an unfettered soul encouraged by beauty tended naturally toward freedom and democracy. By attending to the genius of the place he at the same time encouraged the human soul to follow the contours of its character. His goal was not tranquility for tranquility's sake—his work was subversive; it was a rejection of the urban confinement and materialism that he saw as so detrimental to the social fabric. From the beginning he had been an activist dedicated to fulfilling democracy's highest callings. His first tools were words, but later came the public park and the suburban landscape. Through his art he hoped to bring people of all races and classes together to experience a common appreciation of beauty, thereby releasing the free flow of imagination that lays at the heart of all freedom. In the thrall of beauty there is no place for tyranny, hate, or oppression. Olmsted was "seeking social reform by achieving individual psychological change through the aesthetic impulse. He was attempting to change society by indirection."[66] In Olmsted's art, politics, ethics, and nature are bound together by the democratizing, ordering, and inspirational power of beauty.

---

65. Olmsted, *Mount Royal Montreal,* 59.
66. Fisher, "Frederick Law Olmsted," 271.

TWELVE

Eros Unbound

Despite Olmsted's belief that the city was the seat of civilization, he nonetheless tended to perpetuate the Romantic antithesis between nature and the city. With his public parks he attempted to bring nature to the city, but the city itself was not thought of as natural. Nature always existed elsewhere, "out there" beyond the urban bustle, buildings, commerce, streets, and sewers. Even he distinguished between nature in its raw, given state and the artistic manipulations of landscape gardening and architecture.

When the first settlers arrived on the shores of America there were instantly two, distinct "American" views about nature. Although there is no single "Native American" view of nature, there are some common themes. Indigenous people existed in a reciprocal relationship with nature, respecting it as a place of spiritual and ancestral presences. Humans were part and parcel with nature, not separate, and so were filled with the same spirits that imbued other living creatures and the elements. The proper attitude toward nature was one of reverence and humility. Animals could be killed for survival, but they could not be taken for granted. There were rituals to propitiate the hunt and every effort was made to use the animals killed in the fullest way possible. The land did not belong to individuals but was settled and cared for by the tribe. Nature was a sacred place that itself provided tutelary and guiding spirits—animal spirits were essential to the natures of humans, giving them their temperaments and character.

The "new" Americans saw nature through a Christian lens.[1] The Pilgrim leader William Bradford described the Cape Cod shoreline that

---

1. The following historical sketch of the purported separation of humans from nature appears in a different form in my *Return to Beauty: Restoring the Ecology of Imagination.*

he saw from the deck of the *Mayflower* in 1620 as "a hidieous and desolate wilderns, full of wild beasts and wild men."[2] The Christian doctrine of the early Americans was that nature was Satan's domain and therefore something to be resisted and overcome. Not only did this view attach to the land and water, it also applied to the indigenous peoples who the early settlers thought of more as wild beasts than humans.

The disgraceful treatment of the Native Americans by mostly white, Christian Europeans mirrors the long-standing attitude toward nature itself. God made nature and then put Christians in charge. Humans have dominion over nature; it is there to be used by us however we see fit. It is godless, indeed fallen, and therefore deserves no moral status. We have already commented in Chapter One how the Christian view of an existential separation between humans and nature persisted and was concretized through Descartes, the scientific revolution, and the Enlightenment. The Romantics really fared no better—their hyper-idealized and transcendental view of nature only accentuated its essential difference from humanity. But at least they recognized that nature was beautiful.

Jedediah Purdy, in his book *After Nature,* provides a useful outline of how non-indigenous Americans have viewed nature over time. The *providential* view was that nature was there to provide humans what they need and want, and so there is a moral imperative to own and develop the land to the European ideals of "best use." This view provided the justification for the expropriation of Native American lands because from a European perspective the Native Americans were not putting the land to its best and fullest use. Thus, the Biblical grant of human dominion over nature gained a new moral and political impetus that declared humans had a duty to alter nature to meet human needs. The *Romantic* view saw nature as place for inspiration and transcendence. This was the nature that appeared in the pristine and idealized landscapes of Frederic Church, Ashur Durand, and other painters from the Hudson River School, and in the writings of Henry David Thoreau and Ralph Waldo Emerson. It would later reappear in the creation of the

---

2. Quoted in Leo Marx, "The Idea of Nature in America," *Daedalus* 137, no. 2 (April 2008): 10.

national parks, all chosen, at least in part, because they represented the ideals of the Romantic vision of nature. But here, too, the separation of human and nature remained. According to this view, humans can go to nature to commune with God, but they cannot be part of that nature. And the brighter the light, the darker the shadow. Purdy points out that there was no place in the Romantic landscape for indigenous people. John Muir supported removing the Miwok from Yosemite because he considered nature to be at its best when it was people-free.

Next, as the frontier pushed relentlessly westward, the *utilitarian* view took hold, a view of nature as a resource to be managed for maximum benefit. National forests were managed by the Bureau of Land Management and vast areas of the West were irrigated by the ironically named Bureau of Reclamation. Nature became something to be managed by experts. Lastly comes the more familiar *ecological* view where nature is seen as a network of complex and interpenetrating systems. This view began to coalesce in the 1960s and by the 1970s "nature" was increasingly replaced with "environment." In an attempt to avoid the ambiguities inherent in "nature," "environment" referred to the entire biophysical surround that we inhabit, making no distinction between human and other forms of life. The environment encompasses all that is built and unbuilt, the human-made and the simply present things of the world.

With the ecological view, steps were at least made to see humans finally as direct participants in the natural world. Unfortunately, this recognition was in part forced upon us as a result of human exploitation and recklessness with regard to nature and its resources. The first Earth Day was in 1970, the same year that Congress enacted the National Environmental Policy Act, the Clean Air Act, and the act establishing the Environmental Protection Agency.

Although the ecological perspective offered an alternative to earlier views that kept humans and nature apart, in the last part of the twentieth century the very idea of nature was deemed suspect. Postmodernism and deconstructionist views claimed that nature was a cultural construction having no actual referent in the real world. Nature is simply a concept that is seen as mere discourse. According to this view, not only are humans separate from nature, the very idea that humans could have any direct, unmediated knowledge of the material world is naïve if not laughable.

In 1989 Carolyn Merchant declared nature "dead" because of the widespread acceptance of a mechanistic, male oriented, Newtonian-Cartesian worldview. "The removal of animistic, organic assumptions about the cosmos," wrote Merchant, "constituted the death of nature."[3] Despite this bleak conclusion, Merchant held out hope that the harsh realities of an ecological crisis might drive humans to restore a more organic view of nature. That same year, in *The End of Nature*, Bill McKibben concluded that nature came to an end when the earth's atmosphere was altered by greenhouse gases and other manufactured chemicals. For McKibben, the all-pervasive, globe-encircling presence of humankind's detritus made the very idea of nature meaningless. This idea continues today in the increasing use of "Anthropocene" to refer to a new epoch in which humans have become the defining force shaping the planet. Purdy advances this idea in his aptly titled *After Nature*.

So long as humans continue to believe that we are separate from nature and that nature exists only where we are not, we will be cursed by ideas and conduct that encourage and reinforce catastrophic behavior toward nature. Elemental decay and ecocide through anthropogenic climate change, scarcity of water, pollution, deforestation, and the sixth extinction with its dramatic loss of biodiversity are all sustained because of our pathological ideas about the relationship between humans and the things we make, and the natural world that exists beyond our manipulation. And, if we are now indeed irreversibly in the Anthropocene, the latter no longer exists.

Which brings me back to the city. After all, the alleged separation of the city from nature is just a restatement of the alleged separation of humans from nature. "Nature" as such therefore cannot exist within a city, only facsimiles or imitations of nature in the forms of landscape gardening and landscape architecture can offer us partial glimpses of what must forever lay beyond the city. Even though these human-made creations might be beautiful, and to some degree and in some manner distill nature's essence in ways that are not available in nature itself,

---

3. Carolyn Merchant, *The Death of Nature: Women, Ecology, and the Scientific Revolution* (San Francisco: Harper, 1989). Quoted in Marx, "The Idea of Nature in America," 18.

they still are not "the real thing." Nature cannot be in the city because nature, according to our reigning ideas, must be "out there."

What is it, though, that draws us to nature? What hold do the snow-capped peaks, the flowing prairie, and the bluing sea have on our soul? What makes us long to leave the city so that we can re-create ourselves in the hills and valleys? It is, of course, beauty. Whether we find it in the tranquil rustlings of a forest or the sublime, breath-taking extravagance of mountain peaks, it is beauty that attracts us to nature. More, it is the particulars of nature that most strike us—a fox that appears suddenly in the woods, or the sun glistening off an icicle—nature is constantly presenting us with exquisite, particular displays of beauty. Even the panorama of a mountain range or the infinite blaze of the night sky are given to us as precise images of beauty. Olmsted might have eschewed things that draw attention to themselves and that stop us in our tracks, but nature's beauty does not. Heraclitus said that nature loves to hide, but I think the opposite, that nature loves nothing more than to show itself in all of it incredibly diverse beauty.[4] Remember that Olmsted was striving for a particular effect on the soul, a soothing tranquility that he believed would release a suppressed poetic and aesthetic sensibility. But nature can have a vast range of effects on the soul precisely because of its seemingly endless variety.

So here we have stumbled upon another issue. If we place beauty with nature and nature outside the city, is the city to be left bereft of beauty? To this we can answer, of course, that beauty is not limited to nature, that beauty can also appear in things that are human made. Beauty manifests in the many products of the fine arts, in the smooth precision of tools, and in the majesty of the city skyline. And yet we differentiate this human-made beauty from that of nature. Why? Does not the effect of beauty on the soul share common purchase in both the art museum and the forest? Think how we walk softly with hushed voices in both. Think how particular things, be they animal or sculpture, can arrest our forward push, catching our breath, racing our pulse. What if we are wrong about this alleged separation between the human city and non-

---

4. Wheelwright, *Heraclitus,* 20.

human nature? If beauty can so easily bridge them, is there in fact a gulf between them?

One commentator writes that "nature" is "perhaps the most complex word in [the English] language...[and that] any full history of the uses of nature would be a history of a large part of human thought."[5] We should not be so quick, then, to simply accept our common notion of nature as synonymous with the literal wilderness and its physical constituents. "Nature" is an idea of great depth and variability, and it is when we make it into a grand abstraction, what Purdy calls "capital-N" Nature, that we lose both its particularity and its beauty. There is no "Nature" apart from the elements, animals, and plants that constitute its physical, spiritual, and psychological reality.

"Nature" derives etymologically from the Latin *natura,* from a root in the past participle of *nasci*—to be born. The same root lies within *nation, native,* and *innate.*[6] As we noted in Chapter One, the oldest meaning of nature referred to the essential quality or characteristic *of* something—as when Aristotle said that humans are by nature political animals. It was used in the sense of "the nature of" something in particular. Only later did it acquire the more abstract meanings of "the inherent force which directs either the world or human beings or both [or] the material world itself, taken as including or not including human beings."[7] This shift from calling attention to the qualities of particular things to asserting an abstract, overarching concept that includes all things was "structurally and historically cognate with the emergence of *God* from *a god* or *the gods.*"[8] Echoing this insight, Owen Barfield notes that "At the beginning of the seventeenth century we find the word *Nature* employed in contexts where medieval writers would certainly have used the single word *God.*"[9]

The monotheistic conflation of Nature and God goes hand in hand with the internalization of the cosmos into human subjectivity. When

---

5. Raymond Williams, *Keywords: A Vocabulary of Culture and Society* (New York: Oxford University Press, 1985), 219.

6. Ibid.

7. Ibid.

8. Ibid., 220.

9. Owen Barfield, *History in English Words* (Great Barrington, Mass.: Lindisfarne Press, 1988), 173.

God and Nature become One, and when we declare that we are defined by and limited to a wholly subjective self that is radically different and apart from nature then we are stranded on an island that no bridge can reach. We cannot discern the nature of particular things because they are essentially not like us—we feel no connection because there *is* no connection. We are alone in ourselves and all else is dead matter, soulless, inanimate. We lose our ability to discern and appreciate particular things when we reject the vibrancy of an animistic or polytheistic worldview in favor of monotheism's unifying—and deadening—concepts. The ancient Greeks said that "all things are full of gods," and it is precisely when we deny the gods in things that we lose both. The many things of the world, and the many gods that animate them, are forsaken when we erect an idealized and transcendent Nature that remains forever out of our reach. Nature becomes an abstraction for something that exists forever elsewhere than where we are, a symbol for an inaccessible reality that evaporates with our presence.

The abstraction of Nature from its actual presence in and among the nature of things is the ideational dissonance that lies at the heart of the paradox that leads people to say that they are part of nature while simultaneously defining nature as places that are devoid of humans. The separation we feel from nature is because of how we think about nature; it is our *idea* of nature that gives rise to our abiding sense of dislocation, confusion, and loneliness. An idea of nature that places it always elsewhere means that for us it is nowhere. And with nowhere to call home we are left alone in our secret selves, unable to break free from the eddies and whirlpools of subjectivity and introspection.

When Nature becomes an abstraction that excludes our presence, both we and the many things of the world suffer. "Capital-N" Nature is a pathological idea that isolates humans from our proper place in the order of things, and in our isolation we begin to have delusions of superiority and grandeur, standing atop the ladder of creation with all of nature at our feet. From this transcendent and elevated position, we cannot help but see the other things of the world as being there for our use and disposal and believe that we have dominion over them. How could they be otherwise? After all, it boils down to Us and Them, and there is nothing in between to bind us together. History has shown what this kind of thinking does to us and to nature.

But what if we reject the idea of nature as "capital-N" Nature and return our attention to the particulars that actually constitute the natural world? Isn't that what the beauty of nature is trying to get us to do anyway, to pay attention and have appreciation for what is actually there? From this humbler perspective, nature is not transcendent but rather exists everywhere and is immediately available by opening our imagination and senses to the natures of particular things that are all around us. William Cronon sees the same overarching abstraction of "capital-N" Nature in the idea of "wilderness," and suggests that by focusing on "wildness" instead of "wilderness" we leave the spiritual haze of transcendence and are regrounded in the nature of things. "[W]ildness can be found anywhere: in the seemingly tame fields and wood-lots of Massachusetts, in the cracks of a Manhattan sidewalk, even in the cells of our own bodies."[10]

When we forgo abstractions that draw us away from the particular displays of nature we can once again begin to appreciate the natures of particular things as full of portents and potentialities, displaying qualities and characteristics that attract us to them, and embodying attributes that are waiting to be discovered and discerned. Peter Wohlleben tells the story of how he changed when he stopped looking at trees in term of their commercial value and began looking at them as individuals with intrinsic value. He says his love of nature was "reignited," and he suddenly became aware of "countless wonders."[11] This is the erotic power of beauty. Each thing an each, just as it is, but never alone. Each thing always present in a broader aesthetic array of other things, a thriving, animated context of relationships, microcosm and macrocosm always together, penetrating and implicating one another.

---

10. William Cronon, "The Trouble with Wilderness; or, Getting Back to the Wrong Nature," in *Uncommon Ground: Rethinking the Human Place in Nature*, edited by William Cronon (New York: W.W. Norton, 1995), 79–80.

11. Peter Wohlleben, *The Hidden Life of Trees: What They Feel, How They Communicate* (Vancouver: Greystone Books, 2015), xiv.

With Eros unbound comes the reanimation of our imagination. Our natural senses and skills are released from their internal prison within our alleged subjectivity so that they may fully engage the world in which we live. The tired and false divides between objectivity and subjectivity, outer and inner, nature and human are then seen for what they are—imaginal perspectives foisted upon the mind by the crushing weight of monotheism and Cartesian dualism.

When beauty ignites love, soul also returns. This is the mythical trinity given to us in the old story by Apuleius, where Aphrodite (Beauty), Eros (Love), and Psyche (Soul) (or more precisely in his Roman telling, Venus, Cupid, and Psyche) all belong together, require one another, and implicate one another.[12] When guided by their examples, we approach the world as a place to be appreciated, loved, and deepened. Beauty, love, and soul give us a world that is sensate, sensual, and sensible, and together they evoke and sustain our insatiable curiosity for the many things of the world. And, as we discover and learn more about the natures of particular things, we cannot help but feel a growing kinship. No longer enclosed within our own minds, our desires suddenly take wing, lifted by an empathy that eviscerates the alleged separation between humans and nature.

When beauty teaches us to appreciate the nature of things as they appear to, and in, the imagination, the wall that separates the city from nature falls. Nature no longer appears "out there" but rather exists in our relationship to beauty, whether it be a sparkling stream or a Picasso or the undulating, magical buildings of Jeanne Gang. To make cities "natural" would mean to make them beautiful and to respect and abide the genius of place.

With the wall between city and nature removed, we can now see that the city does not have to imitate nature to be beautiful. Or, rather, the manner of imitation would change. If we want to incorporate the feelings we get from nature into the nature of the city, we can imitate the processes of nature instead of the things of nature. Hillman gives as an example that

---

12. Apuleius, *Metamorphoses* (*The Golden Ass*), vol. 1: Books 1–9, edited and translated by J. Arthur Hanson, Loeb Classical Library 44 (Cambridge, Mass.: Harvard University Press, 1996).

instead of planting trees along a sidewalk we could build the sidewalk so that it meanders like a forest path.[13] Olmsted used exactly this process both in his parks and in the planning of Riverside. It was his goal to unconsciously lead the viewer from one scene or vista to the next, mimicking the sense of discovery and exploration that we experience in nature.

Hillman also suggests another way to eliminate the false divide between city and nature. He suggests that we could "come to a more psychological notion of wilderness." Respect for wilderness is summed up in the motto of "leave no trace." When we are in the wild, we try to disturb nothing and pollute nothing; we want to leave it as we found it, unscarred by our presence. Hillman extends this by recognizing its aesthetic basis. "When we move with senses acute, listening, watching, breathing in tune with the world around us, recognizing its priority and ourselves as guests, witnessing its god-givenness, then we have made a wilderness area or moment. The restoration of the pristine starts in a fresh attitude toward what is—whatever and wherever it is, not necessarily out there in nature."[14] Rilke said that beauty is everywhere; following Hillman and Cronon's lead, nature and wildness are too.

Riverside has two straight streets that parallel train tracks that go straight east to Chicago. The streets, Burlington and Quincy, were not part of Olmsted's design but from the beginning of Riverside they were the central business district of the village. In 2014 the village received a grant to renovate the central business district on Burlington Street. The old, exposed aggregate sidewalk was in its last days and the street in general had a dilapidated, somewhat neglected look. After some prodding, the village board agreed to move forward with a dramatic, comprehensive renovation of the entire streetscape. The plan for Burlington went through extensive review by village commissions, the chamber of commerce, village organizations, and the public in general. But throughout the entire planning and design process we relied on the artistic vision of the senior landscape architect for the village's engineering firm. The plan evolved organically, and from the beginning beauty was the key. We

---

13. "Natural Beauty without Nature," in *Uniform Edition of the Writings of James Hillman,* vol. 2: *City and Soul,* 161.

14. Ibid., 163–64.

wanted something that tied the business district to the historic nature of the village and that in its own way would complement Olmsted's vision for the village. At the same time, though, it was a business district, so we wanted a plan that would benefit our local businesses while being vibrant and friendly to pedestrians, cyclists, and vehicles.

The final plan included a complete redesign of the street—sidewalks made from permeable pavers, raised planters constructed of native limestone and given organic, flowing curves (built to a height that would encourage people to sit on their edges and filled with native perennials), park-like benches that were situated at angles to one another to allow people to easily converse, beautiful lighted bollards that marked crosswalks of contrasting color with the newly-paved street, and bump-outs that added curvature while also protecting pedestrians.

Great care was given in choosing the materials for the streetscape. Everything was done with an eye toward making the new streetscape look like it had been there all along. The native limestone tied the streetscape to the natural environment and the pavers gave an English garden feel to the sidewalks. The one detail, though, that changed everything was a meandering ribbon that wove its way down the sidewalk (my wife's idea!). Its river-like, wandering path within a path transformed the sidewalks. Although they were still straight, they no longer felt straight. The ribbon touched the imagination of everyone who saw it. There were of course the usual naysayers who just wanted to put in a regular, concrete sidewalk and be done with it, but the vast majority loved the new design. Special bike racks were designed, along with attractive trash and recycling cans that themselves added to the design. The renovation was huge success and I feel even Fred himself would have been pleased.

Within a little over a year after its completion, the business district had three new restaurants and all of them mentioned the renovated streetscape as a factor in their decision to open in Riverside. It was the village's commitment to beauty and its respect for the genius of the place that revived Burlington Street. What had been a somewhat desolate place now brimmed with motion and vitality.

A few years later, with more grant money in hand, the village was able to carry the design to other parts of the business district and to our historic train station. We had set out to make our business district a work of art and being able to continue the design was like the final brush strokes. The entire business district had a new sense of completeness, a coherence that it had lacked prior to the project. It was as if it was more fully itself, that it had realized something that had always been there but not revealed. And it was beauty that did it.

THIRTEEN

Animal Aesthetics

In 2018, my wife Jill, who is a professor of evolutionary biology and animal behavior, and I started a Facebook page devoted to Riverside nature. We encouraged people to post photographs, questions, and comments about the flora and fauna of Riverside, its natural beauty, scenery, sunsets, etc. Our goal was to encourage people to open their senses more to the natural setting of our village and to recognize and honor the many non-human inhabitants with which we shared our community. The page was well received, and the number of members grew steadily over time. And then the pandemic hit. Suddenly people were at home and one respite from the isolation of the pandemic was taking walks. Membership in the page increased exponentially as more and more residents discovered, many for the first time, the natural richness and diversity present in our suburban forest, greenspaces, and riparian areas.

The overwhelming number of photographs on the page, and this was true from the beginning, are of animals. Birds get the biggest play, but pretty much all of our local animal neighbors show up. Coyote, fox, deer, beaver, woodchuck, squirrel, chipmunk, skunk, and muskrat have all made their way to the page. And the comments by the members on the page to these photographs repeatedly share a common response—that the animals are beautiful.

Human fascination with the other animals is ancient, and it seems that from the beginning the other animals have touched us both aesthetically and spiritually. Some of the earliest prehistoric art depicted animal forms, some real and some imagined. Henri Frankfort, writing about the ancient Egyptian view of animals, comments on the "underlying religious awe felt before all animal life," and that for ancient Egyptians *"animals as such* possessed religious significance."[1] Ancient Egyptians perceived animals as divine, says Frankfort, because of "their inarticulate wisdom, their unhesitating achievement, and above all their static reality. With animals the continual succession of generations brought no change...The animals never change, and in this respect especially they would appear to share—in a degree unknown to man—the fundamental nature of creation."[2]

The ancient Greeks, perhaps not to the extent of the Egyptians, also felt the divine aspect of animals. The Greek relationship to nature was not one of dominion, as with later Christian ideas, but of reciprocity— the shepherd and his flock lived in a symbiotic state, relying upon and caring for one another. The Greeks also believed that animals possessed magical, therapeutic powers. In the Asclepius cult, dogs licked invalids back to health, and it was a sure sign of a cure if a sick person dreamt about a dog. So, too, the Greeks recognized the superior speed, power, agility, and senses of animals. They believed that animals could control the fertility of crops and flocks, and that they could hold the key to conversing with the immortal gods. The actions of animals were read as portents and omens, indicators of divine intent and action.[3] A long Greek tradition from Pythagoras (570 to c. 490 BCE) through Plutarch (45–120 CE) and Porphyry (234–305 CE) "hold man and beast close together."[4] Plato admonished that a hunt should entail no cruelty, and supposedly one of the three moral precepts of Eleusis was "do not be cruel to animals."[5]

---

1. Henri Frankfort, *Ancient Egyptian Religion: An Interpretation* (New York: Columbia University Press, 1948), 12–13.

2. Ibid., 13.

3. Steven H. Lonsdale, "Attitudes toward Animals in Ancient Greece," *Greece & Rome* 26, no. 2 (October 1979): 149–52.

4. "The Animal Kingdom in the Human Dream," in *Uniform Edition of the Writings of James Hillman,* vol. 9: *Animal Presences* (Putnam, Conn.: Spring Publications, 2008), 34.

5. Plato reference is in Lonsdale, "Attitudes," 153; Eleusis reference is in Hillman, "Animal Kingdom," 34.

This reverential and respectful attitude toward animals did not persist.[6] Already in Roman times, attitudes toward non-human animals became more callous. We have already seen how Christian doctrine subjugates animals to human dominion, stripping them of ethical and moral status. Augustine believed that nothing could be perceived without reason, which is needed to judge and classify sensations, and that because nonhuman animals lacked reason they therefore "lack understanding or sensation or life altogether."[7] The lack of moral status for animals was also made clear by Augustine, who wrote that "Christ himself shows that to refrain from the killing of animals and the destroying of plants is the height of superstition, for, judging that *there are no common rights between us and beasts and the trees,* he sent the devils into a herd of swine and with a curse withered the tree on which he found no fruit."[8] (Emphasis added.)

Descartes carried this religious theme into his philosophy. He and his followers granted animals no consciousness, no soul; they were mindless automata, mere machines. Malebranche, who was deeply steeped in the thought of both Augustine and Descartes, summed up the more extreme view saying that in animals "there is neither intelligence nor a spiritual soul in the usual sense. They eat without pleasure; they cry without pain; they believe without knowing it; they desire nothing; they know nothing."[9] If animals seem to act in an intelligent and purposive

---

6. The following historical sketch about animal consciousness appeared in a different form in my *Return to Beauty.*

7. Augustine, *City of God,* 12.4, translated by Philip Levine, Loeb Classical Library 414 (Cambridge, Mass.: Harvard University Press, 1966), 17.

8. Augustine of Hippo, *The Catholic and Manichean Ways of Life,* translated by Donald Gallagher and Idella Gallagher (Washington, D.C.: The Catholic University of America Press, 1966), 102. Augustine refers here to two biblical stories. The first is an account of Jesus calling demons out from a man into a herd of swine that then are drowned in a lake. Mark 5: 1–20; Matthew 8: 28–34; Luke 8: 26–36. The second is an account of Jesus cursing a fig tree that bears no fruit and is commonly taken to be a symbol directed at the Jews for not accepting Jesus as king. Mark 11: 12–25; Matthew 21: 18–22; Luke 13: 6–9. This is in turn based on the symbolic representation in Jewish scripture of the people of Israel as figs on a tree. Hosea 9: 10, Jeremiah 24. Both stories have also been taken to mean that Jesus was sent by God to redeem human souls and has little interest in their bodies or their "property," including animals.

9. *Méditations Métaphysiques et Correspondance de Nicolas Malebranche,* edited by Félix-Sébastian Feuillet de Conches (Paris: H. Delloye, Libraire-Editeur, 1841),

manner, it is only because "God has made them fit to survive, and has constructed their bodies in such a way that they can organically avoid—without knowing that they do so—everything that might destroy them and that they seem to fear."[10]

Descartes's view of nonhuman animals took hold as an acceptable answer to both the emerging scientific sensibility and the orthodox theological tradition. It has proven remarkably resilient and still has adherents today. Nevertheless, it also sparked considerable disagreement, especially among people who had close contact with animals both wild and domestic. As the naturalist John Ray wrote in his *The Wisdom of God Manifested in the Works of Creation* (1691), if "beasts were *automata* or machines, they could have no sense, or perception of pleasure, or pain and consequently no cruelty could be exercised on them; which is contrary to the doleful significations they make when beaten, or tormented, and contrary to the common sense of mankind."[11] Thomas Hobbes adopted a thoroughly materialist view to counter Cartesian dualism, and although granting non-human animals a degree of consciousness, he maintained that they lacked the ability of self-consciousness, which belonged only to humans. Thus, non-human animals could understand and act upon words spoken by humans but did not understand the words as words—only humans could understand their own "thoughts and conceptions."[12]

This basic split between the Christian/Cartesian view that animals were soulless machines having no moral or ethical status and the "common sense" view that animals were conscious, could feel pain, and therefore warranted at least some moral and ethical consideration pretty much sums up the debate over animal consciousness for the next two centuries. Indeed, many of these same issues still occupy the field of animal consciousness. Notably, during the period before Darwin, the discussion

---

75–76. Translated and quoted in Cartmill, "Animal Consciousness: Some Philosophical, Methodological, and Evolutionary Problems," *American Zoologist* 40, no. 6 (December 2000): 838.

10. Ibid.

11. John Ray, *The Wisdom of God Manifested in the Works of Creation* (London: William Innys and Richard Manby, 1735), 55–56.

12. Thomas Hobbes, *Leviathan: Parts One and Two* (Indianapolis: The Bobbs-Merrill Company, 1958), 32.

remained primarily within philosophy and theology while the scientific interest in animals focused on taxonomy and zoology, neither of which engaged in any significant way with the idea of animal consciousness or the relationship between human and nonhuman animals.

The discussion changed with Darwin, who decisively moved (or at least tried to) the question of the relationship between human and nonhuman animals away from theology and philosophy to what we today would call comparative psychology. For Darwin, the difference between humans and the other animals "is one of degree and not of kind." He maintained that the "senses and intuitions, the various emotions and faculties, such as love, memory, attention, curiosity, imitation, reason, etc.," of which humans boast are found in an incipient, or even sometimes in a well-developed condition, in the lower animals. He even proposed that it was "extremely doubtful" that the formation of general concepts and self-consciousness did not appear in some form in at least some nonhuman animals.[13]

It is important to remember that Darwin was not proposing a philosophical or religious theory. What mattered more to Darwin was that consciousness was part of his larger theory of evolution that proposed a continuity of mind from lower to higher organisms—a difference in degree, not kind. His theory embedded humans inextricably within nature and alongside the other animals. We were different, perhaps, but not separate. We were akin to, not opposed to, the other living creatures of the world and it was not clear where that kinship stopped, if it did. Evolution, not the Bible, told the story of creation and its incremental development through time.

As he fully expected, Darwin's views drew fire from all sides. Despite the ground laid by precursors of evolutionary thought like Georges-Louis Leclerc, Comte de Buffon, and Jean-Baptiste Lamarck in the preceding century, the orthodox science, philosophy, and theology of Darwin's time still clung tenaciously to the Christian/Cartesian view of the immutability of species and a difference in kind, not degree, between human and nonhuman animals. The orthodox view that nonhuman

---

13. Charles Darwin, *The Descent of Man and Selection in Relation to Sex,* 2nd ed. (London: John Murray, 1874), 101–2.

animals were driven by instinct and humans by reason merely restated the old Cartesian divide. Additional resistance to Darwin's sympathetic and humbler views of an indelible bond between humans and non-human animals arose in America where they ran counter to overweening desires that needed nature to be separate, amoral, and providentially given for human use and exploitation.

Denying nonhuman animals their due part of soul is a seminal insult of which our species is responsible. It is true that since the 1970s at least science has begun to shift away from the shameful degradation of non-human animals, but the shadow of the Christian/Cartesian view remains. As a seminal insult, denying animals soul gave spawn to other denigrations that still widely persist. It is worth pausing before we review some of them to focus on the fact that it was and is only humans that deny the presence of soul in the world and in nonhuman animals. Denial in psychoanalytic thought (and Freud himself was no friend to nature) is a defense mechanism used to separate from and defend against ideas or situations that we find uncomfortable or threatening to our preferred sense of things. Denial rests on a fundamentalist ideology that uses two primary tools to achieve its ends—rejection of fact and projection of undesirable traits upon others. As we review the following list of how we denigrate and degrade animals we need to keep in mind that our denial says little about them and much more about ourselves. The purpose of oppression is to grant the oppressor preferred status—denial at its base is an act of hubris.

First is anthropomorphism. Because we deny animals soul, consciousness, imagination, and the range of mental abilities pointed to by Darwin, we must then find a way to account for the appearance of those very attributes that so obviously exist in animals. There is a part of us, even in those who persist in the Christian/Cartesian insult, that knows other animals are conscious beings capable of emotion, imagination, thought, and feeling. But because our denial says otherwise, we must therefore claim that we are projecting these "human" attributes onto animals. Anthropomorphism is therefore an ideological fallacy because despite what we directly perceive it nonetheless insists that what we perceive cannot be real or true. Our denial preordains that result.

It is certainly true that we can anthropomorphize animals—just turn on the Saturday morning cartoons or watch the Disney creations from Bambi to Nemo. In themselves these might not do any harm, but they do train us to look at animals in terms of human characteristics. Bambi is not a deer, but he does influence how we look at deer. Whenever we consider animals in human terms, we distance ourselves from them, ignoring their uniqueness and authenticity.

The alleged fallacy of anthropomorphism rests on the assertion that humans are projecting thoughts and feelings onto non-human animals. This assumes, in classic Western style, that human and non-human animals are qualitatively different, that the only relevant standard for thoughts and feelings are human, and that we already know that non-human animals are incapable of thoughts and feelings.[14]

But what if anthropomorphism is not a projection? What if it is an attempt, given our anthropocentric limitations of thought, feeling, and language, at recognizing and articulating consciousness in non-human animals? Can we not imagine, as did Darwin, that the differences between us and nonhuman animals are of degree, not kind? A dog does not have to be happy in the same manner that a human is happy for the word "happy" to make sense when applied to a dog. Whatever inaptness might appear in the word is our problem, not the dog's. It is we who are struggling to give voice to a direct and tacitly grasped awareness of a conscious state in a fellow creature. From this perspective, anthropomorphism is not a projection but a concession, a confession of the limitations of our methods and terminology, and of our inability to meet nonhuman animals on their terms. The psychological lesson here is simple—whenever we posit a trait or characteristic as a projection, as in anthropomorphism, we are in a state of denial. And when we are in a state of denial, we commit the basic human sins of pride and prejudice.

---

14. For a careful analysis, and refutation, that anthropomorphism is always a categorical fallacy, see John Andrew Fisher, "The Myth of Anthropomorphism," in *Readings in Animal Cognition,* edited by Marc Bekoff and Dale Jamieson (Cambridge, Mass.: The MIT Press, 1999), 15: "Without a plausible argument that ascribing mental states to non-human animals is a categorical fallacy the most basic assumptions of critics of anthropomorphic thinking is seen to be untenable."

Second on our list of insults to non-human animals, and closely related to the first, is symbolism. Here our denial is achieved through rejecting the inherent power and integrity of animals by translating them into meanings and interpretations. Remember Frankfort's comment that for the ancient Egyptians animals *as such* were considered divine, that is, they were not symbols or representations that pointed to a divinity removed from them but rather were divinities present in animal form. Similarly, for the ancient Greeks, the tip of a spear did not represent Ares as a symbol, but rather *was* Ares, just as the owl *was* Athena who was herself described as "owl-eyed."

When we take animals as symbols, as in religious painting where a dove is instantly taken to represent the holy spirit, we devalue their intrinsic value as individuals worthy of respect and admiration. As soon as an animal is taken as a symbol, we no longer need the animal because we have replaced it with an interpretation, an abstract meaning that appeals to our understanding. Symbolism is yet another example of how we deny animals their proper share of soul. Because we are incapable of staying with the mystery that is in inherent in the animal itself, we deny its mystery by replacing it with a symbol that we can define and catalog. Symbols keep the rational mind safe from recognizing its limitations, but they insult what is being symbolized. Just think how offended we get when somebody tries to "explain" us. We rebel because we are being translated out of our actual, embodied reality. We don't want to be explained, we want to be seen, heard, and appreciated. Our fellow animals deserve no less.

The third insult on our list is a tricky one—sentimentality. At first blush, sentimentality seems to suggest an affection for and affinity with nonhuman animals. We watch videos online and are overcome by the cuteness of the otters and kittens and puppies. Or we see the lone polar bear on a patch of ice and are filled with despair, angered beyond words at the abuse it is suffering due to human neglect and ignorance. These emotional, sentimental reactions to what we see are useful because they elicit direct responses to animals and their circumstances. The problem, though, lies in the placement of those emotional and sentimental reactions.

Sentimentality shares borders with anthropomorphism and symbolism because it moves away from the animal and into our feelings and responses. That "Awww," that we express when we see the kittens all cuddled has nothing to do with the kittens and everything to do with our abstracted reaction to the kittens. The videos are not for them, they are for us, and are directed toward our emotions and sentimentality—they are purposefully cute and are meant to manipulate our feelings. They are propaganda.

It is certainly possible to see the polar bear and have legitimate and heartfelt empathy for its plight, but sentimentality does not stay with the animal, it reflects back onto us. Sentimentality is inherently narcissistic because we replace the animal with our feelings about the animal and what it means to us. The polar bear neither needs nor cares about our empathy for its plight. It has no blame in its heart for our heartlessness. Its suffering is its own and our sentimental feelings for it do it no good. The proper, and better, response would be to direct our anger and outrage for its plight to those who are causing it. If we can make our species behave properly toward nature then the other animals will have nothing to fear from us.

Sentimentality depowers animals in the same way that the pristine and idealized landscapes of Frederic Church, Ashur Durand, and other painters from the Hudson River School depower the landscapes they purport to depict. Romanticism and transcendence do the same thing that sentimentality does by making nature and the other animals about us, about our feelings and reactions, turning them all into glorified pets. Nature becomes preserved for us in parks and scenic overlooks, places that we pay fees to drive through, stopping at approved vistas that are intended to match the idealized view of nature that we already hold in our postcard imaginations. Even worse, sentimentality evokes nostalgia—that pitiable state that was first and rightly seen as pathological— leaving us to long for a simpler, more Edenic time. Such feelings leave us limp and weepy when what is needed is resolve to live rightly in the world that we share with our fellow inhabitants.

Denial, anthropomorphism, symbolism, and sentimentality all seek to protect us from the other animals. What is it that we fear? Could it be that our fear is justified precisely because of what the ancient Egyptians so readily recognized, that animals *as such* possess religious significance, that they bring us face to face with the otherness of the divine, reminding us of our limitations and our actual place within the cosmic order. The other animals do not need us, but we desperately need them because it is through them that we can learn about the actual natures of things. They are our teachers, our guides, and our mentors but we can only learn from them if we give up our hubris and anthropocentrism. We can learn from them by appreciating them in their own right without reference to our thoughts and feelings. They are important because *they* are important; they deserve our respect and reverence because of "their inarticulate wisdom, their unhesitating achievement, and above all their static reality."

Portmann maintained that animal forms exist to be seen. Although convinced of the fact of evolution, he nonetheless cautioned that by interpreting animals only through the principles of adaptation and fitness we risk missing a fuller appreciation of them. He draws our attention to the aesthetic power and significance of the manifest living form, a power and significance that can be overlooked in pursuit of hidden meaning. He urged that the "preservation of both individual and species preserves precisely the rich existence of manifold forms, and all of them are, without exception, more than bare carriers of preservative functions."[15] For Portmann, appearance and display are basic characteristics of being alive. And is it not the animal's appearance and display that most takes our breath away?

This idea that appearance needs no other purpose suggests an aesthetic basic to animal life and to nature itself. This is not the aesthetics of prettiness or cuteness, but rather claims aesthetics as an ontological necessity, perhaps even an ontological ground. This is what we see so clearly in the other animals. The aesthetic eye *is* the animal eye, an eye that sees things as they are, free from abstraction or ideas. Beauty lies first in authenticity, that state where there is no distinction between inner and outer, where what we see is what we get, the animal's essence fully present in its presentation. Animals seem to share with the gods a kind of intelligence that escapes the human mind, a kind of knowledge that seems

---

15. Adolf Portmann, *Essays in Philosophical Zoology: The Living Form and the Seeing Eye,* translated by Richard B. Carter (Lewiston: The Edward Mellen Press, 1990), 154.

unhesitating and certain because it is unmediated and direct. Animals "do not need the mediation of reason because they immediately perceive, and thus know."[16] Here the ethologist has much to teach the psychologist because the animal eye is content to observe without judgment and to appreciate without asking for meaning. The animal eye has no need for the dreams of interpretation.

Animals are wholly present, and it is this that makes them feel at once familiar and wholly different from us. We, like the other animals, are aesthetic animals, but we struggle to remain in our animal state, forever being deceived by our hubris. The political goal would be to establish human society in relation to the other animals as at least equals, fully recognizing their share in soul. We are not made in God's image any more than they are, and only when we accept this can we begin to treat them in the manner they deserve. This is the way to get past our denial and to free the animals, and ourselves, from our anthropomorphism, symbolism, and sentimentality. To restore our aesthetic eye we must restore our animal eye so that we can appreciate the natures of things as they present themselves. If we can once again see the divine powers that appear to us daily in animal forms, then we might escape our anthropocentrism and find our place in the natural order of things.

In our house we have a gift that Jill's mother gave to her many years ago. Jill's mother has a deep, and blessedly unsentimental, love for animals. The gift is a quote from the naturalist writer Henry Beston, and it is a fitting close to this chapter.

> We need another and a wiser and perhaps a more mystical concept of animals. Remote from universal nature, and living by complicated artifice, man in civilization surveys the creature through the glass of his knowledge and sees thereby a feather magnified and the whole image in distortion. We patronize them for their incompleteness, for their tragic fate for having taken form so far below ourselves. And therein we err, and greatly err. For the animal shall not be measured by man. In a world older and more complete than ours they move finished and complete, gifted with the extensions of the senses we have lost or never attained, living by voices we shall never

---

16. James Hillman, "Cosmology for Soul," 27.

hear. They are not brethren, they are not underlings; they are other nations, caught with ourselves in the net of life and time, fellow prisoners of the splendour and travail of the earth.[17]

---

17. Henry Beston, *The Outermost House: A Year of Life on the Great Beach of Cape Cod* (New York: St. Martin's Griffin, 1992 [1928]), 24–25.

FOURTEEN

Inanimate Nature, or the Big Mistake

What do we mean when we say something is "inanimate"? The dictionary says it means "not alive, especially not in the manner of animals and humans." This is the usual meaning, and so we easily consider plants and rocks and fire hydrants as inanimate. We might pause a bit on plants, because they are obviously alive in their own way, but we are likely firm on rocks and fire hydrants.

The word itself, of course, literally means "no anima" or "no soul." An inanimate object is a soulless object. In the Christian and Cartesian traditions, the matter is clear—all things other than humans are inanimate. Only humans "have" a soul. We have already seen the fallout of this kind of thinking in terms of how we treat the other animals, but what does this perspective do in terms of how we imagine and relate to the vast range of nonhuman things?

When elected officials spend tax dollars on maintenance and construction, they have to be able to explain and defend their expenditures to the taxpayers. There is always a cost-benefit analysis regarding materials and designs, where a balance is struck between the quality of materials, their longevity, the frequency and cost of maintenance, and the like. Where things get more complicated is when design and aesthetics come in. Convincing taxpayers that it is worth spending more on beauty than on mere functionality can be difficult because of the dominance that economics has over policy discussions and decisions. Because we have defined beauty as an accessory instead of a necessity, we consider spending money on beauty as optional, an add-on. When form follows function, form is reduced to functionality, to what "works" best, where "best" is judged solely by efficiency and cost.

I want to suggest that our Western tradition of considering the nonhuman world inanimate and the repression and degradation of beauty go hand in hand. When we consider a mountain side or a police station inanimate, we no longer have any aesthetic, or ethical, responsibility to them. The mountain can be stripped, and the police station clad with cheap brick because ultimately they are dead to us, just as we are anesthetized to them. When the styrofoam cup in my hand, and the sidewalk on which I walk are both dead and mere *res extensa,* then what matter does it make if I toss the cup on the sidewalk? The only ethical reason to not litter has ultimately to be because people don't like it, not because the sidewalk objects, or that the cup would rather be in a trash can with other cups. Such talk is anthropomorphic nonsense because we have deemed all of nature other than ourselves to be inanimate.

Lynn White, Jr., an historian of medieval science and technology, wrote that "until [the man-nature dualism] is eradicated not only from our minds but also our emotions we shall doubtless be unable to make fundamental changes in our attitudes and actions affecting ecology. *The religious problem is to find a viable equivalent to animism.*"[1] (Emphasis added.) White goes on to pose the question "Do people have ethical obligations toward rocks?" and points out that "to an ancient Greek, to an American Indian, or perhaps certain kinds of Buddhists, the question would have meaning."[2] Indeed, not only would it have meaning, "for quite different reasons they would probably reply 'Yes.'"[3] But "to almost all Americans, still saturated with ideas historically dominant in Christianity (although perhaps not necessarily so), the question makes no sense at all."[4] White concludes that only if we are able to reach a point where we no longer consider such a question ridiculous will we have any hope of answering the ecological crises we face.

We need to hear White's comments in terms of ideas we have already addressed in this book. I have maintained that the polis, both in terms of human society and the actual construction of cities, is as much a part of nature as open prairies and mountain ranges. And I have maintained

---

1. Lynn White, Jr., "Continuing the Conversation," in *Western Man and Environmental Ethics: Attitudes toward Nature and Technology,* edited by Ian G. Barbour (Reading, Mass.: Addison-Wesley Publishing Company, 1973), 62.

2. Ibid., 63.

3. Ibid.

4. Ibid.

that both politics and ethics rest on an aesthetic foundation and that it is through our aesthetic sensibilities as aesthetic animals that we come to know the world and one another. When we appreciate things in terms of their beauty, we are attracted to them, care about them, perhaps even come to love them. This aesthetic attachment to the many things of the world can provide us White's "viable equivalent to animism." In the last chapter I argued for a respectful and even reverential attitude toward the other animals. Now I ask if we can extend this attitude toward rocks and fire hydrants.

When Thales wrote that all things are full of gods, he was simply acknowledging that all things have their share of soul, what we have alluded to as the *anima mundi* or world soul. White correctly identifies that the solution to Cartesian dualism is a religious one, but it is not one that requires religious belief. The problem for the Christian mind is that it cannot apprehend myth and soul in the absence of belief. To speak of gods must mean literal gods, actual divine beings. But that is not how the poetic, imagining mind works. Appreciation of beauty requires no belief, just as perceiving the world as animate does not proclaim a literal belief in soul. The big words of this book—beauty, soul, love, nature, myth, poetry—all exist beyond the realm of tight definitions and literal meanings. They are wholly imaginal, arising from the imagination and speaking to the imagination. They cannot be reduced to concepts, roped and tied by rationality, or delineated by logic. And yet they remain the most real and practical aspects of our lives and deaths.

We cannot appreciate the many things of nature without recognizing their share of soul. They need not walk to be animate. Remember that it is Aphrodite that makes the world available to our senses, her smile that enlivens the appearance and presence of all things, even rocks and fire hydrants. And remember, too, that Plotinus said that Aphrodite *was* soul, was anima (*Enneads* 3.5.4). This suggests that beauty and soul are inseparable, and that ugliness arises when soul is denied.

Here we come to back to the practicalities associated with declaring the nonhuman world inanimate, what Hillman calls "the cost of ugly." First, we must re-establish a connection that we as Westerners have mostly lost by declaring soul or anima as belonging only the human. Indeed, the notion of "belonging to" is itself a denigration of both soul and world that leaves us in a situation where soul exists only in personal subjectivity and interpersonal relationships. At the same time that soul is denied to the nonhuman world, so, too, psychology is separated from that world. We might attend to the world in terms of how the world affects the human soul, but we have no interest in caring for the souls of animals, rocks, trees, or the built environment. This puts an impossible burden on humans because we are forced to carry all that is soul within our subjectivity—the microcosm is divorced and exiled from the macrocosm.

A concrete example. When Riverside was looking at a design for a new public safety facility, the architects and engineers focused mostly on functionality, efficiency, and cost. They were not blind to the aesthetics of the building, but that was, at best, a secondary concern. My view was different. I was concerned about what the building was being expected to do. It was to house first responders who daily confront pressures and sometimes horrors that most of us cannot imagine. Those pressures cannot be self-contained but would naturally emanate outward into the facility itself. The building needed to be designed so that it was prepared for this daily outpouring of pathos—it had to be inherently therapeutic not only for the first responders, but for itself. The first responders would come and go, but the building would endure for generations. It needed to be designed with its soul in mind, with spaces that allowed for its perpetual healing.

In the end, we were not able to find a suitable location for the facility, but the point remains—buildings, too, can be depressed. Anxiety and depression are endemic to American society, but we fail to make the connection between free floating fear, melancholy, and a sense of being overwhelmed and insufficient with our declaration of the nonhuman world as lacking soul. When nature—both wildness and built nature—are denied soul then the weight of soul-care coalesces in us alone. It is too much to bear. And because our relations with all nonhuman things is denied through anthropomorphism, symbolism, and sentimentality, we are left alone in our secret, isolated selves.

An alternative would be to learn again to love. When we appreciate the beauty of nature (and again I emphasize both wildness and the built environment) we cannot help but recognize the presence of its soul. The anima is right there in the animal, given with its display, just as we sense soul in a well-crafted table, or a building that is constructed to be compatible with and complementary to its placement and neighbors (the genius of the place). As I have said repeatedly in this book, when you appreciate beauty love often follows, and when you love something, you care about it, you want to care for it, you want to help it fulfill its destiny in ways that would not be possible absent your love.

In discussing love, Plotinus wrote that "there is a strenuous activity of contemplation in the Soul; there is an emanation towards it from the object contemplated; and Eros is born, the Love which is an eye filled with its vision, a seeing that bears its image with it; Eros taking its name, probably, from the fact that its essential being is due to this *horasis*, this seeing" (*Enneads* 3.5.3). There is much wisdom here. Plotinus begins with contemplation as a "strenuous activity," much as I have emphasized that appreciation of beauty is neither passive nor naïve. He then notes that there is an emanation *towards* the soul from the object contemplated. I take this to be similar to Bushnell and Olmsted's idea on unconscious influences that we receive from the psychic power inherent in nature. Significantly in both views, it is the world itself that reaches out toward soul, like treating like. The things of the world are intentional in their appearance and display, being at once sensate, sensual, and sensible. Finally, Plotinus tells us that Eros is born from an eye filled with Love's vision. Rodin had a similar view when he said that for the artist "the only thing is to see... [with an] eye, grafted on his heart." Such an eye sees by and through images, and in so doing "reads deeply into the bosom of nature."[5]

Imagine a world in which our relationship to nature (wild and built) was premised upon and facilitated through love and its appreciation of beauty. Every ordinance, building, road project, bureaucratic organization, defense plan, and, especially, educational system would have as their first priority the furtherance of beauty and the refinement of love. In such a world we would recognize that the primary and enduring goal of education ("leading out") is to cultivate imagination. As a core cur-

---

5. Auguste Rodin, "Art and Nature," in *Artists on Art from the XIV to the XX Century,* edited by Robert Goldwater and Marco Treves (New York: Pantheon Books, 1945), 325.

riculum, beauty would teach that appreciation requires arrested motion, careful attending, and precise articulation through rhetoric and poetic language. If we approached education in such a manner, would we have over six million children diagnosed with attention deficit and hyperactivity disorders?

Declaring the nonhuman world inanimate—on no basis other than our own declaration—has profound political, ethical, psychological, even metaphysical consequence because, as Plotinus understood, they all rest on aesthetics. When our aesthetics are disordered, when beauty is repressed and denigrated and love sentimentalized, we make an error of cosmic significance. The big mistake affects microcosm and macrocosm alike because they have been severed from their natural interdependence and reciprocity based on reverence and respect. And so, the animals, the rock and trees, the prairies and mountains all suffer; the air and water are polluted, the West ablaze. Meanwhile our children grow increasingly neurotic, our adults are anxious and depressed, our politics is infantile, ethics is derailed by ideology, our marriages fail, and suicide, like the seas, rise with each passing year—the great dark swallowing the living.

So, what are we to do? Clearly calls for morality, duty, and responsibility are not enough—they have been tried and failed. And love, which has the power to address the afflictions that our hubris has created, cannot be summoned at will. What we need is a way to restore our connection to Eros and Aphrodite, those gods that we have neglected and thereby insulted. Mere supplication will not do because we lack the humility to convince them of our request. No, we must prove ourselves once again worthy to be in their presence.

Hillman offers a possibility, certainly not for redemption, but at least as a way re-engage our aesthetic, and thereby political, ethical, psychological, and metaphysical sensibilities. Because our Western tradition has anesthetized us to beauty, we are limited in our ability to sense the emanations that beauty sends to soul. So, instead we can begin with what does get through to us—the ugly.[6]

---

6. I am indebted to Hillman for this account taken from his "The Cost of the Ugly," in *Uniform Edition of the Writings of James Hillman*, vol. 2: *City & Soul*, 195–97.

We begin again with Plotinus, who tells us that an ugly thing (by which he includes "evil, bad, turpitude, shameful, and obscene")[7] is something that has not been "entirely mastered by pattern" (*Enneads* 1.6.2). Hillman takes this to mean that "an ugly thing has no encompassing and profound idea of what the thing wants to be." The ugly lacks "contemplative thought about itself," or what I would term an appreciation for the destiny of its unfolding beauty. "It therefore cannot be truly what it is. It is not true to itself, and consequently it cannot be beautiful or good."[8] (Note here again that aesthetics and ethics are inseparable.)

Elsewhere, Plotinus says that we "possess beauty when we are true to our own being; our ugliness is going over to another order" (*Enneads* 5.8.13). Here Hillman takes Plotinus to mean that "we move toward the ugly when we desert the aesthetic position." Thus, when we repress or denigrate beauty, or subjugate aesthetics to other things, be it bureaucratic restrictions, cost-benefit analyses, or political ideologies, we fall into ugliness.[9] When we lack contemplative thought and respect for the destiny that strives to live through us we are ugly, and when are true to destiny, and thereby true to ourselves, we are beautiful.

The last statement from Plotinus that Hillman cites we have already seen. Plotinus wrote "let the Soul fall in with the Ugly and at once it shrinks within itself, denies the thing, turns away from it, not accordant, resenting it" (*Enneads* 1.6.2). Here Plotinus, and Hillman, call upon us to have the courage of our aesthetic convictions. We have a political, ethical, psychological, and metaphysical duty to trust, and defend, our immediate (that is unmediated by thought or reflection) recoil from what assaults and insults our aesthetic sense. Each of us can come up with our own list of ugliness—drab buildings with tacky and tacked-on art, inhumane and uncivilizing urban design (I say uncivilizing because just as Olmsted thought beauty could further social well-being, so, too ugliness can weaken and fray the social fabric), anthropogenic climate change and its devasting impact on the world soul, toxic partisanship, manipulation of education to serve ideological ends, the embrace and

---

7. Ibid., 195.
8. Ibid.
9. Ibid., 196.

celebration of ignorance, the snarling face of bigotry—I could continue, but I ask instead that you make your own list of what sets you off, of what tries to take you "over to another order."

Your list identifies for you where you sense the aesthetic, animate world being disrespected, insulted, and hurt. But because we have declared that world to be lacking in soul, we can only feel these sufferings as our own. We are unable to feel the suffering of an anorexic building or an oppressed history curriculum and therefore lose our ethical responsibility to them. People think they are bringing personal problems and difficulties to therapy when what they are really bringing are souls lost in a cosmos, adrift and detached because we have turned away from a world that we have allowed to become "disagreeable and alien."

Hillman posits that the "other order" for which beauty and soul are at best secondary and contingent, if not irrelevant, is economic monotheism. Certainly, when I was in office, it was this voice that was the loudest—no matter the beauty of a design or the elegance of a plan the final arbiter, the last and deciding voice heard would "but what does it cost?" But here "cost" has been reduced to its most barren of meanings, where "cost" has no relation to "value" or "worth." This is the cost of the spreadsheet and the money changers, and it is precisely their tables that need to be overturned.

If there are two things that throughout history have instilled courage, they are beauty and love. Ask yourself—for whom or what would you fight; for whom or what would you die? For many the answer will be family, for others the answer might be flag, but all answers will be based in beauty and love. This is important because your list not only tells you what offends you, it also tells you where you must resist. The affront of ugliness is a call to political action and such action could not be more necessary and important. Political action is embodied action, it means standing up and stepping forward, not shrinking back and turning away. Like the heroes we admire, the aesthetic warrior heads toward the ugly, refusing to succumb to repulsion or fear. And this very act of drawing closer to that which offends us enlivens the aesthetic spirit. The blood rises and the heart quickens. Like an animal in the woods or deep in the sea, our reactions to beauty and ugliness help to restore our place in the cosmos because the world "is primarily and always an aesthetic phenomenon

201

with which our animal senses and innate reactions are attuned."[10]

The question, really, is who and what are you going to trust? I suspect that if you have read this book this far then you already know full well that the nonhuman world is not inanimate. You know that Descartes was wrong, as is the Christian reduction of soul to belonging only to the human and the denigration of nature as fallen and satanic. You know that when you see a sparkling, happy stream in a meadow, or a graceful and confident building in a cityscape that you are not projecting or anthropomorphizing. These are examples of things that have been mastered by pattern, that have not gone over to another order, that do shrink back or turn away from the other things of the world. Beauty is manifest, and, as Rilke said, is everywhere. And if beauty is everywhere, then so, too, love. Whenever we attend to beauty through love, we attend to the soul that is inherent in all things and push back against the ugliness that afflicts so much of what we have done with and to the world.

We always have to be careful when we speak of beauty, love, and soul because these words tend to give us wings and lift us aloft in transcendent bliss. But that is not how these words are used in this book. For us these words are worldly, not transcendent, and they are always connected to particular things. Being worldly, they also give rise to ethical obligations and inspire political and practical action. Even the most mundane thing can hold the potential to spark careful attention and loving interaction.

Allow me an example that many would find far removed from beauty, love, and soul. When I took office as president of Riverside one of our goals was to encourage new businesses to come to the village. Other towns were advertising and offering economic incentives to try to draw new businesses, but Riverside simply did not have the resources to spend on such endeavors. So, we asked ourselves, what do businesses look for when they are considering a new location? Some things were obvious like demographics, ease of access, and parking. But they also want a welcoming and encouraging environment and a predictable and efficient governmental process. When we looked at our village code, we realized it was too complicated and burdensome. Our commission structure was cumbersome and had far too many hoops that new businesses had to

---

10. Ibid., 197.

jump through. The code, in this regard, was not "mastered by pattern," it was directed inward toward its own demands and expectations instead of outward toward the world that it was intended to serve. The code was not true to itself. It was ugly.

We did a comprehensive overhaul of our code as it related to both new and existing businesses with an eye toward making the process of opening and running a business in Riverside easy and inexpensive. There were still necessary safeguards in place, but the foremost concern was making the code conform to the needs of the businesses we hoped to attract. Riverside does not lend itself to large, big-box stores given its size, but it is a perfect destination spot for smaller, more boutique style businesses and restaurants. In the end, not only did the code modifications make Riverside more desirable for business, but it also made governmental oversight more efficient and cost-effective for the village itself. Simply combining our planning and zoning commissions into one entity eliminated unnecessary meetings and expense. We changed our sign ordinance to encourage more creative and inviting signage. By uncluttering our code, using less bureaucratic language, and eliminating outdated and unnecessary rules and regulations, we made it more useful and accommodating. In so doing we made the village code more true to itself and therefore more beautiful.

If we find it odd to attach beauty, love, and soul to drafting a village ordinance it is because we have failed to follow Rilke in recognizing that beauty is everywhere. Whenever we turn to a task with care and attention, whether it is cooking a meal or making a painting, we awaken the aesthetic relationship that is latent in all things. When we strive to help something, or someone, to be more fully realized and true to themselves we advance the cause of beauty, love, and soul. Each of us can be an agent for soul-making when we recognize and embrace an ensouled world. From such a perspective we would immediately acknowledge that we have an ethical obligation to rocks. We would move through the world like we move through a pristine forest, striving to leave no trace that would be detrimental to it. If all things are full of gods, then all things hold the potential for epiphanies, each thing an alter providing an opportunity for devotion and service to the greater part of soul that lies beyond the person.

Once we release ourselves from the big mistake of thinking that the non-human world is inanimate, we are restored to our natural place in the order of things. We begin to be interested in things in their own right and not only in terms of their use or significance for us. Politics becomes refocused on service instead of power, and economics returns to its etymological roots as "home management." Economics thus imagined is restored to its relationship with its sister word "ecology" and sees the world with caring and loving eyes instead of seeking dominion and control. Cooperation replaces, or is at least co-equal with, competition. We might even move beyond thinking of life as a struggle for survival and see it also as an opportunity to appreciate and create beauty. As aesthetic animals that really is all the world asks of us anyway.

FIFTEEN

Return to Nature

Throughout this section on beauty and nature we have again and again touched on how our ideas about nature tend to separate us from our place in the natural order. And we have suggested various ways that we might overcome that separation and return to nature. It is important to be clear that nature does not share our problem. The separation is of our own making. The other animals, the wind and sea and land, the weather, the sky in all of its shades and starriness, the sun and the moon, the plants—the list of all the particulars that nature comprises is infinite and all of them have their place in the cosmic order. Only we are displaced. I want to gather the threads and review how we might return to nature.

One of the courses Jill teaches is animal behavior. As part of that course, she has her students create an "ethogram," which is an inventory or descriptive catalog of the behavioral motor patterns displayed by a given species. So, for example, an ethogram for a generic "bird" might include behaviors such as wing flapping, pecking, scratching, or probing with the bill. The point of the assignment is to teach observation, and one of the slides she uses for this assignment says that "If it seems really hard to be descriptive *without* interpreting the function of the behaviors, then you're doing it right!" To observe without interpretation. It sounds so easy, but it goes contrary to our usual mental habits.

One reason we have so much trouble observing without interpreting is that we tend to think of the appearance of something as superficial. When we say that "beauty is only skin deep," our repression of beauty is revealed in that insidious word "only." Beauty is only on the surface, a façade that is but the thin skin that covers, and hides, the true, inner self or essence of something. This goes hand in hand with how we often think of beauty as the merely pretty, trifling, and effete. By keeping beauty on the surface, we deny it depth and parrot the Cartesian mistake of dividing the inner from the outer. And yet we freeze, awe struck, when faced with an animal in the wild precisely because its entire being is right there in front of us, fully revealed in its "static reality" (Frankfort).

Portmann, as we have already noted, refused the Cartesian divide, and maintained that the appearance of an animal gives us the animal in its entirety in self-presentation. I would extend this to all things, with each thing appearing as it is within an ecology of imagination. The things of the world do not exist to be interpreted or translated into meanings; they exist first to be appreciated. That is one of the great gifts of nature, that it refuses to be reduced to human constructs and exists beyond our quest for meaning. It simply is, in all of its glorious diversity; all things content in themselves, mastered by pattern.

To return to nature does not require a literal return. We do not need to retreat to Walden Pond to find nature because nature is everywhere. Nature is as much in the cup of my morning coffee as the wildflowers in the woods. Nature is everywhere when we drop our judgments, expectations, and narcissism. Again and again in this book we have tried to move our imaginations from the transcendent and abstract "capital-N" Nature to the particulars of everyday, beautifully mundane life. I love the capabilities of the intellectual mind as much as anyone, but it is incapable of grasping the eachness that is given with the nature of particular things. Understanding asks us to stand under, assuming that what matters most lies in a transcendent and abstract reality that is above and apart from the immediate (un-mediated) facticity given by beauty.

Throughout this book we have touched on various aspects of beauty, love, and soul that contribute to re-establishing our connection to the natures of particular things. From Portmann we have the respect for appearance as its own purpose, without need of evolutionary theories of struggle, strife, and selfish genes. He tells us that to observe nature we must pay attention to details lovingly. By drawing our attention to details, he encourages us to set aside desires for the big picture and instead perceive the significance of smallness. And he also says that we must dwell upon things instead of rushing from one thing to the next. This latter point is also made by beauty itself in the way it arrests motion, bringing us to a standstill. To restore our place within nature we must stop our headlong rush and learn to pause, to turn back and retrace our steps, to linger and listen.

The primatologist and ethologist Frans de Waal similarly writes that "[t]he maestro of observation, Konrad Lorenz, believed that one could not investigate animals effectively without an intuitive understanding grounded in love and respect."[1] This intuitive understanding "is not self-focused but other-oriented. Instead of making humanity the measure of all things, we need to evaluate other species by what *they* are."[2] This, too, is a key to restoring our place within nature. We must approach the other things of the world with humility and with sincere interest in them as having their own self-worth and integrity.

As ourselves political animals, one way we can show our respect for nature is through political action that places the needs of nature before our needs. When Riverside removed the dam in the Des Plaines River, or incorporated sustainable features in its stormwater management, or educated its residents through its coyote policy, those were political acts intended to respect and further nature's own independence. Removing the wall that we have erected between city and nature helps to return us to nature by restoring the city's own natural proclivities and recognizing the ethical obligations that the city has to its natural brethren.

It is certainly true that there are qualitative differences among the many things of nature. The ocean is different than a rock-skipping pond. But, as Darwin said, these are differences in degree, not kind. And because there are so many differences within nature, so, too, our aesthetic discernments must be varied. There is no one single way to appreciate nature any more than we can have just one way to engage with our fellow human beings. This alludes back to how we started this chapter and the difficulty we have in not interpreting nature. Nature is an excellent teacher for our imaginations because it resists being translated into concepts. As soon as we move from appreciation to abstraction we step away from nature. To return to nature requires that we first return to our aesthetic sensibilities.

---

1. Frans B.M. de Waal, *Are We Smart Enough to Know How Smart Animals Are?* (New York: W.W. Norton, 2016), 19.
2. Ibid., 275.

This is why we have to avoid the idea that to return to nature we have to literally go into the wild which we conceive of as "out there." When we think of nature only in terms of the pristine wilderness we too easily slide into romanticism, which in its own way also removes us from nature. When we slip into rhapsodies about the sublime, as did the upper-class young men on their Grand Tours in the eighteenth century, we find ourselves focused primarily upon our emotional reactions to nature instead of remaining with nature itself. We have seen how anthropomorphism, symbolism, and sentimentality separates us from the other animals. Romanticism, too, with its lofty thoughts, separates us from nature by taking us aloft. Transcending nature leaves nature behind, and below. To return to nature we must stay attached to nature, dwelling as Portmann told us, attending to details lovingly.

Plotinus can once again help us here. "We do not habitually examine or in any way question the normal: we set to doubting and working out identifications when we are confronted by any display of power outside everyday experience: we wonder at a novelty and we wonder at the customary when anyone brings forward some single object and explains to our ignorance the efficacy vested in it. Some such power, not necessarily accompanied by reason, every single item possesses; for each . . . in its kind has partaken of soul" (*Enneads* 4.4.37). Here Plotinus makes the point that the beauty of each thing disappears only when we take it for granted. But even the most ordinary of things has its share of soul and therefore the power to elicit wonder.

To return to nature we might try seeing beauty in the everyday things of life. Taking time to savor a meal, a moment to breathe in the freshness of a spring rain, listening to the wind and how it sounds differently in forest leaves and prairie grass, touching the bark of a tree and tracing the contours of its limbs, or looking, really looking, at those we love—appreciation needs time to deepen and so reveal what is around us. Or we can practice using different senses in unusual ways to help refine and cultivate them. The great chef Jacques Pepin, for example, can tell when mushrooms have properly sauteed by how they sound in the pan. The more we open our senses to the world, and the more time we take to pay attention to the world, the more nature will reveal itself to us.

Here we can recall Hillman and Cronon's advice on ways to return to nature. From Hillman we have the idea of a more psychological notion of nature. "When we move with senses acute, listening, watching, breathing in tune with the world around us, recognizing its priority and ourselves as guests, witnessing its god-givenness," we find that nature is everywhere and not only in the wild.[3] And from Cronon we have the shift from wilderness to wildness, from a grand abstraction to finding nature "in the seemingly tame fields and woodlots of Massachusetts, in the cracks of a Manhattan sidewalk, even in the cells of our own bodies."[4] Both men are suggesting that by changing how we imagine and think about nature we can find our way back to nature.

We can return to nature, too, by finding ways to de-industrialize ourselves. We can try eating when we are hungry instead of when the clock tells us it is time to eat. We can feel, and obey, our natural rhythms throughout the day, the night, and the seasons. We are not the same in the morning and the evening, or in the summer and the winter. Trying to maintain a steady output in the name of efficiency is a work against nature that takes us outside the ebb and flow of life. So, too, the pressures of constant progress and development, of moving ever forward and advancing, disorders our relationship with nature. We must let ourselves stop, regress, repeat, and lie dormant and avoid the manic rush urging us forever onward. Nature is constantly teaching us this lesson and we ignore it at our peril. How many of the ailments of the modern malaise arise from the pressure of the clock and the relentless drive to do more, faster?

To return to nature we might also try to surround ourselves with objects of beauty and quality. I am convinced that Bushnell and Olmsted's unconscious influence comes from far more than natural scenery. A well-made piece of furniture, a sturdy Dutch oven, or a beautiful lamp are all part of nature and have their share of soul. Beauty, as Plotinus told us, emanates outward from things, reaching toward and touching the souls of others. If one goal of psychology is to make the unconscious

---

3. "Natural Beauty without Nature," in *Uniform Edition of the Writings of James Hillman,* vol. 2: *City and Soul,* 163–64.

4. "The Trouble with Wilderness; or, Getting Back to the Wrong Nature," in *Uncommon Ground: Rethinking the Human Place in Nature,* edited by William Cronon (New York: W.W. Norton, 1995), 89.

conscious, then the more we attend to the beauty in things the more we educate our erotic connection to them, feeling their impressions on our souls. By appreciating the aesthetic power in other things, we become more conscious of them. But this consciousness is of a different order, a consciousness "not necessarily accompanied by reason." Rather it is an animal consciousness that adheres to the root meaning of "conscious" as to "to know with." Our human, rational style of consciousness sets us apart from nature because it wants to have knowledge *of* things. But we are also capable of an animal style of consciousness that connects us *with* things. Once we restore our animal sense of the soul connection between us and other things, we will naturally give them more attention and take greater care in how we relate to them. We will seek out kind and decent people as friends, treat our homes as vessels for soul-making, and choose belongings to which we wish to belong.

This brings us to perhaps the most basic, and difficult, shift that we must make if we are to return to nature. We must recognize the animate nature of all things. There is a divine nature in all things that partake of soul, and all things partake in soul. The *anima mundi* is the world of the indigenous peoples who know that they share in nature because they share in soul. A polytheistic or animistic style of consciousness—not religious belief—is a natural style of consciousness. The animal, aesthetic eye sees the divine manifested in all things. And so we can restore our animal sensibilities through our aesthetic sensibilities, and our aesthetic sensibilities through our animal sensibilities.

If we recognize and embrace that nature is ensouled and that all things are full of gods, then we naturally relate to things with reverence and respect. The many atrocities that we commit on nature would become literally unthinkable—our minds would lack the hubris that these atrocities rely upon. The idea of dominion over nature would be replaced with the idea of service to nature. Our ethical stance toward nature would be to care for it as we care for ourselves, like treating like with our intentions guided by love, not profit. We would still use the things of nature, just like all other living creatures do, but we would do so with an attitude of thankfulness and a frugality based on respect. We cannot help but leave a trace, but we would do so mindfully and with an effort toward minimizing negative effects.

By re-establishing our aesthetic/animal relationship with the other things of nature we would have no need for anthropocentric denial of their inherent integrity. We would accept what we already, deep down, know—that non-human animals are sentient beings, graced with their own manner of feeling, intelligence, and imagination. Our science of animal studies, as Beston suggested, would admit a degree of poetry and mysticism, recognizing that there will always be a mystery in animal life beyond our reach. Just as my wife tries to teach her students, our attitude toward nature would be as observers and not interpreters, we would attend to our fellow inhabitants with interest and appreciation, attending to them so as to make sure our presence does them no harm.

It is possible, of course, that we simply cannot do what I am suggesting. It is naïve to think that we can step out of the millennia of traditions that have led to our current state. But where the mind is incapable the soul is not. The return to nature begins, and likely can only be accomplished, through imagination. The ideas that have taken millennia to become habitual will take a long time to break, but the direct appreciation of nature goes on daily in imagination. The aesthetic response to nature connects us to the timeless embrace that precedes our ideas and traditions. And so, the return to nature can proceed along parallel paths. We can follow our sense of what is ugly and try to alter our ideas and practices so as to realign ourselves with a reverential and respectful relationship with nature. At the same time, we can educate and refine our aesthetic sensibilities, turning to the animal spirits and the genius of the place to show us the way forward.

Because the return to nature requires a shift toward a psychological appreciation of nature, the other place that we can turn to for guidance are dreams. All manner of natural things appear to us in dreams, but dream animals are perhaps the most enlivening and impactful. Dream animals can help us learn how to observe real animals because when dream animals appear they are wholly psychic events. Dream animals are not ours even though they appear in our dreams. They are not part of us and do not signify anything about us. They are not symbols for something else and do not portend anything about our personalities or traits. A fox in a dream has nothing to do with my foxiness or my cunning nature. The fox is just the fox, and to do right by the fox we have to be interested in what the fox is doing, precisely doing, in the dream. The fox has to be limned against and with the other things that are happening in the dream so that it is seen within the context of its ecology of imagination. The dream fox is always a particular fox, and if the same fox reappears to us in other dreams it will be immediately apparent to us.

The same insults we apply to real animals—anthropomorphism, symbolism, and sentimentality—similarly insult dream animals. As with real animals, these insults are attempts to deny the dream animal its inherent integrity and to avoid its presence and power. That is why interpretations of dream animals are always so lame and uninteresting. The interpretation leaves the dream animal in favor of an abstraction, and our abstractions never have the vitality and depth of the actual dream animal.

Dreams are wholly imaginative and appear to us as autonomous psychic facts. All of our senses are present in dreams, but they are not our literal senses. Accordingly, when we meet dream animals the meeting takes place in and through imagination. The emotions we feel in the presence of the dream animal are imaginal and yet they impact us as if real. The terror and recoiling from a snake in a dream awakens us with a pounding heart, or we cry out while still asleep. Sometimes we not sure if we are asleep or awake, within a dream or the waking world.

This last statement is yet another key in returning to nature. Dream animals teach us that there is not always a clear distinction between what is real and what is dream. That suggests that we should rely primarily on imagination in our dealing with the many things of nature. The imagination tacitly grasps that the nature of things is revealed in how each thing manifests its share of soul. Grasping this particularity, what Willam James called "eachness," is where we return to nature. When we attend to the eachness of things with the full power of our aesthetic sensibilities then we have returned to nature, whether this occurs in a forest, or a meeting room, or a dream.

SIXTEEN

The Beautiful and the Good

Although we moderns struggle to hold the ideas of politics, ethics, and nature together within the broader and deeper images of beauty, love, and soul, the ancient Greeks found the connection obvious. The connection appears in their use of the words *kalon,* beautiful, and *agathon,* good. Of the two terms, *kalon* has given rise to the most disagreement among philosophers as to its meaning. These philosophical disagreements over the meaning of *kalon* are reflected in the difficulties that translators have had, and continue to have, in translating the term into English. One difficulty is that the ancient Greeks used *kalon* to apply to a much wider and deeper range of things and experiences than do the modern meanings of "beauty" or "beautiful."[1]

Generally speaking, translators have followed the lead of Liddell, Scott, and Jones (LSJ) in assigning three possible meanings to *kalon:* 1) beautiful, especially as applied to persons or parts of the body in the sense of "fair" or "shapely," although this meaning is also applied to clothes, arms, armor, buildings, and manufactured articles; 2) good, in the sense of functional or utilitarian, or of fine quality (a well-made, sharp knife is a "good" knife); and 3) beautiful in the moral sense of noble, honorable, moral beauty, or virtue.[2] The philosopher Terence Irwin summarizes these three meanings of *kalon* as: "(*a*) Aesthetic, for various kinds of beauty; (*b*) Functional, where something is *kalon* for a

---

1. See, e.g., articles and essays collected in *Looking at Beauty to Kalon in Western Greece: Selected Essays from the 2018 Symposium on the Heritage of Western Greece,* edited by Heather L. Reid and Tony Leyh (Sioux City, Iowa: Parnassos Press, 2019); *Classical Philology* 105, no. 4 (October 2010), Special Issue: Beauty, Harmony, and the Good, edited by Elizabeth Asmis.

2. H. G. Liddell, Robert Scott, and H. S. Jones, *A Greek-English Lexicon,* 9th ed. (Oxford: Clarendon Press, 1940), s.v. "κάλος."

task or purpose...; [and] (*c*) Moral, referring to people and actions."[3]

Although the first meaning of the *kalon* given by LSJ is "beautiful," it has become the habit of translators to avoid translating *kalon* as "beautiful." Most use the word "noble," while one, Paul Woodford, prefers the word "fine." Woodford explains his choice thusly:

> Like beauty, *to kalon* is something splendid and exciting; and in women or boys it is the loveliness that excites carnal desire. But the use of *kalos* [beauty] or that quality is embraced by its use as a quite general term of commendation in Greek. "Noble," "admirable," and "fine" are better translations, and of these "fine" is best of all in virtue of its great range. Different sorts of things are commended as *kala* for different sorts of qualities: boys for their sex appeal, horses for their speed, fighting cocks for their spunk, families for their lineage, acts of war for their courage, speeches for their truth, and so on. Our "beautiful" translates *kalos* in only a few of its many uses, and is wholly inappropriate for the word as Socrates uses it.[4]

Thus, because many translators conceive of *kalon* as encompassing meanings that extend beyond what we nowadays think of as beauty or the beautiful, *kalon* has largely been subsumed under the context of moral discourse by translating it as noble, admirable, and fine. This traditional viewpoint has become the dominant viewpoint and now strongly resists simply translating *kalon* as "beautiful."[5] The sources of this resistance are varied, but as one commentor puts it, "[t]he issues of translation...are less literarily specific, and therefore reveal deeper cultural and philosophical patterns of meaning."[6] In other words, the resistance toward

---

3. Terence Irwin, *Plato's Moral Theory: The Early and Middle Dialogues* (Oxford: Clarendon Press, 1977), 290 n.29.

4. Plato, *Hippias Major,* translated by Paul Woodruff (Indianapolis: Hackett Publishing Company, 1982), 110.

5. For discussion of this traditional view and arguments against it, see Aryeh Kosman, "Beauty and the Good: Situating the Kalon," *Classical Philology* 105, no. 4 (October 2010): 341–57; Gabriel Richardson Lear, "Response to Kosman," ibid., 357–62; Nicholas P. Riegel, "Beauty, To Kalon, and its Relation to the Good in the Works of Plato," (PhD diss., University of Toronto, 2011), 13–21; Jonathan Fine, "Beauty on Display: Plato and the Concept of the Kalon" (PhD diss., Columbia University, 2018), 2–10.

6. Kosman, "Beauty and the Good," 351.

translating *kalon* as "beautiful" points less to a confusion about what the term meant for the ancient Greeks and more about how we moderns have so greatly limited the range of meaning for the words "beauty" and "beautiful." I would go further and say that the resistance to translating *kalon* as "beautiful" derives from the deeper cultural resistance to, and indeed repression of, beauty that we have seen repeatedly throughout this book.[7] Discussing his translation of Aristotle's *Nicomachean Ethics,* Joe Sachs is more blunt and concludes that "the translators are afraid to give it to you straight...The word the translators are afraid of is *to kalon,* the beautiful."[8]

Here are two examples of how different translators treat *kalon.* The first is from Harris Rackman and follows the more common modern approach (the translations for *kalon* are in italics):

> Persons therefore who are exceptionally zealous in *noble actions* are universally approved and commended; and if all men vied with each other in *moral nobility* and strove to perform the *noblest deeds,* the common welfare would be fully realized, while individuals also could enjoy the greatest of goods, inasmuch as virtue is the greatest good.[9]

In a note on his translation, Rackman acknowledges two meanings for *kalon*: "(1) bodies well shaped and works of art or handicraft well made, and (2) actions well done...it thus means (1) beautiful, (2) morally right."[10] Despite this acknowledgement, however, he gives no explanation for not using "beautiful." Compare the same passage as translated by Joe Sachs:

> Everyone, then, approves of and praises those who are exceptionally zealous about *beautiful actions,* and if they all competed for *the beautiful,* and strained to the utmost to perform the *most beautiful actions,* then for all in common there would be what is needful, and

7. For additional discussion and examples of how we have repressed beauty, see my *Return to Beauty.*

8. Aristotle, *Nicomachean Ethics,* translated by Joe Sachs (Indianapolis: Hackett Publishing Company, 2002), xxi.

9. Aristotle, *Nicomachean Ethics,* translated by H. Rackham, Loeb Classical Library 73 (Cambridge, Mass.: Harvard University Press, 1926), 1169a8–11.

10. Ibid., 7n.*b.*

for each in particular there would be the greatest of goods, if indeed virtue is that.

Comparing these two versions, Sachs's translation is more in line with the way the ancient Greeks understood *kalon* as "beautiful" as including ethical dimensions, while the Rackman translation avoids any implication that "noble actions," "moral nobility," and "noblest deeds," may be properly imagined *aesthetically* as "beautiful." Again, this points to a limitation in the modern usage and understanding of "beautiful."

Still another translator, C. D. C. Reeves, also translates *kalon* as "noble," even though he confirms that the primary meaning of the term is "beauty." He says that the connection between the aesthetic meaning and ethical meaning of *kalon* is reciprocal, "connecting what is ethically *kalon* to what is aesthetically noble, lending the former too an aesthetic tinge."[11] But despite acknowledging that what is "ethically kalon "has an "aesthetic tinge" he still chooses not to translate *kalon* as "beautiful."[12]

Translators have an enormously difficult task. Not only are they trying to express the style and rhythm of a text in a different language, but they are also trying to convey a different mode of thought and imagination into a different language and time. But in the case of *kalon,* what we see is a predisposition, perhaps largely unconscious, against "beauty" and "beautiful." Because of the way the modern mind conceives of beauty and the beautiful, it cannot readily grasp the ethical dimensions that the ancient Greeks effortlessly saw as inherent to beauty and the aesthetic dimensions they saw in ethics.

As you can see, while translators struggle to express the range of meaning of *kalon* through various formulations, the Greeks were quite comfortable with "beauty" and "the beautiful." *The problem of the translators is our problem.* From the eighteenth century onward, our Western minds have held beauty and ethics apart.[13] We ascribe beauty primarily

---

11. Aristotle, *Nicomachean Ethics,* translated by C. D. C. Reeves (Indianapolis: Hackett Publishing Company, 2014), 261 n. 20.

12. For more examples of this resistance to translating *kalon* as "beautiful," see Fine, "Beauty on Display," 4–5.

13. While we have largely confined beauty to art or the fine arts, that was not the ancient Greek conception: "Whether we can speak of aesthetics in the case of Plato,

to art and to nature, or as being a subjective response to people and things that we find attractive or pleasing. Ethics, for its part, belongs to rational and moral determinations of what is good or just, fair or equitable. But we cannot in our modern minds hold beauty and ethics together as does *kalon*. We find it difficult to consider customs, laws, sciences, or even wisdom beautiful, whereas all were considered by the ancient Greeks capable of being *kalon*.[14] In short, the three meanings of *kalon* described in LSJ, and adopted by traditional views of the *kalon* are *our* meanings, not those of the ancient Greeks, who found no ambiguity is using *kalon* in the multitude of ways that they did. Our resistance and repression, indeed denigration, of beauty belong to us, to our "deeper cultural and philosophical patterns of meaning." It is our disordering of the meanings and significance of beauty and ethics that leaves us unable to see them intimately connected to one another and to politics and nature. Our minds have cast asunder what for the ancient Greeks were simply part and parcel of a well-ordered *kosmos*.

All manner of things could, for the ancient Greeks, be *kalon*—bodies, colors, artifacts, shapes, sounds, laws and activities, studies, men, pictures and sculpture, sounds and music, souls, knowledge, animals.[15] Another consistent theme in their use of *kalon* was pairing it with *agathon*, usually translated as "good." It is important to note, though, that the Greeks meant "good" in the sense of beneficial or useful. Good was connected to virtue, which is how we tend to use "good" in a moral sense, but the connection was that *agathon* was good because it was useful or

---

Plotinus or Augustine will depend on our definition of that term, but we should certainly realize that in the theory of beauty the consideration of the arts is quite absent in Plato and secondary in Plotinus and Augustine." Paul Oskar Kristeller, "The Modern System of the Arts: A Study in the History of Aesthetics (I)," *Journal of the History of Ideas* 12, no. 4 (October 1951), 500.

14. See, e.g., Plato, *Symposium, 210b–d.*

15. Edvard Pettersson, "The 'Kalon' and the 'Agathon' in Plato's Socratic Dialogues" (PhD diss., University of California, Irvine, 1996), 7; and sources at 8n.6: "In the three dialogues that discuss the *kalon* in detail, the *Gorgias,* the *Hippias Major,* and the *Symposium,* we find lists of *kala*. These include bodies, colors, shapes, sounds, laws and activities, studies (*Gorgias*), men, pictures and sculpture, sounds and music, activities and laws (*Hippias Major*), and bodies, souls, laws and activities, knowledge (*Symposium*), as well as many individual instances of *kala*."

beneficial to a virtuous person. This benefit, however, *was not subjective,* that is *agathon* was not good for a virtuous person because it made them *feel* good. Rather, *kalon,* as beauty, inspired a desire *(eros)* for *agathon* that constituted a virtuous person's character, driving them to live a virtuous life. It was not virtuous acts that were *agathon,* it was the erotic activity of virtue that was *agathon,* and the end toward which virtue was directed by *agathon* was *kalon.*

Kalon, then, *brings together the three activities that are constitutive of our lives as aesthetic animals—appreciating beauty, creating beauty, and being beautiful.* It begins with our appreciation of beauty that gives rise to an erotic desire to virtuous conduct with an eye toward creating yet more beauty. It is through this appreciation and love for beauty that we can ourselves become beautiful and virtuous. The Greeks referred to such a person as *kalos kagathos,* beautiful and good. The intimate and inexorable connection between beauty and the good, between aesthetics and ethics if further revealed by what the Greeks considered to be the opposite of *kalon—aischros,* which means both ugly and shameful.[16]

Our inability to hold aesthetics and ethics together stems from a love disorder. For us, beauty and good belong to different states of mind. We take beauty to be something that we apprehend directly through sense perception, while the good is a matter of rational reflection. The apprehension of beauty is an "emotional reflex more than a reflective or mediated response."[17] But precisely in this false divide do we lose our way. The ongoing, generative force of the virtuous life in service of beauty, is *eros,* not *logos.* The good is not hypostatized in actions but rather is embodied in the character of a person that is *kalos kagathon. It is the erotic desire for virtue that is itself virtuous.* And if it is love that sustains a life well-lived, it is beauty that calls forth that love. Once we see that beauty and good converge through *eros* the wall that our minds have erected between *kalon* and *agathon* falls away. They are not the same, but through *eros* they implicate one another.

---

16. Fine, "Beauty on Display," 3.

17. Lawrence Kimmel, "Eros/Kalon/Agathos: Love, the Beautiful, and the Good," *Analecta Husserliana* 97 (2008): 5

For the Greeks, *kalon* was not an abstract concept but rather appeared immediately to the senses. But here we encounter another difference between the modern, cramped view of beauty, and the expansive, deeper notion of *kalon*. The ancient Greek understanding of appearance differs vastly from our own, which is largely a product of the eighteenth and ensuing centuries. For us, appearance is usually related to something being visible to sight. Moreover, as we saw in the last chapter, appearance usually refers to the surfaces of things, appearance as a façade, something superficial. This is where our attitudes about appearance coincide with our diminutive view of beauty as only skin deep, cosmetic in a trivial or even deceptive sense, something "made up." For the Greeks, on the other hand, appearance is "the manifestation or presence to immediate awareness of the thing's being."[18] Aryeh Kosman makes a similar point, suggesting that if we think of appearance "as presentation to subjective awareness" then we might better understand the Greek notion of *kalon* as beautiful.[19] Kosman goes on to say that for Plato:

> appearance is not something separate from being, but simply the presentation of what is to a subject: being, as we say, making its appearance. It is not therefore essentially deceptive; the phenomenological is not standardly the illusion of being. It becomes illusory only in the context of something going wrong, a failure of uptake. Standardly, appearance is being's presence to subjectivity: face not as façade, but as organic expression. The *kalon* in turn reveals the integrity of being and its proper appearance; it constitutes the virtue of proper and expressive appearance... What appears well, we might say, appears in the mode of beauty.[20]

By expanding and deepening our idea of appearance we can expand and deepen our idea of beauty. We might remember here that it is Aphrodite who makes all things appear, not only to the visual sense but to

---

18. Gabriel Richardson Lear, "Response to Kosman," *Classical Philology* 105, no. 4 (October 2010): 358. Lear attributes this view to Kosman and largely agrees with it. She disagrees with his view that *kalon* and beautiful are different, though connected, concepts and instead suggest that the "the difference is not so much a difference in concepts as it is in philosophical theories of those concepts."

19. Kosman, "Beauty and the Good," 353.

20. Ibid., 354.

the imagination. Kosman, then, almost has it right but falls into the trap of subjectivity. Things manifest and present their being directly not to "subjective awareness" but to the soul. Further, "the Greek *kalon* reveals a thing's goodness and is not limited to the sensible surfaces of things."[21] Note here that a "thing's being" is the same as a "thing's goodness." This is because for the ancient Greeks "goodness" refers to the moral virtue inherent in all things *kalon*; they are *kalon* precisely because they appear (manifest, present) as they are. The immediate recognition of a thing as it appears in itself reveals *kalon,* ignites *eros,* inspires the good, and aims toward beauty. For the Greeks, appearance, and beauty, are not superficial but reveal through imagination the totality of a thing's being. The being and goodness of a thing is displayed, presented, manifested, appears in its image. And, as Jung insisted, "image *is* psyche."[22]

The appearance of things evokes visceral aesthetic and ethical responses. *Kalon* presents the *kosmos* of each thing as well-ordered, fitting, and appropriate. We respond with admiration, approval, pleasure, and desire, deeming them good and virtuous. *Aischros* presents a disordered *kosmos* that is not "mastered by pattern" (Plotinus). Because of this lacking, ugly things are not true to themselves and "consequently...cannot be beautiful or good."[23] Here we are repelled, the soul shrinks back, denies the thing, disapproves of it, resents its lack of proper order and the shamefulness of its display and conduct. Thus, our aesthetic and ethical responses "are cosmological, not merely personal. They are signs that [we] are here and taking part in the entire world order, which is from the beginning set out as a pleasing aesthetic display."[24] This active engagement with the *anima mundi* helps also to free us from our habitual fall into subjectivity. Aphrodite shows us the divine radiance of the world as

---

21. Lear, "Response to Kosman," 358.

22. *The Collected Works of C.G. Jung,* vol. 13: *Alchemical Studies,* edited and translated by Gerhard Adler and R.F.C. Hull (Princeton, N.J.: Princeton University Press, 1983), par. 75. Hillman has a similar view that images are "the psyche itself in its imaginative visibility." "A Brief Account," in *Uniform Edition of the Writings of James Hillman,* vol. 1: *Archetypal Psychology* (Putnam, Conn.: Spring Publications, 2013), 17.

23. Hillman, "The Cost of the Ugly," 195.

24. Hillman, "Aesthetics and Politics," 148.

full of gods, and this calls forth our aesthetic and ethical responses. "It is not through turning inward that man experiences deity but by proceeding outward, seizing, acting."[25]

Notice how nicely this view of *kalon* and appearance comports with Portmann's view discussed above in Chapter Three that appearance is "self-presentation" in which the display of things includes their interiority. *Kalon* ignores the tired dualism between inner and outer and instead honors a thing's presence in its entirety. Here is how Hillman puts it:

> Beauty...means the form of what is presented, that which is breathed in, *aisthesis,* and by which the value of each particular thing strikes the heart, the organ of aesthetic perception, where judgments are heartfelt responses, not merely critical, mental reflections. Reflection takes on another sense than our usual one. For the thought of the heart...reflection refers to the aesthetic quality of any event, its sheen and shape, the luster of its skin. Event itself as image. An event reflects itself in its *Selbstdarstellung* ["self-presentation"] as an image. Aesthetic reflection is immediately given with sensation, and the aesthetic response foreshortens reflection into reflex, the spontaneous reactions of the heart's taste.[26]

I take Hillman to mean that through beauty we appreciate the being and goodness of things by valuing them according to how they strike the heart (*eros*), and by judging them not through mental concepts but through heartfelt responses. As Kimmel noted, the apprehension of beauty is an "emotional reflex more than a reflective or mediated response." This is the ethical dimension of *kalon,* the aesthetic reflection "immediately given with sensation" that releases the ethical reflex revealed in the "spontaneous reactions of the heart's taste."

This latter point, the "reflex" and "spontaneous reactions" engendered by *kalon,* brings us back to nature. Aristotle tells a story that when visitors found Heraclitus in his kitchen, they were reluctant to enter. But Heraclitus beckoned them, telling them "Come in; don't be afraid;

---

25. Walter F. Otto, *The Homeric Gods: The Spiritual Significance of Greek Religion,* translated by Moses Hadas (Boston: Beacon Press, 1964), 174.

26. James Hillman, *The Thought of the Heart,* 34.

there are gods even here." Aristotle uses this story as a prelude to declaring that even the most seemingly insignificant animal also shared in the divine and could properly be called *kalon*:

> In like manner, we ought not to hesitate nor to be abashed, but boldly to enter upon our researches concerning animals of every sort and kind, knowing that in not one of them is Nature or Beauty lacking.
>
> I add "Beauty," because in the works of Nature purpose and not accident is predominant; and the purpose or end for the sake of which those works have been constructed or formed has its place among what is beautiful.[27]

I would extend this to all aspects of what we today call nature. Because the many things of the world present themselves as they are and not otherwise, because they are "fully mastered by pattern," they are *kalon*, beautiful, and, because each of these things is "fully and properly itself," they are *agathon*, good.[28]

Just as *kalon* brings together the human propensities for appreciating beauty, creating beauty, and being beautiful, it also brings together politics, ethics, and nature. All strive for the beauty of a well-ordered, fitting, and appropriate *kosmos*. Indeed, when guided by beauty, politics and ethics become self-fulfilling. Recall the translation with which we began this chapter, that if "all competed for the beautiful, and strained to the utmost to perform the most beautiful actions, then for all in common there would be what is needful." From this perspective, the aim of politics is to create beauty through ethical activity grounded in and sustained through love. All of the things that we seek for the polis—justice, truth, equality, fairness, freedom—are all available to those who compete for the beautiful. The more we strive for beautiful actions the more we build a polis through which our natures can be fully realized as aesthetic and political animals. But, as Hillman puts it, "ethics alone is not enough to make a change in the world. Alone, ethics without aesthetics doesn't hold...We must first be moved by beauty. For then, love is aroused."[29]

---

27. Aristotle, *Parts of Animals,* translated by A. L. Peck, Loeb Classical Library 323 (Cambridge, Mass.: Harvard University Press, 1937), 645*a*20–27.

28. Sachs glossary entry on "the good," in Aristotle, *Nichomachean Ethics,* 205.

29. Hillman, "Aesthetics and Politics," 148.

The ancient Greeks thought that a virtuous life, a life well-lived granted the soul *eudaimonia,* which we usually translate as "happiness." But Hillman offers a beautiful twist that we touched on at the end of Chapter Ten. The word *eudaimonia,* means "a well-pleased daimon."[30] If we take *kalon* to refer to the beauty that allows things to appear as they are, and if it is beauty that gives rise to the erotic desire for *agathon* that is in service to beauty, then our ethical responsibility is to help the daimon that lives us to become *kalos kagathon,* beautiful and good:

> Maybe the human task is to bring our behavior into line with [the daimon's] intentions, to do right by it, for its sake. What you do in your life affects your heart, alters your soul, and concerns the daimon. We make soul with our behavior, for soul doesn't come already made in heaven. It is only imaged there, an unfulfilled project trying to grow down.[31]

To do the right thing, to be true to ourselves, means to be true to the daimon, and the pursuit of happiness means helping the daimon to become *kalon.* That is why ethics so stubbornly resists being standardized or codified. Ethics is an aesthetic activity inspired by love to do right by the daimon, which although pointing back to the invisibles, is itself striving to fully appear as it is in all of its being and goodness (*agathon*).

To reunite *kalon* and *agathon* we must restore our faith in our aesthetic sensibilities as trustworthy guides to a virtuous life. By turning to and trusting in beauty, love blossoms and goodness ensues. We are released from our insular views of self and subjectivity and replaced in a vibrant world that we naturally approach with a heart devoted to serving its well-being (this is the virtuous desire we saw in volunteerism in Chapter Three.) By appreciating the beauty that is radiant in the world we are inspired to add to its beauty, thereby becoming ourselves beautiful as we align our lives in terms of the daimon and the powers that live us. Whatever destiny it is that our daimon calls us to fulfill, then, let us begin in beauty.

---

30. James Hillman, *The Soul's Code,* 83.
31. Ibid., 260.

Agora and the Political Soul

The ancient city-states of Greece had a meeting place called the agora. The agora was the center of political life in the city, and included all manner of athletic, artistic, business, social, and spiritual activities. The word itself means "gathering place" or "assembly." These dual meanings are significant because they connect the actual, physical place of the agora with the people who gathered there—the relationship was symbiotic and reciprocal. The agora was a sacred space in which governmental meetings, athletic events, and rituals all took place. Merchants sold their wares, artists and artisans had their workshops and studios nearby, and philosophers gave public speeches and taught their ideas. (From "agora," two Greek verbs were derived that meant "I shop," and "I speak in public.") The agora had a special significance for women. Women merchants worked alongside men. The many rituals that took place in the agora provided opportunities for women to leave their homes and interact with people beyond family. Some rituals that took place in the agora could only be performed by women.[1]

The agora was also a place of great beauty. Excavations at the Athenian agora show that it was filled with statues and marblework. This coming together, largely out of doors and close to nature, of all facets of the polis in one sacred and beautiful place gives living form to the ideas of this book. Politics, ethics, and nature all share a common ground because they all belong to beauty. Because they all have their share of soul, they require one another. Just like the Greek gods, whenever one appears the others are implicated. It is not coincidence that nearby the hustle and

---

1. Susan I. Rotroff and Robert D. Lamberton, *Women in the Athenian Agora* (Athens: American School of Classical Studies at Athens, 2005), 18.

bustle of the Athenian agora, if not indeed within it, stood the statue that Pausanias told us about—Aphrodite Pandemos.

The agora is both a place within a literal city and a place within our imagination. We can each have an agora within the polis of our imagination. There can be a place where the many facets of our lives gather to shop and play, to enjoy the company of many voices and faces, and to pay reverence to the gods. We can find there, too, the many wares and creations of the soul that is constantly producing images and fantasies, lining the market tables with weavings, and sending us animals while we sleep. We go to our imaginal agora to consider the necessities of politics and governing, to conduct business, to mull philosophy, and to propitiate the gods. By providing a common space for these things, the agora enlivens our spirit and prepares us for action. The agora teaches us that the polis is inspired by the heart and modeled by the hands.

In the agora of imagination stand the founding pillars of beauty, love, and soul—pillars that provide places where we might rightly revere these necessary gods of the polis. Here, too, within the imaginal agora, myth provides the structures for governing, the impetus for ethics, and the manifest patterns of nature. Because there are always lots of things going on at once in the imaginal agora, it protects us from single-mindedness, reminding us of the necessity of diversity and differentiation. The agora is interesting and so our imaginations stay involved, paying attention as we make our way through the flowing crowd as each passing thing unconsciously influences our souls. Just as the real agora was a space that connected the life of the polis with nature and the *anima mundi,* so, too, the imaginal agora provides a communal space that connects the polis that lives through us, the "powers we pretend to understand," and the greater part of soul that lies beyond us.

My time as village president has passed, and new public servants have taken the helm of leadership. Looking back over my time in office, I am pleased with what we as a community accomplished. The village is more beautiful than before, and I believe its soul has deepened as it has become more fully realized. Our residents have a deeper connection to nature, in part due to the Covid-19 pandemic, but also because we made concerted attempts to emphasize the significance of our natural beauty.

Our local government remains for the most part free from the rancor that characterizes too much of our political life and is civil in its manner and open-minded in its thinking. The seeds we planted by crafting a more beautiful village code are blossoming with more businesses coming to town, drawn by a welcoming governmental structure that furthers their needs while also protecting the village. The many infrastructure changes that we made have blended in with their natural surroundings and now seem to have been here always. The success of beautifying a part of our village's agora has given rise to other aesthetic goals yet to be achieved—the tapestry continues to be woven. The village's residents, old and new alike, seem to intuitively understand the need to balance development and adapting to new technologies alongside the need to maintain the beauty and historical legacy that makes Riverside a place special unto itself. Where there once was a kind of rigidity that sought to hold Riverside in the past, that has given way to newer perspectives that see that from the beginning Olmsted *intended* Riverside to be different. The proper respect for any legacy is to live it forward. In Riverside's case, that means constantly finding creative ways to unconsciously influence society so as to create a more perfect polis, relying on beauty to stimulate our natures as political animals, igniting in the polis a desire for virtue in service to beauty. In Riverside, beauty remains a civic necessity.

I began this book by saying that it was intended as an act of civil disobedience. My intent has been to destabilize existing notions of politics, ethics, and nature so that other, more civil, alternatives might emerge. Civil disobedience upsets the status quo by proposing other ways of ordering or arranging things. It attempts to show, through its actions, that civility can be better served through other means. By showing how the current ways of doing and imagining things are deficient, or even ugly, it hopes to promote more satisfying and beautiful ways of doing and imagining. Its subversion is purposeful, but always done in service to a greater ideal.

By looking at politics, ethics, and nature as essentially aesthetic, I hope I have persuaded you that their beauty always exists in their particulars, in a well-drafted ordinance, being touched by a kindness, rebelling against an unjust act, or gazing into the eye of a tiger. When we realize that life is an ongoing encounter with the particulars of imagination as presented to us by beauty, then even the things that we tend to belittle as mundane and tedious become vessels for soul-making. How we do politics, or think about ethics, or interact with nature all become aesthetic opportunities, chances to make the world more beautiful.

We live in a time of political decay and upheaval, where being ethical is said to be weak and naïve, and where our accumulated atrocities to the planet may have pushed us irretrievably beyond the brink. There is little cause for hope, and hope itself might be, as the tale of Pandora tells us, the last evil that prevents us from doing what must be done. Perhaps we can attempt to revision our politics, ethics, and nature as an ethologist might, withholding judgment as we try to observe and discern precisely what is happening. This aesthetic eye, this animal eye grafted to the heart might reveal where things stand by seeing *how* they stand, the manner of their presentation, the degrees to which they manifest as true to themselves or as having gone over to another order. Appreciation does not mean acceptance; appreciation tells us how we must act within the reality and practicality of our ecology of imagination.

In the context of politics and ethics, the polis will not be served nor justice restored until we return to beauty. If we can restore politics and ethics to their aesthetic foundations, then our return to nature would naturally follow. The only thing that the things of nature need from us is for us to be true to our natures as aesthetic and political animals. If we accept that we exist to appreciate beauty, to create beauty, and to be beautiful, and that the world needs nothing more from us, then we will naturally treat the world with reverence and respect. Beauty will give us the world in all of its well-ordered diversity, each thing befitting itself, at home in a supporting *kosmos*. Love for the world in all of its ensouled radiance will grow new wings as find news ways to serve the *anima mundi.* Soul, with its images and myths, will grow us downward, deepening us with its spontaneous creativity and quiet certainty. Perhaps we might still yet do our part in helping to restore the cosmic order. And perhaps, just perhaps, Aphrodite will smile.

ACKNOWLEDGMENTS

The idea for this book began many years ago in Dallas, Texas. I was a graduate student at Southern Methodist University and was lucky enough to have Thomas Moore as a teacher and advisor. Tom became a mentor and friend, and he introduced me to James Hillman, who was teaching at the University of Dallas and became a seminal figure in the founding of the Dallas Institute of Humanities and Culture. From those early days, the idea that the city was a natural place and that the true function of the polis was to enrich the imagination took hold. This book would not be possible without that early work and the ensuing decades of friendship and collegiality I have enjoyed with both men. It was Tom who encouraged me to pursue a life devoted to soul, and James who gave me, among many life-changing ideas, the idea of the *anima mundi* and the foundational importance of beauty. Decades later, I was able to put these ideas into practice in my public service in Riverside. I am indebted to the many public officials I have worked with, but special mention belongs to Jessica Frances, the village manager that I worked alongside as village president, Orion Galey and Doug Gotham, Riverside's village engineer and landscape architect, Michael Collins, village forester, and Ed Bailey, director of public works. All of these people knew that I was trying to govern on the basis of beauty and soul, and they contributed greatly to that effort. I also thank the other elected and appointed officials with whom I served. I appreciate their skill, talent, and dedication to public service. Because of them Riverside deepened its soul and more fully revealed its beauty. Thank you to Doug Pollock and Aberdeen Marsh-Ozga for reading and commenting on an early draft of the chapter on Olmsted. Thank you to the Riverside Public Library and its enormously helpful Frederick Law Olmsted Collection. Lastly, I am indebted beyond words to my wife (who is also a public servant), Jill Mateo. This book belongs as much to her as to me. In ways I can never express, she has opened my eyes to see the world anew, and through her brilliance and love she has sophisticated my political sense, deepened my ethics, and quickened my return to nature.

Aeschylus, *Oresteia: Agamemnon. Libation-Bearers. Eumenides,* translated by Alan H. Sommerstein, Loeb Classical Library 146 (Cambridge, Mass.: Harvard University Press, 2009)

Anderson, Ross. "Nature Has Lost Its Meaning," *The Atlantic,* November 30, 2015 (online at *https://www.theatlantic.com/science/archive/2015/11/nature-has-lost-its-meaning/417918/*)

Apuleius, *Metamorphoses (The Golden Ass),* vol. 1: Books 1–9, edited and translated by J. Arthur Hanson, Loeb Classical Library 44 (Cambridge, Mass.: Harvard University Press, 1996)

Aristotle, *History of Animals,* vol. 1, translated by A. L. Peck, Loeb Classical Library 437 (Cambridge, Mass.: Harvard University Press, 1965)

—. *Nicomachean Ethics,* translated by H. Rackham, Loeb Classical Library 73 (Cambridge, Mass.: Harvard University Press, 1926)

—. *Nicomachean Ethics,* translated by C. D. C. Reeves (Indianapolis: Hackett Publishing Company, 2014)

—. *Nicomachean Ethics,* translated by Joe Sachs (Indianapolis: Hackett Publishing Company, 2002)

—. *Parts of Animals. Movement of Animals. Progression of Animals,* translated by A. L. Peck, Loeb Classical Library 323 (Cambridge, Mass.: Harvard University Press, 1937)

—. *Politics,* translated by H. Rackham, Loeb Classical Library 264 (Cambridge, Mass: Harvard University Press, 1932)

Auden, W. H. *The Collected Poetry of W. H. Auden* (New York: Random House, 1945)

Augustine, *City of God,*, vol. 4: Books 12–15, translated by Philip Levine, Loeb Classical Library 414 (Cambridge, Mass.: Harvard University Press, 1966)

—. *The Catholic and Manichean Ways of Life,* translated by Donald Gallagher and Idella Gallagher (Washington, D.C.: The Catholic University of America Press, 1966)

Barfield, Owen. *History in English Words* (Great Barrington, Mass.: Lindisfarne Press, 1988)

Bekoff, Marc and Dale Jamieson, ed. *Readings in Animal Cognition* (Cambridge, Mass.: The MIT Press, 1999)

Bekoff, Mark, and Jessica Pierce. *Wild Justice: The Moral Lives of Animals* (Chicago: The University of Chicago Press, 2009)

—. "Wild Justice Redux: What We Know about Social Justice in Animals and Why it Matters," *Social Justice Research* 25, no. 2 (2012): 122–39

Bellah, Robert; Richard Madsen, William Sullivan, Ann Swider, and Steven Tipton, *Habits of the Heart: Middle America Observed* (London: Hutchinson, 1985)

Berry, Patricia. "An Approach to the Dream," *Spring: An Annual of Archetypal Psychology and Jungian Thought* (1974): 58–79. Reprinted in Patricia Berry, *Echo's Subtle Body: Contributions to an Archetypal Psychology* (Thompson, Conn.: Spring Publications, 2017 [1982])

Beston, Henry. *The Outermost House: A Year of Life on the Great Beach of Cape Cod* (New York: St. Martin's Griffin, 1992 [1928])

Beveridge, Charles E. "Olmsted—His Essential Theory" (online at *https://www.nps.gov/frla/learn/historyculture/flo.htm*)

Bradbury, Jack, and Sandra Vehrencamp. *Principles of Animal Communication* (Sunderland, Mass.: Sinauer Associates, 1998)

Brosnan, Sarah F., and Frans B. M. de Waal. "Fairness in Animals: Where to from Here?," *Social Justice Research* 25, no. 3 (2012): 336–351

—. "Monkeys Reject Unequal Pay," *Nature* 425 (2003): 297–99

Bushnell, Horace. *Building Eras in Religion* (New York: Charles Scribner's Sons, 1881)

—. *Christian Nurture* (New York: Charles Scribner, 1861)

—. *God in Christ* (New York: Charles Scribner's Sons, 1876)

—. *Unconscious Influence: A Sermon* (London: Partridge and Oakey, 1852)

—. *Work and Play: or Literary Varieties* (New York: Charles Scribner, 1864)

Cartmill, Matt. "Animal Consciousness: Some Philosophical, Methodological, and Evolutionary Problems," *American Zoologist* 40, no. 6 (December 2000), 835–46

Cronon, William, ed. *Uncommon Ground: Rethinking the Human Place in Nature* (New York: W.W. Norton, 1995)

Darwin, Charles. *The Descent of Man and Selection in Relation to Sex,* 2nd ed. (London: John Murray, 1874)

Dawkins, Melody Buyukozer, Stephanie Sloane, and Renée Baillargeon, "Do Infants in the First Year of Life Expect Equal Resource Allocations?," *Frontiers in Psychology* (19 February 2019): 1–19 (online at *https://www.ncbi.nlm.nih.gov/pmc/articles/PMC6389704/*)

Fine, Jonathan. "Beauty on Display: Plato and the Concept of the Kalon," PhD diss., Columbia University, 2018

Finkelberg, Aryeh. "On the History of the Greek κοσμοσ," *Harvard Studies in Classical Philology* 98 (1998)

Fischer, David Hackett. *Fairness and Freedom: A History of Two Open Societies—New Zealand and the United States* (New York: Oxford University Press, 2012)

Fisher, Irving David. "Frederick Law Olmsted and the Philosophic Background to the City Planning Movement in the United States," PhD diss., Columbia University, 1976

Ganczarek, Joanna, Thomas Hünefeldt, and Marta Olivetti Belardinelli, "From 'Einfühlung' to Empathy: Exploring the Relationship between Aesthetic and Interpersonal Experience," *Cognitive Processing* 19, no. 2 (2018): 141–45

Hesiod, *Theogony. Works and Days. Testimonia,* edited and translated by Glenn W. Most, Loeb Classical Library 57 (Cambridge, Mass.: Harvard University Press, 2018)

Hillman, James. "*Anima Mundi*: Return of the Soul to the World," *Spring: An Annual of Archetypal Psychology and Jungian Thought* (1982): 71–93. Reprinted in *Uniform Edition of the Writings of James Hillman,* vol. 2: *City and Soul,* edited by Robert J. Leaver (Thompson, Conn.: Spring Publications, 2018 [2006])

—. *Uniform Edition of the Writings of James Hillman,* vol. 9: *Animal Presences* (Putnam, Conn.: Spring Publications, 2008)

—. *La Guistizia di Afrodite/Aphrodite's Justice* (Capri: Edizioni La Conchiglia, 2017)

—. *Uniform Edition of the Writings of James Hillman,* vol. 1: *Archetypal Psychology* (Putnam, Conn.: Spring Publications, 2013)

—. "Cosmology for Soul: From Universe to Cosmos," *Sphinx: A Journal for Archetypal Psychology and the Arts* 2 (London: London Convivium, 1989), 17–33. Reprinted in *Uniform Edition of the Writings of James Hillman,* vol. 8: *Philosophical Intimations,* edited by Edward S. Casey (Thompson, Conn.: Spring Publications, 2021 [2016])

—. "An Inquiry into Image," *Spring: An Annual of Archetypal Psychology and Jungian Thought* (1977): 62–88. Reprinted in *Uniform Edition of the Writings of James Hillman,* vol. 4: *From Types to Images,* edited by Klaus Ottmann (Thompson, Conn.: Spring Publications, 2019)

—. *Kinds of Power: A Guide to Its Intelligent Uses* (New York: Doubleday, 1995)

—. "The Practice of Beauty," *Sphinx: A Journal for Archetypal Psychology and the Arts* 3 (1992): 13–28

—. *The Soul's Code: In Search of Character and Calling* (New York: Random House, 1996)

—. *The Thought of the Heart and the Soul of the World* (Thompson, Conn: Spring Publications, 2021 [1992])

Hobbes, Thomas. *Leviathan: Parts One and Two* (Indianapolis: The Bobbs-Merrill Company, 1958)

Howe, Daniel. "The Social Science of Horace Bushnell," *The Journal of American History* 70, no. 2 (1983): 305–22

Hume, David. *Essays, Moral, Political, and Literary, Part 2* (1752) (online at *https://davidhume.org/texts/empl2/oc*)

Izenberg, Gerald. *Identity: The Necessity of a Modern Idea* (Philadelphia: University of Pennsylvania Press, 2016)

John of Salisbury. *Policraticus: Of the Frivolities of Courtiers and the Footprints of Philosophers,* edited and translated by Cary Nederman (Cambridge: Cambridge University Press, 1990)

Keats, John. *The Letters of John Keats, 1814–1821,* edited by Hyder Edward Rollins, 2 vols. (Cambridge, Mass.: The Harvard University Press, 1958)

Kerényi, Karl. *The Religion of the Greeks and Romans,* translated by Christopher Holme (New York: E. P. Dutton, 1962)

Kimmel, Lawrence. "Eros/Kalon/Agathos: Love, the Beautiful, and the Good," *Analecta Husserliana* 97 (2008): 3–12

Kosman, Aryeh. "Beauty and the Good: Situating the Kalon," *Classical Philology* 105, no. 4 (October 2010): 41–57

Kristeller, Paul Oskar. "The Modern System of the Arts: A Study in the History of Aesthetics (I)," *Journal of the History of Ideas* 12, no. 4 (October 1951): 496–527

Lao-tzu. *Tao Te Ching,* translated by Stephen Mitchell (New York: Harper Perennial, 2006)

Lear, Gabriel Richardson. "Response to Kosman," *Classical Philology* 105, no. 4 (October 2010): 357–62

Liddell, H. G., Robert Scott, and H. S. Jones, *A Greek-English Lexicon,* 9th ed. (Oxford: Clarendon Press, 1940)

Lonsdale, Steven H. "Attitudes Toward Animals in Ancient Greece," *Greece & Rome* 26, no. 2 (October 1979): 146–59

Marx, Leo. "The Idea of Nature in America," *Daedalus* 137, no. 2 (Spring 2008): 8–21

Merchant, Carolyn. *The Death of Nature: Women, Ecology, and the Scientific Revolution* (San Francisco: Harper, 1989)

Moore, Thomas. *The Re-Enchantment of Everyday Life* (New York: Harper-Collins Publishers, 1996)

Murdoch, Iris. *The Sovereignty of Good over Other Concepts: The Leslie Stephen Lecture* (Cambridge: Cambridge University Press, 1967)

Nicholson, Carol J. "Elegance and Grass Roots: The Neglected Philosophy of Frederick Law Olmsted," *Transactions of the Charles S. Peirce Society* 40, no. 2 (Spring 2004): 335–48

Nisker, Wes. "The Soul of the Matter: James Hillman in Conversation with Wes Nisker," *Inquiring Mind* 11, no. 2 (Spring 1995) (online at *https://www.inquiringmind.com/article/1102_8_hillman-soul-of-matter/*)

North, Helen F. "Emblems of Eloquence," *Proceedings of the American Philosophical Society* 137, no. 3 (1993): 406–30

Olmsted, Frederick Law. *Civilizing American Cities: A Selection of Frederick Law Olmsted's Writings on City Landscapes,* edited by S. B. Sutton (Cambridge, Mass. and London, England: The MIT Press, 1971)

—. *A Consideration of the Justifying Value of a Public Park* (Boston: Tolman and White, Printers, 1881)

—. *Forty Years of Landscape Architecture,* vol. 2: *Central Park,* edited by Frederick Law Olmsted, Jr. and Theodora Kimball (Cambridge, Mass. and London, England: The MIT Press, 1973)

—. *Mount Royal Montreal* (New York: G. P. Putnam's Sons, 1881)

—. *Olmsted: Writings on Landscape, Culture, and Society,* edited by Charles E. Beveridge (New York: Library of America, 2015)

—. *The Papers of Frederick Law Olmsted,* vol. 1: *The Formative Years,* edited by Charles E. Beveridge and Charles Capen McLaughlin (Baltimore: The John Hopkins University Press, 1977)

Onians, Richard Broxton. *The Origins of European Thought: About the Body, the Mind, the Soul, the World, Time, and Fate* (Cambridge: Cambridge University Press, 1989)

Otto, Walter F. *The Homeric Gods: The Spiritual Significance of Greek Religion,* translated by Moses Hadas (Boston: Beacon Press, 1964)

Parke, H.W. *Greek Oracles* (London: Hutchinson, 1967)

Pausanias, *Description of Greece,* translated by W.H.S. Jones, Loeb Classical Library 93 (Cambridge, Mass.: Harvard University Press, 1918)

Pettersson, Edvard. "The Kalon and the Agathon in Plato's Socratic Dialogues," PhD diss., University of California, Irvine, 1996

Pizan, Christine de. *The Book of the Body Politic,* edited and translated by Kate Langdon Forhan (Cambridge: Cambridge University Press, 2007)

Plato, *Laches. Protagoras. Meno. Euthydemus,* translated by W.R.M. Lamb, Loeb Classical Library 165 (Cambridge, Mass.: Harvard University Press, 1924)

—. *Republic,* edited and translated by Chris Emlyn-Jones and William Preddy, Loeb Classical Library 276 (Cambridge, Mass.: Harvard University Press, 2013)

—. *Symposium,* edited and translated by Chris Emlyn-Jones and William Preddy, Loeb Classical Library 166 (Cambridge, Mass.: Harvard University Press, 2022)

—. *Hippias Major,* translated by Paul Woodruff (Indianapolis: Hackett Publishing Company, 1982)

Plotinus. *The Enneads,* translated by Stephen MacKenna (Burdett, N.Y.: Larson Publication, 1992)

Poland, Donald J. *Unconscious Influence: Olmsted's Hartford,* manuscript prepared for the Amistad Committee, New Haven, Connecticut (October 2020) (online at *https://portal.ct.gov/-/media/ DECD/Historic-Preservation/03_Technical_Assistance_Research/ Research/Frederick-Law-Olmsteds-Hartford2020.pdf*)

Portmann, Adolf. *Animal Forms and Patterns: A Study of the Appearance of Animals,* translated by Hella Czech (London: Faber and Faber, 1948)

—. *Essays in Philosophical Zoology,* translated by Richard Carter (Lewiston: The Edward Mellen Press, 1990)

Purdy, Jedediah. *After Nature: A Politics for the Anthropocene* (Cambridge: Harvard University Press, 2015)

Ray, John Ray. *The Wisdom of God Manifested in the Works of Creation* (London: William Innys and Richard Manby, 1735)

Reid, Heather L., and Tony Leyh, *Looking at Beauty to* Kalon *in Western Greece: Selected Essays from the 2018 Symposium on the Heritage of Western Greece* (Sioux City, Iowa: Parnassos Press, 2019)

Riegel, Nicholas P. "Beauty, To Kalon, and its Relation to the Good in the Works of Plato," PhD diss., University of Toronto, 2011

Rilke, Rainer Maria. *Letters of Rainer Maria Rilke 1892–1910,* translated by Jane Bannard Greene and M. D. Herter Norton (New York: W. W. Norton, 1945)

Robinson, Gerard, and Maury Giles. "America Divided: Why It's Dangerous That Public Distrust in Civic Institutions Is Growing," *USA Today* (15 March 2021, online at *https://www.usatoday.com/story/opinion/2021/03/15/why-americans-growing-distrust-civic-institutions-warning-column/4668616001/*)

Rotroff, Susan, and Robert Lamberton. *Women in the Athenian Agora* (Athens: American School of Classical Studies at Athens, 2006)

Ruskin, John. The Works of John Ruskin, vol. 4 (London: George Allen, 1903-12)

Scarry, Elaine. *On Beauty and Being Just* (Princeton, N.J.: Princeton University Press, 1999)

Scheper, George. "The Reformist Vision of Frederick Law Olmsted and the Poetics of Park Design," *The New England Quarterly* 62, no. 3 (1989): 369–402

Sells, Benjamin. *Return to Beauty: Restoring the Ecology of Imagination* (Thompson, Conn.: Spring Publications, 2022)

—. "Answers and Explanations: Fundamentalism as a Variety of Rational Experience," *Spring: An Annual of Archetypal Psychology and Jungian Thought* 68 (2001): 1–16

Shelley, Percy Bysshe. *Selected Poems, Essays, and Letters,* edited by Ellsworth Barnard (New York: Odyssey Press, 1944)

Solomon, Robert. *A Passion for Justice: Emotions and the Origins of the Social Contract* (Lanham, Md.: Rowman & Littlefield, 1995)

Sussman, Robert, and Audrey Chapman. *The Origins and Nature of Sociality* (New York: Aldine De Gruyter, 2004)

—, Paul Garber, and Jim Cheverud. "Importance of Cooperation and Affiliation in the Evolution of Primate Sociality," *American Journal of Physical Anthropology* 128, no. 1 (2005): 84–97

Tocqueville, Alexis de. *Democracy in America,* translated by Henry Reeve, 2 vols. (New York: Vintage Books, 1990)

de Waal, Frans B. M. *Are We Smart Enough to Know How Smart Animals Are?* (New York: W. W. Norton, 2016).

Warden, C. J. "The Development of Modern Comparative Psychology," *The Quarterly Review of Biology* 3, no. 4 (December 1928): 486–522

Watkins, Mary. "In Dreams Begin Responsibilities: Moral Imagination and Peace," in *Facing Apocalypse,* edited by Valerie Andrews, Robert Bosnak, and Karen Walter Goodman (Thompson, Conn.: Spring Publications, 2021 [1987])

Weil, Simone. *Waiting for God,* translated by Emman Craufurd (New York: Harper and Row, 1951)

Whyte, Lancelot Law. *The Unconscious before Freud* (New York: Basic Books, 1969)

Zimmermann, Johann Georg von. *Solitude Considered, with Respect to Its Influence upon the Mind and the Heart,* translated by J. B. Mercier (New London: Cady & Eells, 1807)